✓ B&T
2/3/84
16.95

# THEOLOGY AND PHILOSOPHICAL INQUIRY

D0140948

# Theology and Philosophical Inquiry

AN INTRODUCTION

by
Vincent Brümmer

THE WESTMINSTER PRESS
Philadelphia

Wingate College Library

© Vincent Brümmer 1982

All rights reserved. No part of this publication
may be reproduced or transmitted, in any form or
by any means, without permission.

Published by The Westminster Press ®
Philadelphia, Pennsylvania

PRINTED IN HONG KONG
9 8 7 6 5 4 3 2 1

**Library of Congress Cataloging in Publication Data**

Brümmer, Vincent.
  Theology and philosophical inquiry.

  Includes bibliographical references and index.
  1. Philosophical theology.   2. Philosophy and
religion.   I. Title.
BT40.B69          230'.01          81-11557
ISBN 0-664-24398-3                 AACR2

093390

# Contents

# Contents

The illustration on the front of the book represents: *'Philosophia ancilla theologiae'*: Aristotle between the saints on the *Portail Royal* at Chartres cathedral (12th century).

# Preface

ONE of the difficulties in doing theology, is that the theologian is required to master the basic tools of various other disciplines. Thus he should be a philologist and master the elements of Greek and Hebrew in order to do Biblical exegesis; he ought to be a historian and master the methods of historiography in order to study church history and the history of religions; he should be able to deal with the sort of questions asked by cultural anthropologists and social scientists in order to study comparative religions; and, as I shall argue in this book, he should master some of the basic tools of conceptual inquiry as practised by philosophers, in order to do systematic theology.

Since these requirements are rather comprehensive, theologians often try to take short cuts, for example, by doing exegesis without an adequate knowledge of Greek and Hebrew, or systematic theology without an adequate ability to deal with conceptual issues. Furthermore, a Barthian prejudice against philosophy (conceived of in a certain way) combined with a lack of clarity about the nature of conceptual inquiry and its relation to the sort of issues dealt with in systematic theology, often tends to make theologians wary of using philosophical tools. I shall argue that this is to the detriment of systematic theology.

This book is aimed at introducing theology students with no previous knowledge of philosophy, to some of the basic equipment of conceptual inquiry. As such it is not an introduction to the philosophy of religion even though some of the most fundamental issues in the philosophy of religion are dealt with. Those chapters dealing more specifically with theological issues are not the main aim of the book. They are intended rather as illustrations of the way in which the conceptual apparatus developed in the other chapters, is applicable to theological problems.

Like most textbooks, this one grew out of some teaching syllabi written and rewritten a number of times in the course of years, and used (in this case) for teaching philosophy to theology students. I am grateful to my students for always insisting that I make my argument perfectly clear, that I produce arguments and illustrations for the points I wish to make, and that I show how the philosophical tools which they have to acquire are of use to them as theologians. I would like to thank my colleagues in Utrecht as well as Donald Hudson, John Hick and Stewart Sutherland, for their encouragement and helpful comments on the manuscript of this book. I am also very grateful to all my colleagues in Holland who criticised the earlier Dutch version published a few years ago. Their comments and criticism contributed in making this version so different.

VINCENT BRÜMMER

# 1 Introduction

## 1.1 PHILOSOPHICAL QUESTIONS

ACADEMIC disciplines often differ by being concerned with differing fields of knowledge. Thus the biologist, the geologist and the astronomer are interested in different fields of study. But such disciplines often also differ from each other in the kind of questions they ask. The mathematician, the philologist and the historian, for example, ask quite different kinds of questions in the pursuit of their respective disciplines.

What characterises philosophy is not so much its field of interest. In fact, there is no field of human knowledge about which philosophy would ask no questions. What distinguishes philosophy is, rather, the kind of questions asked by philosophers. But what kind of question is characteristic of philosophy? Unfortunately philosophers themselves have quite different views on this matter. As a result all kinds of people call themselves philosophers although they are concerned with widely differing kinds of questions.

All this becomes even more complicated if one considers that the distinctions between philosophy and the sciences and between the various sciences themselves are fairly recent. The modern philosopher does not regard all questions as philosophical questions, whereas the classical philosopher took an interest in intellectual problems of any kind. Aristotle, for example, wrote books on botany, zoology and metaphysics, and the Pythagoreans practised mathematics as well as cosmology.

The intellectual problems with which classical philosophers concerned themselves may be divided into three main groups: they asked questions about the factual nature of the world, about the meaning or significance of life and of the world in which they lived, and about the function of the most fundamental concepts we use in our thinking and speaking. We could say that they asked *factual questions, questions of meaning,* and *conceptual qustions.* An example may serve to illustrate the difference between these three kinds of questions in a preliminary way.

Suppose I became seriously ill. I could then ask the following questions about my illness: What disease have I? What are the causes of my illness? Is my disease contagious? Are there any legal requirements that would apply to me if my disease were contagious? These and similar questions are all *questions of fact*. But the following questions which I could ask about my illness are of a quite different nature: What does my illness mean to me? Should I see it as punishment or as some form of trial, or simply as an unfortunate interruption to my studies? Why should it happen to *me*? How should others treat me now that I am ill? If my disease is contagious, should I submit to the legal requirements for people with contagious diseases? Why? These and similar questions are all *questions of meaning* in the sense that they inquire into the meaning or significance of an event, and the meaning of something also has a bearing on the attitude I should adopt towards it and on the way I should behave.

Such questions of fact and of meaning are all questions I could ask about my illness. But there are also questions I could ask about these questions. For example: How do questions of meaning differ from factual questions, and how are they related? What is the difference between being ill and being well? What does one mean when one says that legal requirements apply? When I say this, am I stating a fact or doing something else? These and similar questions are all *conceptual questions* because in answering them I have to examine a number of *concepts* (meaning, fact, ill, well, applicable, law, etc.).

A question about the relationship between these three kinds of questions is in itself a *conceptual question*, and one on which there is no agreement among philosophers. Thus, there are some philosophers who hold that the distinction between these questions is in itself dubious; they hold that these are all questions of fact, even though they deal with facts of different kinds. In this book we shall try to show that such a view is both confused and confusing, since these three kinds of questions cannot be answered by the same procedures. On the other hand it would be absurd to maintain that these three kinds of questions are in no way related to each other. Anyone who applied himself to questions of meaning without considering the facts would be an uninformed moraliser. Anyone who inquired into the facts without taking an interest in the meaning or significance of his own inquiry and of the facts that he examines would fall a victim to amoral neutrality. Amoral boffins are even more dangerous than uninformed moralisers: Those who concentrate one-sidedly on questions of meaning or on factual questions risk conceptual confusion and invalid arguments should they pay no attention to the function of their concepts. Anyone who tried to deal with conceptual questions, with no regard for questions of fact and of meaning, would lapse into futile theorising. He would have to examine the function of concepts *in* our discussions about facts and meaning, or else he would be like somebody practising swimming strokes without entering the water. Because these three questions are so closely related one can understand why philosophers have not always drawn sharp distinctions between them.

In the course of history the various academic disciplines have expanded to such an extent that it has become impossible to be a *homo universalis* like Aristotle. Anyone who takes an interest in intellectual pursuits has to confine himself to a particular field of human knowledge. Thus the asking and answering of factual questions about the various areas of knowledge have been taken over by the various sciences, whereas philosophy concentrates on questions of meaning or significance and on conceptual questions. To the modern philosopher factual questions are of interest only in so far as they are relevant to the answering of questions of meaning and conceptual questions.

If it is assumed that *questions about the meaning* of life and the world are the 'truly' philosophical questions, the philosopher's primary task becomes the construction of a philosophical system in terms of which all such questions of meaning can be answered. This is how St Augustine, for example, saw the task of philosophy. Theology, which has the task of systematising the Christian faith in order to answer questions about the meaning of life in terms of this system, was the *philosophia christiana*. Karl Barth, too, sometimes takes this view of philosophy when he argues that a philosophy which attempts to answer such questions in terms of some criterion other than the Christian faith, is nothing but bad theology.

Philosophy assumes a rather different character if the philosopher concerns himself primarily with conceptual issues. Instead of constructing large systems of ideas in the light of which the meaning of life and the world is to be determined, he examines the function and the implications of the various concepts we employ in our thinking and speaking in various intellectual pursuits and in everyday life. This distinction is often expressed by saying that such philosophers *do philosophy* but do not *produce philosophies*. Doing philosophy in this sense is what Socrates did in the market place when he discussed with his pupils questions concerning the *concepts* of knowing, perceiving, justice, piety, goodness, virtue, and so on.

## 1.2 THE AIM OF THIS BOOK

In this book we propose to provide an introduction to conceptual inquiry, primarily for the sake of theologians. But why should theologians be introduced to the practice of conceptual inquiry? In a preliminary way, we could say two things in reply to this question.

(1) Since all academic disciplines are themselves conceptual activities, conceptual inquiry is to some extent a meta-inquiry, that is an inquiry about the nature of every inquiry. Thus the philosopher could examine how the basic concepts and arguments function within some academic discipline. What kind of problems are involved in physics, for example? And what demands would a theory have to meet in order to be useful in the solution of these problems? How do men set about constructing such theories? And how are they tested? And what is the function of the fundamental concepts employed in physical theory? In this way it belongs to the task of a philosopher to inquire into the nature of all academic inquiries – including that of philosophy itself.

In the middle ages it was fairly commonly held that philosophy was an *ancilla theologiae* – a handmaiden to the queen of the sciences! According to some, the task of this handmaiden was to demonstrate, on rational grounds, the truth of the Christian faith. Philosophy was to provide a *praeambula fidei*, a rational basis for belief. It is doubtful whether the handmaiden is qualified, or even able, to perform this task. However, in pursuing meta-inquiry, the philosopher does render an important service to theology as much as to all intellectual disciplines: he must help the theologian toward a better understanding of the nature of his own activity and the meaning of his own fundamental concepts.

(2) Conceptual inquiry is not merely a useful ancilla to theology since, as we shall argue later, systematic theology is itself a form of conceptual inquiry, that is, an inquiry concerning the basic concepts of the Christian faith. As such, familiarity with conceptual inquiry is not only useful but essential for the pursuit of systematic theology.

The Christian faith (with which Christian theology is concerned) is not an esoteric affair, remote from ordinary life and from other human pursuits. Hence, too, most of the fundamental concepts employed in expressing the Christian faith are ordinary everyday concepts. Very few, if any, are really technical terms. Religious language is not some form of glossolalia: The concepts we shall examine in this book are therefore ordinary everyday concepts, even though in expressing the

Christian faith we use them in a religious context.

Thus, for example, the Christian maintains that in the final analysis his faith determines what things are of value to him, what meaning his life and the world he lives in has for him, what things are good or bad, and what actions right or wrong. 'Good', 'bad', 'right', 'wrong', 'valuable', 'valueless', 'meaningful' etc. are the fundamental concepts of axiology or theory of value. In Part Two of this book we shall examine these axiological concepts and see how they are related to religious belief.

The Christian maintains that his religious beliefs are true, and that he has adequate grounds for holding them. He would even go as far as Job did and say: 'I know that my Redeemer liveth! 'Knowing', 'believing', 'true', 'grounds' etc. are the fundamental concepts of epistemology or theory of knowledge. In Part Three of this book we shall examine these epistemological concepts and see how they function in a religious context.

The reality of God is a fundamental presupposition of the Christian faith. For the Christian it is a fact that God exists in reality. 'Exist', 'fact', 'real' etc. are fundamental concepts in ontology, or theory of being. In Part Four of this book we shall examine these ontological concepts and see in what sense they could be applied to God.

There are of course many other concepts apart from axiological, epistemological and ontological concepts which also have an essential function in expressing the Christian faith. In order to keep this book within manageable proportions, we will, however, limit ourselves to an examination of these. At any rate, as an *introduction* to conceptual inquiry for theologians, this selection will suffice.

Before we can set about this examination, however, we shall have to get a clearer idea of the nature of concepts and conceptual inquiry in general, and its relation to theology. This we shall do in Part One of this book.

# PART ONE

# CONCEPTUAL INQUIRY

# 2 Saying and Doing

## 2.3 INTRODUCTION

WHY is conceptual inquiry important for theology and why, therefore, is an introduction to this sort of inquiry essential for a theologian? How we reply to this question depends on what we mean by conceptual inquiry. But what sort of inquiry is a conceptual inquiry? What sort of questions do philosophers ask about concepts and how do they set about finding answers? What we say to these questions depends in turn upon what we mean by 'concepts'. What are concepts? How do concepts differ from words and how are they related to words and to things? A reply to these questions presupposes a theory of language: what do we do when we say things and how do words and concepts enter into what we do?

In this chapter we propose to develop a theory of speech acts. In chapter 3 we will discuss the nature of concepts and their relation to words and the world, and in chapter 4 we will examine the nature of conceptual inquiry and its relation to theology. First of all, then: what do we do when we say things?

## 2.4 SPEECH ACTS

A human act or deed is something we *do,* not something that *happens to* us or is *done to* us. As 'doers' we are *active* in our actions, not passive. Catching someone, for example, is an act; being caught is not an act. Jumping off the stairway is an act; falling down the stairs is not an act. In short a doer always takes the initiative in his own actions.

Human acts are performed for a *purpose.* We try to achieve or establish something and our attempts may succeed or fail. Because of this, one and the same act may be described in more than one way: either as doing *x*, or as bringing about *y*. I could, for instance, report one and the same act by a centre-forward during a game of football as follows: (a) he kicks the ball; (b) he makes the ball go into the net; (c) he scores a goal; (d) he pleases his supporters. In this way an act is often 'complex', so that we may distinguish between various aspects of what is done in one and the same act.

An act may be related to its purpose in two ways: (a) There may be a *causal* relationship between my doing $x$ and my bringing about $y$. For instance a causal relationship between our centre-forward's kicking the ball and its going into the net. Whether or not I succeed in bringing about $y$ by doing $x$ is a matter of causal effectiveness. (b) There may also be a *conventional* relationship between my doing $x$ and my bringing about $y$. Thus the relationship between someone's kicking the ball into the net and his scoring a goal is conventional and not causal. It is only in terms of the conventional rules of football that his kicking the ball into the net counts as a goal. 'Scoring a goal' is an act that is constituted as such by a rule. In the one case $x$ (kicking the ball) is causally related to $y$ (making the ball go into the net). In the other case $x$ (putting the ball into the net) counts as $y$ (scoring a goal) in terms of the conventions of football.

A *constitutive* rule (by which doing $x$ is constituted as or counted as doing $y$) can usually be formulated as follows: *'Under the factual circumstances $z$, doing $x$ counts as doing $y$.'* For example: if a football player in the course of a football match, when the ball is in play and he is not out of play himself, etc. (circumstances $z$), kicks the ball into the net (doing $x$), this is counted as scoring a goal (doing $y$). Whether or not someone succeeds in performing a conventional act (one constituted by a rule) depends on whether his act fulfils the conditions set out in the rule – namely, whether the *factual circumstances $z$* under which he did $x$ were as required by the rule. Kicking the ball into the net counts as a goal only if the factual conditions are as prescribed by the rule: the ball is kicked into the net during a football match, by one of the players, who was not out of play, the ball was in play, etc. In sum: a *causal* act succeeds only if the desired effect is achieved; a *conventional* act succeeds only if it is performed in accordance with the conventional rules that prescribe under which factual circumstances ($z$) a specific act *($x$)* is or is not counted as a particular kind of act *($y$)*.

Speaking is also a form of action. It is a form of intentional action and therefore complex in the sense indicated above. What kinds of acts do we perform when speaking? Or better: which aspects are distinguishable in the acts we perform with words? J. L. Austin[1] tried to find an answer to this question.

Austin distinguishes between three aspects of the act someone performs when saying something:

(1)   he *utters* a specific sentence, for example, 'please open the door';
(2)   he directs a *request* at his hearer;
(3)   he causes a specific *response* in his hearer, for example, he causes his hearer to open the door.

Austin calls these three aspects a 'locutionary act', an 'illocutionary act' and a 'perlocutionary act', respectively. Let us call them *locutions, illocutions,* and *per-illocutions,* respectively, and then examine the relation between the three in terms of our analysis of human actions.

In a certain sense a *locution* is the basis for the performance of illocutions and per-illocutions, as kicking the ball is the basis for putting the ball into the net and for scoring a goal.

It is *in* performing a locution that I perform an illocution (in uttering a sentence I make a request). It is *by* performing an illocution (and therefore also a locution) that I perform a per-illocution (by making a request – and therefore also by uttering a sentence – I persuade my hearer to open the door). Briefly: illocutions are performed *in* performing a locution, and per-illocutions are performed *by* performing illocutions.

An *illocution* is a *conventional aspect* of the act someone performs in saying something. Illocutions are therefore related to locutions in the same way as scoring a goal is related to putting the ball into the net: a locution is constituted as an illocution (or complex of illocutions) by a constitutive rule of speech. Thus my words, 'please open the door' are recognised, under the rules of our speech, as making a *request,* provided that there is a door, that the door is not open already, that my hearer is capable of opening the door, etc. Briefly: whether or not my uttering of a sentence is recognised as making a request, depends on whether it is done in accordance with the conditions laid down in the illocutionary rules.

A *per-illocution* is a *causal aspect* of the act performed by someone when saying something. We may define the term per-illocution as 'evoking an intended response in a hearer by performing an illocution'. For example, by making a request I persuade my hearer to open the door. Two things that do not fall under this definition are the following. (1) Evoking unintended responses in the hearer. For example, unintentionally, I irritate my hearer by making a request to him. This falls outside our definition because it is not an act. Human acts are intentional and per-illocutions are aspects of a human speech act. (2) Evoking a response by means other than an illocution. For example, I disturb my hearer by speaking (performing locutions) and not by what I say to him (performing illocutions). In this instance we may speak of per-locutions (evoking a response by a locution), but not of a per-illocution (evoking a response by an illocution).

In the structure of our concrete speech acts, the basic aspect (locution) forms the basis for the conventional aspect (illocution) and the latter, in turn, the basis for the causal aspect (per-illocution). This order, which is characteristic of speech acts, does not apply to all our actions. In scoring a goal we find a different order: kicking the ball (basic aspect) forms the basis for putting the ball into the net (causal aspect) which, under the rules of football, is recognised as scoring a goal (conventional aspect).

Briefly: speaking is a form of purposive or intentional action. Like every intentional act, a concrete speech act is analysable into its various elements: a locution in which a number of illocutions are performed, by which, in turn, various per-illocutions are performed. These different aspects of a concrete speech act never occur on their own. They are *abstractions* that we make when analysing a speech act. In our concrete speech they occur only as elements of our concrete speech acts. Yet it may be illuminating to analyse a speech act in all its elements, because by this means we can examine precisely what kind of speech act it is that someone is performing, and what it means.

A concrete human act is complex, comprising a number of distinguishable elements. An act may succeed or fail in any of these elements. Thus a footballer may (on occasion) fail to kick the ball squarely. Or he may succeed in kicking the ball, but not in putting it into the net. He may also succeed in putting the ball into the net, yet fail to score a goal (he was out of play or the ball was out of play). A concrete speech act may also fail in various respects: either the locution, or one of the illocutions or per-illocutions may be flawed.

A speech act fails in its *per-illocutionary* aspect if the speaker does not succeed in bringing about the intended response in his hearer. For example if the hearer does not believe what the speaker alleges, or does not do what the speaker asks of him, or does not rely on what the speaker promises, etc.

*Locutions* are subject to the rules of grammar, and thus to the language in which they are expressed. Thus we have French, German, English, Dutch, etc., locutions. A locution may therefore be judged in terms of these grammatical rules and fails as a locution if it does not comply with these rules.

*Illocutions* are subject to the rules of the 'language game' (that is, the 'game' of human communication by means of language) and not to the rules of grammar (except indirectly, in the sense that they are performed in a locution, which is subject to grammar). We can therefore utter French, English, etc., *sentences,* but we do not thereby perform French, English, etc., requests, orders, assertions. 'Please open the door' and 'Ouvrez la porte, s'il vous plaît' are two *different locutions* in two different languages, formed according to the rules of two different grammatical systems. Nevertheless, I can use them to perform *the same set of illocutions,* that is, a *request* to open the door. In translating from one language into another, we *substitute* a locution in one language for a locution in another (a different language), by means of which we can perform *the same* illocutions. A translation succeeds if we replace a locution in one language by a locution in another language without altering the *illocutionary load* of the speech act that we perform when uttering either of these two locutions.

*Illocutions* succeed or fail only in terms of the rules of the *language game.* This language game is the *social activity* in which people participate when they communicate with each other in questions and answers, predictions and assertions, commands and promises, blessings and curses, judgements and accusations, and so on. All these *kinds of speech acts* differ from each other in their *illocutionary load,* that is, in the specific set of illocutions performed in each speech act. Thus a *statement,* for instance, contains a constative element (a fact is asserted) and an expressive element (the speaker expresses his belief). A *promise* contains *inter alia* an element of commitment (the speaker commits himself to doing something in future) and an expressive element (the speaker expresses his intention). The rules of the language game are *social* and not grammatical rules: they are constitutive rules for the illocutions we perform in our social intercourse by means of speech acts. These rules always have the form: 'the utterance of locution $x$ counts as the performance of illocution $y$ if it is performed under factual circumstances $z$'. For example the utterance of the locution 'Please open the door' counts as a *prescriptive* to open the door, provided that there is a door, that the door is not open already, that the hearer is capable of opening the door, and so on. The conditions for the successful performance of an illocution differ in respect of each kind of illocution. Different kinds of illocutions are constituted by different

Wingate College Library

rules and may therefore fail in different ways.

Let us illustrate the failure of the illocutions in a speech act with reference to the following examples:

(1) There is a tree outside my window.

(2) I promised you my support.

(3) I promise you my support.

(4) I accept responsibility for this.

(5) I take thee to my wedded wife.

(6) I (Elizabeth) appoint you Governor-General of Australia.

(7) I name this ship 'Britannia'.

(8) You must stop smoking within ten days.

(9) I baptise thee in the name of Jesus Christ.

(10) Thank you very much.

(11) I divorce thee.

(12) We praise Thee, O Lord.

(13) Please open the door.

(1) and (2) may fail because they are untrue: there is no tree outside my window and I did not promise you my support.

(3) and (4) may fail because I am not in a position to give support or carry out responsibility.

(5) may fail because I am already married — in which case I am not taking a wife but am simply participating in a ceremony that purports to be a marriage ceremony.

(6), (7), (8) and (9) may fail because I am not authorised to appoint, to name, to order or to baptise (for instance, I am not the Queen or the priest).

(9) may also fail because I am not following the correct procedure (for instance, I am not using the Trinitarian formula).

(11) may fail because I do not live in an Islamic society.

(13) may fail because the door is open already or because there is no door at all, or because the door is inaccessible to my hearer.

In all these instances there is something lacking in the *factual circumstances* in which the speech act is made. These circumstances are not as required by the constitutive rules for the illocutions one seeks to perform in the speech acts in question. The essential factual conditions for the success of an illocution must be met, otherwise it fails.

There are two kinds of illocution that can fail in a further way:

(*a*) Speech acts often contain an *expressive* element; that is, the speaker expresses a certain attitude, intention or belief. He may, however, *abuse* the illocutionary procedure for expressives by pretending to have an attitude, intention or belief when this is not so. In such cases we speak of *abuse* because the speaker has the aim of *misleading* his hearer. He may, for instance, make a promise with no intention of fulfilling it, or praise someone he despises, or thank someone without feeling grateful, or chant 'We praise Thee, O Lord' in church while thinking about last night's party, or allege that there is a tree outside the window and be lying because he knows or firmly believes that there is no tree there. In this way expressives may be *insincere* if the speaker pretends to express attitudes or intentions or beliefs that he does not have at all.

(*b*) Speech acts often contain an *element of commitment*, that is, the speaker commits himself to doing something in future. Such commitments may later be *violated* because the speaker does not meet them.

In sum: a concrete speech act is complex and may therefore fail in various ways. It fails in a *locutionary* respect in terms of grammatical rules, in a *per-illocutionary* respect if the hearer does not respond as the speaker intended him to do, and in an *illocutionary* respect if the speech act is not performed in accordance with the rules of the communicative language game. These rules stipulate what the factual circumstances should be if the illocutions contained in a speech act are to succeed. In addition, expressives may be abused by insincerity, and commitments may be violated.

## 2.5 ILLOCUTIONS

Austin provides a preliminary classification of illocutions into five classes, remarking that he is not fully satisfied with this division and regards it as no more than a first attempt, open to amendment and improvement. His classification is briefly as follows:

(1) *Verdictives*: (evaluative) judgements in which someone (or something) is declared to be good or bad, guilty or innocent, correct or incorrect, etc. The typical example that Austin has in mind is the verdict of a jury.

(2) *Exercitives*: exercises of authority, rights, power, etc. Austin gives the examples of appointments, nominations, commands,

instructions, warnings.

(3)  *Commissives*: utterances in which the speaker commits himself to a future act. Here Austin has in mind promises and expressions of intention.

(4)  *Behabitives*: a somewhat vague group concerned with the expression of attitudes and with social behaviour. Here Austin has in mind certain social customs such as thanking, congratulating, condoling, challenging, cursing, etc.

(5)  *Expositives*: another vague group, concerned with the exposition of points of view, opinions, etc.

From Austin's examples we may conclude that his 'expositives' coincide to a large extent with what elsewhere in his book he calls 'constatives', namely factual assertions or statements.

It is clear that Austin's classification can be improved and refined. In what follows we will distinguish between four kinds of illocution:

*Constatives*: more or less Austin's 'expositives' or 'constatives'.
*Expressives*: a class that includes Austin's 'behabitives'.
*Commissives*: Austin's 'commissives'.
*Prescriptives*: a class that includes Austin's 'exercitives'.

Austin's 'verdictives' are evaluative judgements. In Part Two we shall argue that evaluative judgements should be construed as speech acts with a *complex* illocutionary load, and not as a fifth kind of illocution. The other four kinds of illocution are probably fundamental in the sense that the illocutionary load of all our speech acts are analysable into these four illocutionary elements.

Before we take a closer look at these four kinds of illocution it may be worthwhile pointing out once again the distinction between *illocutions* and *speech acts*. As we use the term here, a *speech act* is a concrete utterance in which various illocutions and per-illocutions are performed on the basis of a locution. An *illocution* is an element in a speech act, that is, one part of the illocutionary load (set of illocutions) performed in the speech act. Various kinds of speech acts (for example, descriptions, promises, exclamations, commands) differ in their illocutionary load, that is, in the specific set of illocutions performed in each kind of speech act. As a rule each kind of speech act has in its illocutionary load one kind of illocution that is formally characteristic of this kind of speech act. Descriptive statements, for instance, are characterised by their constative function, commands by their prescriptive function, and promises by their commissive function. But the illocutionary load of a descriptive statement contains more than merely a constative, that of a command more than a prescriptive, and that of a promise more than a commissive. It is therefore essential that a distinction be drawn between a classification of kinds of speech acts and a classification of kinds of illocution. One of the main sources of confusion in Austin's classification is that he does not draw this distinction.

Let us take a closer look at the four (fundamental) kinds of illocution.

## 1. Constatives

We perform a *constative* in a speech act when we assert in it that a certain state of affairs exists in reality. It is therefore characteristic of all descriptive statements that they have a constative function. For instance, the illocutionary load of the following utterances is characterised by a constative function:

(1) Nelson's column stands in Trafalgar Square.
(2) Nelson's column does not stand outside Westminster Abbey.
(3) We have 112 first-year students.
(4) If water is heated to 100°C it will boil.
(5) All men are mortal.
(6) Some students come from Scotland.
(7) It will rain tomorrow.
(8) It rained yesterday.
(9) God exists.
(10) The Lord is risen indeed.
(11) His conduct is not in accordance with the norms generally accepted in our society.
(12) In current English usage, the verb 'state' means the same as the word 'assert'.

Constatives differ from all other illocutions in that they may be judged to be *true* or *false*: if in reality a state of affairs is not as asserted in the constative, the constative is false. If it is indeed as asserted, the constative is true. This provides us with a test for constatives: if it makes sense to say of a speech act that it is true or false, the constative function is formally characteristic for the illocutionary load of that speech act. Descriptive statements are therefore true or false; promises, commands, expressions of feeling, etc., are not.

In philosophy constatives are also called *propositions*. In logic $p$ is often a symbol for a proposition. It is therefore of propositions (or constatives) that we may say, '$p$ is true', or '$p$ is false'. Propositions form the content of our knowledge and our beliefs – for this reason we may also say of a proposition (or constative): 'I know that $p$' or 'I believe that $p$'. We may also ask with reference to propositions (or constatives): 'How do you know that $p$?' or 'On what grounds do you assert that $p$?' or 'Why do you believe that $p$?'. In this respect, too, constatives differ from all other illocutions.

It thus becomes clear that an examination of the nature of *constatives* is fundamental to the theory of knowledge. In Part Three we shall deal with constatives in detail.

## 2. *Expressives*

The following utterances all contain an expressive element in their illocutionary load:

(1)   'I know that my redeemer liveth' (Job 19:25) – (expression of *belief* or *conviction*).

(2)   'Father, to Thee we look in all our sorrow' (Hymn 538) – (expression of *trust*).

(3)   'How amiable are Thy tabernacles, O Lord of hosts!' (Ps. 84:1) (expression of *praise*).

(4)   'O give thanks unto the Lord; for He is good: for His mercy endureth for ever' (Ps. 106:1) – (expression of *gratitude*).

(5)   'I stretch forth my hands unto Thee: My sol thirsteth after Thee as a thirsty land' (Ps. 143:6) – (expression of *longing*).

(6)   ' O foolish men, and slow of heart to believe all that the prophets have spoken' (Luke 24:25) – (expression of *dissatisfaction* and *disappointment*).

(7)   'The Lord is risen indeed, and hath appeared to Simon' (Luke 24:34) – (expression of *joy* and *wonder*).

(8)   'As for me and my house, we will serve the Lord' (Joshua 24:15) – (expression of *intention*).

The first example contains an expression of *conviction* or *belief*, examples (2) to (7) contain various expressions of *attitude* and example (8) contains an expression of *intention*.

Expressives are always in the first person present tense. In other words: I can always assert or *report* of others (or of myself in the past) that they have certain beliefs, attitudes, or intentions (or that I had these), but I cannot express these beliefs, attitudes or intentions. I can express only my own beliefs, attitudes, and intentions at the moment of speaking. (I could of course express the beliefs, etc., of someone else or of a group *on behalf of them*, but only if he/they accept that what I am saying is an expression of his/their beliefs etc. In this sense such expressives 'in the name of someone else' are also in the first person present tense.)

Expressives are not *autobiographical constatives*. To put it differently, an expression of belief, attitude or intention is not a *statement* about myself to the effect that I now have this belief, attitude or intention. Constative speech acts, such as making statements about something or describing it or commenting on it, are possible only when we have an objectifying detachment from whatever we describe or comment upon or make statements about. For this reason I can describe or comment on the beliefs, attitudes or intentions of others (or myself in the past). I am, however, not detached in the required sense from my own beliefs, attitudes or intentions at the moment of speaking, and without such detachment I cannot treat them as objects which I can describe or comment upon. I can now express (reveal) them or perhaps conceal them, but I cannot describe them, etc. My autobiographical statements, comments or descriptions are thus concerned with my (even if most recent) past, never only with my present at the moment of speaking.

Whereas (autobiographical) constatives are characterised by the fact that they are true or false, expressives are characterised by their being sincere or insincere, not true or false. The statements 'He intends going to Paris' and 'I intended going to Paris' are both true or false. In respect of either we could ask 'How do you know?' (answer: 'He told me' and 'I remember it very well'). My assertion 'I intend going to Paris', however, is neither true nor false, although it may be sincere or insincere: I could be *pretending* that I intend going to Paris. Your statement about me 'He intends going to Paris' is true or false, because you are *stating* (truly or falsely) that I have an intention; you are not *expressing* my intention.

In contrast to (autobiographical) constatives, my expression of intention cannot be met with the question 'How do you know that you intend doing that?' or 'Have you valid grounds for saying that you intend going to Paris?' This applies to other types of expressives as well. Gilbert Ryle[2] explains this with reference to an expression *of boredom or depression*.

> If a person says 'I feel bored', or 'I feel depressed', we do not ask him for his evidence, or request him to make sure. We may accuse him of shamming to us or to himself, but we do not accuse him, of having been careless in his observations or rash in his inferences, since we do not think that his avowal was a report of observations or conclusions. He has not been a good or a bad detective; he has not been a detective at all . . . . That is why, if we are suspicious, we do not ask 'fact or fiction?', 'true or false?', 'reliable or unreliable?', but 'sincere or shammed?' The conversational avowal of moods requires not acumen, but openness. It comes from the heart, not from the head. It is not discovery, but voluntary non-concealment.

A concrete speech act is never *purely* expressive. An expressive function is never more than one element in the illocutionary load of a speech act. The expressive element is often a subordinate element in this illocutionary load. The characteristic illocutionary purpose of a speech act is often not to express my belief, etc., but to do something else, for example, to state a fact, to ask for information, to make a promise, or something of this kind. But *in* doing these things, I also express my belief, attitude, or intention. Of this, too, Ryle[3] gives a neat example.

> If the lorry-driver asks urgently, 'Which is the road to London?' he discloses his anxiety to find out, but he does not make an autobiographical or psychological pronouncement about it. He says what he says not from a desire to inform us or himself about himself, but from a desire to get on to the right road to London.

Some illocutions (other than expressives) are by implication always linked with some or other particular expressive. For example, a *constative* (in which a fact is stated) is always coupled with an expression of belief. A *concrete statement* therefore always contains a constative element (something is stated as a fact) and an expressive element (a factual belief is expressed with a greater or lesser degree of certainty). For this reason, a *concrete statement* can always be both true or false (on account of the constative element) and sincere or insincere (on account of the expressive element). Statements can be both erroneous (false) and lies (insincere). The possibility of judging a speech act as true or false is a criterion for determining whether this speech act contains a *constative* element. The possibility of judging a speech act as sincere or insincere is a criterion for determining whether it contains an *expressive* element.

Expressives are sometimes reduced to mere social formalities, remaining expressive in *form* but without in fact expressing beliefs, attitudes or intentions. This is often the case with apologising, congratulating, thanking, condoling, greeting, and so on.

Saying 'Thank you' is formally an expression of gratitude. However, when I teach a child to say 'Thank you' when he receives something, he (unfortunately!) does not thereby learn to express gratitude (let alone to be grateful!) What he does learn is a social form which he is expected to practise in polite society. I think that Austin had these social forms in mind when he coined the term 'behabitives' for speech acts which 'have to do with attitudes and *social behaviour*.' [4]

We have seen that illocutions are constituted by rules with the form: 'under factual circumstances $z$ a specific locution $x$ counts as the performance of illocution $y$'. Hence, when I perform illocution $y$ I *presuppose* that factual circumstances $z$ exist. In this sense all non-constative illocutions presuppose *facts*. (Constatives *state* facts rather than presupposing them). It is important to know which factual presuppositions are constitutive for each type of illocution. This gives us a criterion for distinguishing various types of illocutions and for determining their success conditions.

In the case of expressive illocutions, the factual presuppositions vary depending on what is expressed. An *expression of belief* presupposes the state of affairs which the speaker believes to be the case. An *expression of intention* presupposes that the speaker is free and able to carry out his intention. An *expression of attitude* presupposes that the intentional object of the expressed attitude exists and has those characteristics which make it worthy of the expressed attitude. If, for example, I express my admiration for Peter, I presuppose that Peter exists and that he has characteristics which make him admirable (and not detestable or pitiable).

## 3. Commissives

In a *commissive* a speaker commits himself, before his hearer(s), to some specific future act(s). In this sense the illocutionary load of the following speech acts contain a commissive element:

(1)    'Tenderer confirms that he will furnish the engineer, the final

arrangement drawings, with all details required for civil design not later than thirty (30) days from the date of the letter of intent.'

(2)    'I Peter take thee Joan to my wedded wife, to have and to hold from this day forward, for better for worse, for richer for poorer, in sickness and in health, to love and to cherish, till death us do part, according to God's holy ordinance; and thereto I plight thee my troth.'

(3)    'I promise to return your book tomorrow.'

(4)    'I intend returning your book tomorrow.'

(5)    'I detest all this pollution of the environment.'

In (1) I commit myself *contractually* to a certain mode of behaviour and accept legal responsibility for following this line of behaviour. In (2) I take a *vow* before God that I will live with Joan in a certain manner and will remain true to her. In (3) I *promise* to do something. In (4) I express my *intention* of doing something, and in (5) I *imply* that I myself will not pollute the environment.

In all these speech acts I commit myself (explicitly or by implication) to do or not to do certain things and I declare myself answerable to my hearers for fulfilling this commitment.

It is characteristic of commissives that they may fail through violation. This provides us with a test for commissives: if it makes sense to say of a speech act that it can be violated, then its illocutionary load contains a commissive element.

In a commissive a speaker accepts an *obligation* towards his hearer(s). This obligation may be more or less binding: in concluding contracts and taking vows a speaker accepts a very strong obligation (in the case of contracts he is even subjecting himself to legal sanctions). In the case of ordinary promises the obligation is less strong, and when it comes to expressions (and implications) of intention there are all sorts of possibilities for violating the commitment without incurring sanctions.

Like constatives, commissives are coupled with an expressive element: in committing myself to doing or not doing something and declaring myself answerable to my hearer(s) for fulfilling this commitment, I am at the same time expressing my *intention* of fulfilling my commitment (expressive). Concrete promises, etc., may therefore fail through *violation* (because they contain a commissive) and through *insincerity* (because they contain an expressive element).

It is part of the factual *presuppositions* of a commissive that one is capable of fulfilling it. It is absurd to promise the impossible – for instance to promise that I will jump over Nelson's column. Secondly, a commitment presupposes the possibility of violation. It must be something I am capable of not doing, otherwise there would be no sense in promising that I will do it. It is therefore equally senseless to promise that I will *not* jump over Nelson's column! (Since similar factual presuppositions apply to prescriptives as well, we shall say more about them in that connection.)

## 4. Prescriptives

In commissives I accept an obligation before my hearer(s). In *prescriptives* I lay upon my hearer(s) or potential hearer(s) the obligation to adopt a certain attitude or follow a certain line of action.

The illocutionary load of the following speech acts contains a prescriptive element:

(1)   'Present arms!'
(2)   'Stand at ease!'
(3)   'I order you to stop smoking immediately' (said by a doctor to a patient).
(4)   'I advise you to stop smoking immediately' (said by a doctor to a patient).
(5)   'Please don't smoke so much!' (said by a wife to her husband).
(6)   'Will you help me?'
(7)   'O Lord, have mercy upon us miserable offenders.'
(8)   'I detest all this pollution of the environment!'
(9)   'I, Elizabeth, appoint the honourable James Murray to be my Ambassador Plenipotentiary at the court of the Prince of Monaco.''
(10)  'I find this man guilty and sentence him to six months' imprisonment.'

In the case of *commissives* the obligation accepted by the speaker may be more or less binding. In *prescriptives* the obligation laid by the speaker upon his hearer(s) may also be more or less binding. Consider examples (1) to (7) above: the commands (1) and (2) are more binding than the command (3). Advice (4) is less binding and pleas (5) or requests (6) still less so. Supplications (7) are the least binding of all prescriptives.

The obligatory nature of a prescriptive is often dependent upon the speaker's authority over his hearer(s) (the greater his authority, the more obligatory the prescriptive). Compare the authority of a military commander over his troops with that of a doctor over his patient, a wife over her husband, someone over his friend, etc. Austin was especially concerned with this aspect in his classification, hence his term 'exercitives' (= exercises of authority). Since this element of authority varies considerably from one prescriptive to another it is perhaps better to speak of 'prescriptives' rather than 'exercitives'.

All prescriptives may be formulated as 'ought' utterances (you ought to do *x*), although this 'ought' is not always equally obligatory. The 'ought' often applies only to the hearer – examples (1) to (7). Often, however, the 'ought' has a more general application: example (8) *implies* a general 'ought': 'Everyone ought to stop polluting the environment'. In example (9) *authority* (to represent the Queen and her government) is vested in someone. In other words, everybody (and in partiular the government of Monaco) *ought* to recognise in their dealings with Mr Murray that he bears the authority vested in him.

Prescriptives have the following factual presuppositions:

(1) Commanding/advising/requesting, etc., someone to do something makes sense only if he is capable of doing it. *Ought* presupposes *can*.

(2) Commanding, etc., someone to do something makes sense only if he is capable of not obeying this command, etc. In other words, *ought* presupposes *'can refrain from'*.

Prescriptives make sense only if they are concerned with what R. M. Hare[5] calls 'practical questions'. Hare illustrated this point with the following example:

> Suppose . . . that I am in a boat sailing in the English Channel, and that it is fair weather. I can then ask 'Shall I land in France?', and this can be a practical question; somebody can say, by way of advice, 'Yes, land in France; we can get a good meal in Dieppe'. But suppose, on the other hand, that I am being driven on the French shore by a gale and that it is obvious that whether I shall land in France is out of my control; then, if I ask 'Shall I land in France?' this cannot be understood as a practical question, but only as a request for a prediction, equivalent to 'Am I as a matter of fact going to land in France?

In such a gale there is no sense asking or commanding the helmsman to land in France (he is incapable of not doing it). Nor is there any sense commanding him *not* to land in France (he is incapable of carrying out this command). Prescriptives (like commissives) presuppose therefore, that the context within which they are uttered is that of a 'practical question'. A *commissive* presupposes that the *speaker* is capable of doing and refraining from doing that to which he commits himself. A *prescriptive* presupposes that the *hearer* is capable of doing and refraining from doing what the speaker requires of him.

Since prescriptives always presuppose that the hearer is *free* in the sense of able to do or to refrain from doing what is prescribed, such prescriptives differ from coercion. A prescriptive places an *obligation* on the hearer but does not force him to fulfil this obligation. In chapter 8 we shall return to this point.

Not all prescriptives presuppose that the speaker has authority over the person(s) to whom he addresses his prescriptive (see examples (4) to (7)). Nonetheless, the speaker always assumes that there is an (often unspoken) 'agreement' between him and his hearer and that he is entitled, by virtue of this 'agreement', to address the prescriptive to his hearer. By virtue of this 'agreement' the hearer is obliged to do what the speaker demands/asks/requests/begs of him. The speaker could appeal to this 'agreement' to justify the prescriptive. The hearer could reject the prescriptive by rejecting or questioning the 'agreement'. In chapter 8 we shall deal in detail with the nature and function of such 'agreements'. We are using the term 'agreement' for a variety of conventional relations by which the hearer is obliged to the speaker. Thus the speaker could base his prescriptive on a *promise* the hearer has made him, on what the speaker *deserves* from the hearer, on the speaker's *authority* over the hearer, etc. He could also appeal to a *norm*. Norms will be dealt with in detail in chapter 8, but here it will suffice to say that the existence of an 'agreement' or conventional relation, by which the hearer is obliged to the speaker, is a third factual presupposition of all prescriptives.

Like constatives and commissives, prescriptives are usually accompanied by an expressive. In a concrete request I oblige my hearer to do something (prescriptive) *and* express the wish that he should do it (expressive). My *concrete request* may therefore fail because the factual presuppositions of its prescriptive element are not in order. Because of the expressive element in its illocutionary load, however, it could also be insincere.

## 2.6 THE STRUCTURE OF A SPEECH ACT

Speech acts are complex. Each speech act contains a number of different elements. In one and the same speech act one illocution may be performed directly and a number of other illocutions performed by implication. A speech act may also be accompanied by a number of parenthetic additions, which serve various purposes. Let us take a closer look at this structure.

### 1. Asserting

We will use the term 'assertion' to refer to the performance of an illocution. Thus in performing a speech act (or saying something) we *assert* a number of illocutions either directly or by implication. We will apply the term assertion to the performance of every kind of illocution and not only to factual *statements* in which constatives are asserted.

In saying something, that is, in asserting an illocution or set of illocutions, we have to take account of the rules that govern *every* assertion as such. These rules, which *determine what counts as asserting*, are the fundamental *principles of traditional logic*, namely the Law of Identity (*principium identitatis*), the Law of Non-contradiction (*principium contradictionis*) and the Law of the Excluded Middle (*principium tertii exclusi*).

(*a*) *The Law of Identity* says that if I have asserted an illocution, it is asserted. For example if I have made a commitment, a commitment has been made; if I have issued a prescriptive, a prescriptive has been issued.

(*b*) *The Law of Non-contradiction* lays down that I cannot simultaneously assert and deny an illocution (or a set of illocutions). For example I cannot simultaneously make and retract a promise. 'I promise you a biscuit but you are not getting it' is not a promise. 'I command you to polish your shoes but I forbid you to polish them' is not a command.

(*c*) *The Law of the Excluded Middle* lays down that I can either assert or deny an illocution (or a set of illocutions), but that there is no third possibility. For example, I can either make a promise or retract it, but nothing in between. I can only assert or deny something, but not something in between.

These three rules apply to *everything* we say, regardless of *what* we say. This, then, is what we call 'saying'. If I break one of these rules I do not succeed in saying something. If, for instance, I say, 'Nelson's column is in Trafalgar Square but it is not in Trafalgar Square', I do utter a number of words, but they do not assert anything. I do not succeed in making an assertion at all. I succeed, at the most, in confusing my hearer!

There are some who deny that the principles of logic always apply. Some theologians, for instance, hold that these principles apply only to assertions about the created universe and that assertions about God transcend our 'human' logic. But this is an untenable position. When talking about God we purport to *say* something, and since the principles of logic are rules that determine what 'saying' is, we cannot *say* anything (even about God) without taking account of these rules. We do not say 'profound things' by means of contradictions; on the contrary we do not succeed in saying anything at all. It is true that *paradoxes* often occur in theology, but a paradox is an *apparent* contradiction. For example, 'From him that hath not, shall be taken away even that which he hath', 'Whosoever will save his life shall lose it: and whosoever will lose his life for my sake shall find it', 'Blessed are they that mourn'. Paradoxical utterances may be very valuable, for instance to set people thinking (as one does with riddles, too), or to ensure that one does not see only one side of a matter without doing justice to the other side as well. But if one asserts a paradox, one is obliged to make it clear that the paradox does *say* something, that it merely contains a *seeming* contradiction, and that the two apparently contradictory aspects of what is said are to be understood in such a way that they do not deny each other.

## 2. Implying

We have distinguished between the following four kinds of illocutions: (1) *Constatives*, in which it is stated of a factual state of affairs that it exists. Constatives may be true or false. (2) *Expressives*, in which the speaker expresses his belief, intention, or attitude. Expressives may be sincere or insincere. (3) *Commissives*, in which the speaker commits himself before his hearer(s) to a certain attitude or line of action in future. Commissives may or may not be violated. (4) *Prescriptives*, in which the speaker, by virtue of an explicit or implicit 'agreement' between him and his hearer, obliges the latter to adopt a certain attitude or perform certain actions in future.

We have seen that a concrete speech act has an illocutionary load in which several logically interrelated illocutions can be distinguished.

One of the illocutions is dominant in the sense that it characterises the *form* of the speech act. In this way factual statements are characterised by a constative, promises by a commissive, commands and requests by a prescriptive, and so on. It may be useful to classify concrete speech acts according to the illocution which is characteristic for the form of the speech act. Thus, statements of fact, descriptions, factual hypotheses, predictions, etc., could all be classified as *constative speech acts*; thanks, condolences, applause, congratulations, etc., could all be classified as *expressive speech acts*; promises, oaths, contracts, etc., could all be classified as *commissive speech acts*; orders, entreaties, requests, questions, commands, supplications, etc., could all be classified as *prescriptive speech acts*.

The illocution characteristic for the form of a speech act, is explicitly asserted, while a number of other illocutions are *implied* in some way or other by the explicitly asserted illocution. When I assert an illocution explicitly in an utterance I, therefore, by *implication* also assert a number of other illocutions that are related to but nonetheless distinguishable from the explicitly asserted illocution. Thus the assertion of a commissive implies the assertion of an expressive (namely an expression of the intention to fulfil the commitment made by the commissive). The assertion of a constative also implies the assertion of an expressive (namely an expression of belief regarding the state of affairs asserted in the constative).

The illocutions in a speech act may imply each other in two ways: either *undeniably* or *contextually*.

*Undeniable implication.* Sometimes the implied illocution is so closely bound up with the asserted illocution that we cannot retract or deny it without at the same time causing the asserted illocution to fail. For example: 'It is a fact that Nelson's column is in Trafalgar Square' (constative) implies: 'I am convinced that Nelson's column is in Trafalgar Square' (expressive). The implication of this expressive is undeniable, because its denial would at the same time mean the denial of the constative. I cannot succeed in asserting my constative if I say: 'It is a fact that Nelson's column is in Trafalgar Square, but I am not convinced that Nelson's column is in Trafalgar Square,' The prescriptive, 'I commend James to you', undeniably implies the expressive, 'I have a positive attitude towards James.' 'I beg you, let me go' (prescriptive) undeniably implies 'I wish you would let me go' (expressive, namely an expression of desire). 'I intend going tomorrow' (expressive of intention) undeniably implies, 'I commit myself to going tomorrow' (commissive).

An important example of undeniable implication is the following. We have seen that every illocution presupposes factual states of affairs by virtue of the rule constituting it. This means that the assertion of the illocution always implies the assertion of a constative in which the relevant facts are stated. 'Please open the door' implies 'There is a door'. This implication is undeniable. I cannot perform a prescriptive by saying, 'Please open the door – but there is no door'! The prescriptive undeniably implies the constative. The reverse does not apply, however: the constative, 'There is a door' does not undeniably imply the prescriptive, 'Please open the door.'

*Contextual implication.* An implication is often dependent upon the context in which a speech act is performed. In such a case the implied illocution does not arise from the asserted illocution alone, but from the asserted illocution in conjunction with the context in which the speech act is performed. The implied illocution may then be denied without denying the directly asserted illocution, provided one puts the context in parentheses or denies that one presupposes that context. For example the constative, 'James is honest and sincere' implies the expressive, 'I am favourably disposed (I have a pro-attitude) towards James'. This implication is, however, *contextual*, because it is valid only within a moral context in which honesty and sincerity are valued positively. If one denied that one presupposed this morality, one could deny the expressive without at the same time denying the constative: 'James is honest and sincere, and (speaking as a gang leader or as an organiser of counter-espionage) I therefore consider him useless for our organisation'. In a moral context in which an obligation must always be fulfilled the constative, 'I ought to go tomorrow', implies the commissive, 'I promise you that I will go tomorrow'. By suspending this moral context one might say, 'I ought to go tomorrow, but I am not going to'. The expressive '(sigh) who will rid me of this turbulent priest!' that King Henry II voiced in the presence of his courtiers implied a prescriptive within the context of the English court of the twelfth century. To Henry's horror Becket was murdered by his courtiers because Henry had not thought of denying the implied prescriptive. One final example. 'Nelson's column is in Trafalgar Square' implies (to us) no prescriptive. But let us imagine a Celtic tribe to whom Trafalgar Square is a holy place. In such a context the constative, 'Nelson's column is in Trafalgar Square' would in fact imply a prescriptive: 'Nelson, as a "denizen of Trafalgar Square",

ought to be treated with due reverence'. In section 9.25 we shall deal
with this last example in detail.

Briefly: there is an *implicative* relation between the various illocutions
in the illocutionary load of a speech act. These illocutions may imply
each other either *undeniably* or *contextually*. In the case of an undeniable
implication the implied illocution follows from the asserted illocution
alone. Denial of the implied illocution is therefore impossible without a
simultaneous denial of the asserted illocution. In a contextual
implication the implied illocution follows from the asserted illocution
in conjunction with the presupposed context. It is therefore possible to
deny the implied illocution by putting the presupposed context in
parenthesis and still to maintain the asserted illocution.

Various kinds of contexts may be presupposed here. One may speak
within the context of a conventional relationship (a husband speaking to
his wife, a king to his courtier), or within the context of a certain moral
system (middle-class morality or gangster morality), or within the
context of an ideology (for example, Marxism), or of a view of life (for
example Biblical faith), or within the context of a normative
'agreement'.

Apart from this implicative relation between the various illocutions in
a speech act we also have to take account of the relations between the
illocutions and the per-illocutions. Since the per-illocutions are
performed through the illocutions, there are certain per-illocutions that
are always performed through certain illocutions. *Constatives* and
*expressions of belief* are always aimed at convincing the hearer of the
truth of the asserted constative or the expressed belief. It would be
absurd to say 'It is a fact that $p$ (or I believe that $p$), but I do not want
you to believe that $p$.' *Commissives* and *expressions of intention* are
always aimed at making the hearer trust that the speaker will fulfil his
intention or commitment. *Expressions of attitude* are often aimed at
evoking the same attitude in the hearer. It would be absurd to say
'James is a splendid fellow, but I do not want you to find him a splendid
fellow too'. *Prescriptives* are aimed at getting the hearer to do what he is
commanded/asked/begged to do. In addition, it is true of every speech
act that the speaker wishes the hearer to understand what is said. This
per-illocutionary aim is the basis of all human communication.

## 3. Parentheses

Our concrete speech acts are often ambiguous because it is not always
quite clear what illocutions are asserted or implied. In such cases it is

necessary to give the hearer extra instructions along with the speech act. Such 'instructions' are not part of the speech act. They are, so to speak, added parenthetically to the speech act to tell the hearer how he should construe the speech act.

(1) It is often not clear what context the speaker presupposes in his speech act. It is then also not clear what contextual implications the speech act contains. In such cases it is necessary to say explicitly in what context the utterance is made.

(2) It is sometimes not clear whether the speaker is suspending a certain context and is therefore also denying a certain number of contextual implications (as in the example of Henry II and Thomas à Becket).

(3) It is sometimes not clear what illocution is explicitly asserted in a speech act, and it is therefore not clear what kind of speech act is being made. Is the utterance, 'I shall deal harshly with him' a prediction, a threat, an expression of intention, a promise, or a warning? In such cases it is necessary to explain parenthetically what the utterance is meant to be. One could say, for instance, 'I foresee that I shall deal harshly with him' or 'I'm warning you, I shall deal harshly with him', and so on.

(4) With *constatives* (and expressions of belief) we may indicate parenthetically with what *degree of certainty* the fact is being stated (or the belief held). For example: 'I think that $p$' or 'I know that $p$' or 'I suspect that $p$', and so on.

(5) With *commissives* a parenthetic indication can be given of how firmly the speaker is committing himself: is the utterance a promise, an expression of intention, a covenant, an oath?

(6) With a *prescriptive* a parenthetic addition may indicate whether it is a command, a request, advice, a supplication, etc. There may also be a parenthetic indication of the kind of 'agreement' to which the speaker is appealing for his right to assert this kind of prescriptive.

(7) Such parenthetic remarks often function as indications of the function a speech act fulfils in the context of a whole argument, for example: 'I conclude that ...', 'to start with ...', 'I notice that ...', 'I deny that ...', 'I accept that ...', 'I concede that ...', 'I put it to you that ...', etc.

Once again such parenthetic words or expressions are *not part of* the speech act they accompany. They are asides or remarks *on* a speech act and make it clearer to the reader how he should construe the speech act.

## 4. An example

In conclusion we could illustrate all these different aspects of the structure of a speech act by means of an example. Let us take the first article of the Apostles' Creed: 'I believe in God the Father Almighty, Maker of heaven and earth.'

(1) The *explicitly asserted illocution* in this speech act is an expression of faith or trust ('believe in ...'). If the words had been 'I believe that $(p)$', it would have been an expression of belief, namely belief that $p$ is true. As it is, however, this speech act is not an expression of belief that some statement is true, but of faith in someone.

(2) The *factual presuppositions* constitutive of expressions of faith are, first, that whoever one trusts exists in reality (it would be absurd to say that one has faith in someone and then to add that the person in whom one has faith does not exist); second, that the person in whom one has faith has characteristics that would make him trustworthy. It is therefore always relevant to ask with regard to an expression of faith: (*a*) In whom do you vest your faith? and (*b*) What characteristics has this person, to make him trustworthy? In the first article of the Apostles' Creed these two questions are answered parenthetically with the expression of faith: (*a*) God, Maker of heaven and earth, is the object of the faith expressed here, and (*b*) He is worthy of faith because He is *almighty* and is therefore able to do that for which one trusts Him, and because He is a *Father* and therefore also *wishes* to do that for which His children trust Him.

(3) Since these factual presuppositions are constitutive of the expression of faith, this expressive undeniably implies the *constative* in which these presuppositions are stated as facts: 'I have faith in $x$' implies undeniably that $x$ exists and that $x$ has characteristics which make him trustworthy. This constative, in turn, implies undeniably the *expressive of belief* that this constative is true. For these reasons it is absurd to say that religious faith is merely an attitude of trust and not a belief that specific factual statements are true.

(4) An expression of faith in someone never undeniably implies the *commissive* that one will persist in such faith in future. If I trust that James will keep his appointment with me in five minutes' time this does not imply undeniably that I shall trust him in other matters too, or that I shall trust him in different situations in future! Whether the speaker commits himself to enduring faith in future and in other situations, is therefore dependent upon the context, the nature and the content of such faith. An expression of faith could therefore *contextually* imply a

commitment to enduring faith. The first article of the Apostles' Creed does not indicate this context parenthetically, but the expression contained in it is made within the context of the Christian faith. One of many attempts to formulate the content of an expression of faith within this context, is contained in the catechist's explanation of what he desires of God in the Lord's Prayer, as set out in the Book of Common Prayer: God is He to whom we pray 'to save and defend us in all dangers ghostly and bodily; and ... keep us from all sin and wickedness, and from our ghostly enemy, and from everlasting death'. If the faith expressed in the first article of the Apostles' Creed is understood in this fashion it is clear that it is an all-embracing faith, valid for all situations. It is faith in protection against '*all* dangers', '*all* sin and wickedness'. In *this context* an expression of faith does therefore imply a commitment to enduring faith.

(5) An expression of faith in someone never undeniably implies a prescriptive that others must also put their trust in him. This implication would, however, be *contextually* present if the grounds for the faith of the speaker were also grounds for faith on the part of others. As I understand the Christian faith it does indeed imply that God is worthy of everybody's trust (even if not everybody puts his trust in God). God's care is promised to anyone who needs this care. 'Come unto me, all ye that labour and are heavy laden, and I will give you rest' (Matthew 11 : 28). If the expression of faith at the beginning of the Apostles' Creed is read *in this context*, the expressive does indeed imply a general prescriptive that all who labour and are heavily laden should put their trust in God. A *confession* of faith (as an expression of trust in God) is therefore also equivalent to a *profession* of this faith (as an appeal to others to put their trust in God).

# 3 Words and Concepts

## 3.7 WORDS AS NAMES

WHAT are concepts and how are they related to words and to things? In the history of philosophy two different models have often been used to explain the relation between words, things and concepts: the model of *names* in which words are regarded as names referring to things, and the model of *tools* in which words are regarded as tools used by us to perform speech acts in relation to things. Our view on the nature of concepts depends upon which of these two models we prefer. In line with the theory of speech acts developed in the previous chapter, we shall argue for the tools model as the more adequate of the two. In the history of philosophy, however, the names model has been the one most commonly used by philosophers in order to explain the relation between words, things and concepts. It is so common, in fact, that we are tempted to regard it as one of the unquestioned presuppositions of Western philosophy. Before turning our attention to the tools model in section 3.8, we shall in this section examine the names model: What were the most important forms this view of language took in the history of philosophy? What can we learn from it regarding the nature of concepts? And in what ways is it inadequate as a theory of language?

One of the first philosophers to put forward a rudimentary theory of language, was *Pythagoras*. According to Pythagoras, the soul gives names to things. These names, Pythagoras maintained, are not given arbitrarily; they are given on the basis of a natural link between the name and the thing – a link somewhat like the correspondence between a mental image and the object represented by such an image. To Pythagoras concepts were, therefore, equivalent to words: they were viewed as names which, like mental images, corresponded naturally to things.

*Parmenides* adopted a similar view. He, too, did not distinguish between words and concepts, and viewed them as names for things. However, he distinguished between true names, corresponding to real things, and false names, which referred to nothing and were therefore meaningless. In this connection he drew no clear distinction between words (or names) and statements. Words, like statements, could be judged to be 'true' or 'false'. Furthermore, Parmenides identified falsehood with meaninglessness and thus disregarded those functions of our speech, like the commissive and prescriptive functions, which do have meaning but cannot be judged as true or false. In terms of this view, only the constative or fact-stating functions of our speech can be meaningful, since only these functions can be judged to be true or false.

In contrast to Pythagoras, *Democritus* maintained that names are conventional signs, not natural ones. A word or name corresponds to a thing, not through some natural link between the two, but by virtue of an agreement among language-users that this word is to be used for that thing. In his dialogue *Cratylus*, *Plato* examined the conflict between a naturalistic view such as that of Pythagoras and a conventionalist one such as that of Democritus. Plato describes a discussion between Cratylus and Hermogenes. Cratylus is a naturalist who, like Pythagoras, maintains that words are names which naturally refer to the things named by them. The problem with this view is that different languages have different words for the same thing. For example, the Greek 'hippos' and the Latin 'equus' are used to refer to the same animal. This fact confronts the naturalist with a dilemma: which language has the true name, corresponding to the thing named, and which has a false and hence meaningless name? Cratylus' opponent, Hermogenes, is a conventionalist of sorts, who maintains that words are names that refer arbitrarily to things. There is no natural link between the word and its referent. We could therefore use any word to fit any object we please. For this reason a Roman is free to use a different word for a horse than that used by a Greek. The problem with this view is that it makes communication between people impossible: if it is a matter of arbitrary choice what name we use for which thing, there is no guarantee that we shall be using the same word for any particular thing, with the result that we have no way of knowing what others are talking about. For instance, if I could use any arbitrary sound to refer to a horse, I could never be sure that my hearer would be able to conclude from my words that I was indeed speaking of a horse.

Through Socrates, Plato now defends a mediating position between the naturalism of Cratylus and the kind of conventionalism put forward by Hermogenes. To understand this position, one has to know something about Plato's theory of ideas. The things we observe about us, Plato maintained, are all divided into classes: horses, cows, trees, people, etc. All members of such a class have certain fundamental characteristics in common and differ from the members of other classes in respect of these characteristics. Plato held that, far from being arbitrary, this ordering or classification of our environment results from the fact that the world is a reflection of a transcendent realm of ideas. Thus all horses have certain fundamental characteristics in common because they are copies or reflections of the one ideal horse in the realm of ideas. The differences between the various classes thus reflects differences between ideas. The differences distinguishing the classes from each other are therefore not fortuitous but *essential*.

We could use a culinary analogy to illustrate this point. In preparing a chicken for the pot we usually cut it at the joints. In this sense a chicken has convenient natural lines of division. A loaf of bread, on the other hand, has no such natural dividing lines so that slices of bread are cut along arbitrary lines. Plato maintains that the world is like a chicken in having natural lines of division which dictate how we classify the things around us. The world is not like a loaf of bread which can be divided along any arbitrary lines. The natural divisions in the world around us reflect the essential differences between the ideas in the realm of ideas.

Before birth, the soul of every human being exists in the realm of ideas, where it observes the ideas. Because of this, all human beings have an innate memory of the ideas. These memories or *concepts* are ideal names that correspond excactly to the ideas. This implies that all people have the same innate concepts reflecting, so to speak, the essential divisions of reality. With regard to concepts, therefore, Plato's stand is similar to that of Cratylus: our concepts correspond naturally to things because they reflect the essential differences between things.

In contrast to his predecessors, Plato distinguished between words and concepts. In respect of words he adopted a conventionalism closer to that of Hermogenes, maintaining that words are conventional signs used for concepts in communication between people. Which words (or signs) people adopt for which particular concepts is a matter of agreement or convention. Different languages are held to be different systems of conventional signs. Thus the Romans agreed to use the word 'equus' for the concept of a horse, whereas the Greeks used 'hippos' for the same concept. Through this kind of conventionalism Plato could account more satisfactorily than Cratylus could for the existence of different languages. Contrary to Hermogenes, however, Plato maintained that it is not a matter of *arbitrary choice* what word we use for any particular concepts. Words are, after all, *conventional* signs: which word we use for which particular concept is determined by agreement between people, not arbitrarily by each individual on his own. Since we agree on which words are to be used for which concepts, we have the assurance that we shall be using the same words for the same concepts, so that communication between people remains possible.

Briefly, then, Plato saw words as conventional signs for concepts, concepts as mental representation of ideas, and ideas as the transcedent essences of the things around us. Our language, therefore, reflects our concepts, which in turn reflect ideas as essential structures of reality. In this regard Plato said, through Socrates, that words are *instruments* that we can use to perform two important tasks. Since words correspond to concepts and thus reflect the structure of reality, they can be used, on the one hand, to teach one another the truth (that is, to say how reality is structured) and, on the other hand, to classify things according to their essential natures. 'A name is an instrument of teaching and of separating reality, as a shuttle is an instrument of separating the web' (*Cratylus* 388B).

For our purposes, three features of Plato's view are of interest:

(1)   Plato distinguished between words and concepts: words are names (conventional signs) for concepts and concepts are mental representations of the essential structures of reality.

(2)   Plato adopted a *realistic* view with regard to concepts: reality has inherent, essential divisions which are reflected in our concepts. Others (e.g. Kant) would later reject this realism.

(3)   Plato spoke of words as *instruments*, but then instruments used for *one* purpose only: to reflect the natural divisions of reality. In this sense Plato took account only of the constative or fact-stating functions of language. Words were held to be instruments, but then instruments of one kind only: *names*.

Aristotle accepted Plato's realism; he, too, maintained that the world about us has natural divisions reflected by our concepts. On the other hand, however, he rejected Plato's theory of ideas: the world about us is not a reflection of some transcendent realm of ideas; nor, therefore, are the divisions of the world reflections of the divisions between ideas. The essential natures of things lies within the things themselves, not in some transcendent realm of ideas. Therefore, we know the essential nature of things, not through memories of a previous existence in a realm of ideas, but by perceiving the things themselves. Through perception, *homoioomata* (images) of things are formed in our minds.

Words are symbols or conventional signs for such images. Different languages are different systems of such conventional signs, all of which can be used to refer to those images and thus also to the things themselves. Briefly, then: words were held to be conventional names for concepts, and concepts were images of the essential nature of things, thus reflecting the natural divisions of reality.

But not all words are names. Aristotle pointed out that when we make assertions (*logoi*), we need more kinds of 'instruments' than names alone. In an assertion we say something about something: of Socrates we say that he is mortal; of a tree, that it is high; of the cat, that it is black; and so on. In order to make such assertions we need, firstly, *names* (for example, 'Socrates', 'tree', 'cat') to refer to the object in reality that we wish to speak of. Secondly we need *predicates* (for example, 'mortal', 'high', 'black') as signs for whatever we wish to ascribe to whatever we are talking about. Thirdly we need connective words to join the other words together in various ways.

*Words* are neither true nor false. According to Aristotle, truth and falsehood relate only to *assertions* in which we state facts about reality – that is, to constative assertions. Aristotle recognised the fact that not all assertions are constative in this sense. Prayers, for example, are not statements of fact and are therefore neither true nor false. Such non-constative assertions he relegated to the study of rhetoric and poetry, confining his attention in his logical works to factual assertions or propositions. Therefore, although Aristotle made the point that not all words are names reflecting the essential divisions of reality, he himself concentrated mainly on the constative uses of language (true and false propositions) and thus on language in so far as it is used to describe reality.

Briefly: Aristotle maintained that reality has an inherent, natural structure, reflected by the concepts in our minds and described in our constative assertions. Yet there are indications that Aristotle sought to break free of the confines of this representational model of language: not all words are names, nor are all assertions constative.

The same double tendency is to be found in the views of Augustine. In his *Confessions* 1 – 8 – 13 he describes how, as a child, he learnt to speak:

My elders did not teach me words according to any set method, as afterwards they taught me the letters, but I did it myself with the understanding Thou gavest me, O my God. Whenever I tried with various cries and sounds and with various movements of my body, to express the feelings of my heart in order to get my wishes carried out, and when I was unable to express all my desires to whomsoever I wished, I remembered those situations where they named some object and moved their body toward it: I noticed this and gathered that the thing they wished to point out was called by the sound they then uttered. That they did mean this was made plain by the motion of the body, as it were the natural language of all peoples: the expression of the face, the glance of the eye, the movement of the other limbs, and the tone of voice which expresses our state of mind when seeking, having, rejecting or avoiding something. So it was that by frequently hearing words used in their proper places in various sentences, I gradually gathered what things they were the signs of, and having formed my mouth to utter these signs, I used them to express my wishes.

Where in this passage Augustine speaks of his *learning* how to use words, he is concerned with words as names used to refer to things. He observed how people used words in naming something or other, or in indicating something, and gradually he came to grasp what things these signs represented. But when he speaks of what he wished to *do* with the words once he had learnt how to use them, he is no longer concerned with the referential use of words; he then deals with the expressive and prescriptive uses of language: expressing the feelings of his heart, in order to have his wishes carried out, expressing his state of mind when he seeks, or possesses, or rejects, or avoids certain things, and expressing his wishes. This clearly shows up the inadequacies of the names model: if words were no more than names used to refer to things, they could not possibly fulfil all these expressive and prescriptive functions of language. To do so, we need more than referential signs.

In the seventeenth century *John Locke* developed a theory of language very similar to that of Aristotle: words, he maintained, are conventional signs for concepts and concepts (Locke called them 'ideas') are our mental images of things around us. Such images reflect the natural divisions of reality and are formed in our minds when we perceive reality about us. In the eighteenth century *Immanuel Kant* argued against theories such as Locke's. Kant held that our minds are not merely passively registering what we see when we perceive reality, but actively structuring it. Perception, he maintained, is not the passive recording of an inherent order in reality: it is an active process of creating order in the chaos of disorderly impressions we receive through perception. Our concepts are not, therefore, reflections of an inherent order in reality, recorded through our perception; they are principles of order which we apply to phenomena as we perceive them. The world we experience has no inherent order, as proposed in the conceptual realism of Plato and Aristotle; its order is brought about by us. That the world has the same orderly structure for all of us is due to the fact that we all cognitively structure the world of our experience in the same way. That all of us structure the world of our experience in the same way is due to the fact that we share the same general mental structure (*Bewusstsein überhaupt*).

In terms of the *realism* of Plato and Aristotle, our concepts reflect the natural divisions of reality. According to Kant's *conceptualism*, our concepts reflect the divisions that we apply to reality as we experience it. If we have to choose between realism and conceptualism, I suppose the latter is to be preferred. In a sense the divisions of reality as we experience it, are made by us rather than being aspects of an inherent structural order in the things themselves. It is doubtful, however, whether there is only one universal conceptual ordering of our experience as Kant seems to suggest. Are there not, rather, alternative ways in which we could order our experience? Are not the differences between the vocabularies of various natural languages a reflection of different ways in which people conceptually organise their experience of reality? In section 3.9 we shall examine these questions in more detail.

What, then, is the relation between language and reality (or between words and things) and how do concepts bear on this relation? According to the names model, *concepts* are mental representations of the structural divisions which according to the realists we read *off* and according to the conceptualists we read *into* the reality we experience. *Words* are names or signs referring to concepts and hence to the structural divisions of reality represented in these concepts.

It is doubtful whether this model provides an adequate basis for a theory of language or for a theory about the nature of concepts. The following are some of the most important objections which can be raised against this model: (1) It is not clear in what sense concepts can be mental representations of things; (2) Not all words are names or referential signs; (3) In order to say something we need more kinds of words than names alone, because saying is more than merely referring; (4) Language has far more uses then merely asserting propositions which represent the structure of reality.

Let us examine these objections more closely.

(1) If words are signs associated with concepts and if concepts are mental representations of reality, then it is quite unclear what is meant by 'mental representation' in this connection. Consider, for instance, the following sentence from Locke's *Essay concerning Human Understanding*[6] in which he stated this view on the relation between words and concepts: 'The use, then, of words, is to be sensible marks of ideas; and the ideas they stand for are their proper and immediate signification.' What distinguishable idea in the sense of mental representation or mental image could we associate with each word in this sentence? What idea is associated with 'use', 'word', 'mark', 'idea', 'signification' (not to mention 'the', 'is', 'to', 'for')? Most words do not stand for any specific idea. Others may relate to such ideas, but such words would be associated with different ideas by different people. For instance 'marks': writing in a letter; footprints in the sand; wheelmarks on a road; bloodstains etc. Briefly, if words are signs for ideas in the sense of mental representations of experience, then most words are not associated with any specific idea. Worse still, this theory cannot even account for the function of words that are clearly related to representations in our minds (for example, 'dog', 'man', 'stove'). A little reflection suffices to show that every time we use a specific word (for example 'bird') with the same meaning, and this word is accompanied by an image in our minds, the image differs: we can use the same word ('bird') for different mental representations (of a pigeon, a lark, a heron, a gull, etc.). Does this imply that the same word has a (completely) different meaning every time, depending on the (quite different) image it refers to in our minds?

Locke's answer to this question was his theory of general abstract ideas: according to him, general words refer to general ideas. But the problem is: how do we acquire such general ideas? To this Locke replies that the human mind forms, by means of abstraction, a general abstract idea from the correspondence between a group of simple ideas. Thus, for instance, I form the idea 'dog' by abstracting the common characteristics of the simple ideas I have of Rover, Fred, Jock, Ripper, Winston, and all the other dogs I know. General words refer to such general ideas, which are their 'proper signification'. What Locke did not realise was that he was giving an entirely new meaning to the word 'idea'. Such general 'ideas' cannot possibly still be images or representations in the mind. I can, for instance, form ideas ( = representations) of individual colours (green, red, blue, yellow, etc.), but not of a colour in general, which is neither green, nor red, nor blue, nor any other specific colour. Since all mental representations or mental images are per definition individual, they cannot be the 'proper and immediate signification' of general words. If words stand for concepts, therefore, these concepts cannot be ideas in the sense of mental representations. But what are concepts then in terms of this kind of theory?

The problem here can also be stated as follows. We saw that Augustine thought of words as being names which refer to particular *things*. We use words to refer to whatever we want to talk about. Aristotle, on the other hand, thought of words as names for *concepts* which reflect the natural divisions of reality into *classes* of things. Locke tried to combine these two views. Simple ideas are representations of individual things and abstract general ideas are representations of what is common between the individuals – that is, what divides the individuals into *classes*. However, it is not possible to interpret both these kinds of ideas as mental *representations* in the same sense: I can form a mental *image*, only of individual things not of sorts or classes of things. In what sense then is a general class-concept to be understood as a mental *representation?* Not in the sense of an image. But in what sense then?

(2) It is not enough to deny that all words refer to concepts in the sense of mental images. We must go still further and deny that all words refer. As we pointed out above, Aristotle already distinguished between names, predicates and connective words, and hence rejected by implication the view that all words are names or referential signs. There are in fact many words, for instance *articles* (a, an, the), *prepositions* (on, in, under, behind), *conjunctions* (but, and, because, then), etc., that have no referential relationship to entities (let alone to ideas or concepts). Words such as 'on', 'and', 'the', etc., never refer to entities. This makes it rather difficult to account for their use on the basis of the names model. Mediaeval logicians tried to solve this problem by distinguishing between two kinds of words: *categoremata* and *syncategoremata*. *Categoremata* are words which have a referential function by themselves. The *syncategoremata* are words such as prepositions, articles, conjunctions etc., which have no referential function if they are isolated from other words. They can, however, be used together with other words, or categoremata, to form phrases that have a referential function. Like categoremata such as 'man' and 'moon', the phrase 'the first man to set foot on the moon' has a

referential function too. Mediaeval logicians spoke of two kinds of names in this connection: *singular names* (that is, categoremata, or words that have a referential function on their own) and *compound names* (that is, phrases consisting of a number of words and having a referential function). Thus syncategoremata have a referential function only when they form part of a compound name. This distinction between categoremata and syncategoremata does not solve our problem entirely, because syncategoremata are not the only words that have no referential function in isolation from other words.

*Referring* is what we do in answer to the question 'what are you talking about?' When performing speech acts we refer to things or persons to make it clear to our hearer what (or whom) we are talking about. When saying something by means of a sentence with a subject-predicate form – for example, 'The cat (subject) is-on-the-mat (predicate)' – it is the subject term that has a referential function. With the *subject term* (the cat) we refer to something (or draw attention to something), and with the predicate term (is on the mat) we say something about the entity to which we refer with the subject term. Therefore, if a term (word or phrase) is to fulfil a referential function, we must be able to use it as subject term of a sentence. For example:

> '*The moon* is made of cheese'
> '*The man in the moon* does not exist'
> '*Trees* have leaves'
> '*My car* has four wheels'
> '*That* is a cat'
> '*He* is not a reliable person'
> '*Inflation* is dangerous to economic development'
> '*Peter* comes from Scotland'.

It is clear that the so-called syncategoremata cannot be used as subject terms in sentences unless they are parts of complete referential phrases (compound names). The trouble is, however, that this applies to most other words as well: (*a*) verbs, adjectives, and adverbs can never be the subject terms of a sentence on their own; (*b*) even singular nouns (for example, dog, tree, town, man) cannot be subject terms. I cannot say 'tree has leaves'; only '*the tree* (or *this tree*, or *my tree*, or *trees*) has (have) leaves.' Isolated from other words, only the following words can function as subject terms in sentences: (*a*) names (Peter, John, Edward); (*b*) indicative pronouns (he, she, it, that); (*c*) plural nouns (trees, towns, people); and (*d*) abstract nouns that have no plural (inflation, virtue, beauty, etc.) Very few words, therefore, can function as referential signs when used by themselves. Such difficulties led Russell to refer to all these words that have no referential function on their own as '*incomplete symbols*', that is, he regarded all of them as similar to the syncategoremata of the mediaeval logicians: on their own they are not symbols or signs for things; only the referential phrases of which they form part ('complete symbols') have a referential function.

The view that all words are names used to refer is clearly untenable. Most words cannot be used to refer at all, unless they form part of some phrase which is used referringly.

(3) If the only words we had were referential signs and referential phrases or expressions, then we would not be able to say anything in the sense of performing a speech act. 'Three is a prime number' is a sentence with which we can say something, but it is neither a referential phrase nor a series of referential terms. 'Aristotle, Plato, my car, the man in the moon' is a series of referential terms, but it is not a sentence with which something is said. Briefly: referential terms are not sentences. They are merely *parts* of sentences, namely the parts in which the speaker indicates what the speech act he is performing with the sentence is concerned with. Words and phrases therefore have more functions in our speech than merely a referential function, and in order to form sentences with which we can perform speech acts we also need words with other than referential functions.

This raises a further important point: words do not refer. *We* refer by means of words. The same applies to all the other functions of words in our speech: all of them are functions of words *as used by people in performing speech acts*. No word or phrase has a referential function or any function whatsoever apart from its use by us as speakers. Separated from what we *do* with words, they are simply sounds or patterns of sound without meaning. It is clear, too, that in saying things, we use words in many more ways than in referring to things or to the classificatory divisions in the reality we experience around us.

(4) According to the names model words stand for concepts and concepts somehow reflect the basic structure of reality as we experience it. This suggests that the fundamental use of language is to represent the structural divisions of reality and in this way to state that reality is structured thus. As we have argued in the previous chapter, it would be a wholly inadequate view of language to reduce all language to its constative functions in this way. Saying cannot be reduced to referring,

nor can all speech acts be reduced to the assertion of constatives.

In his *Philosophical Investigations* I,3 Wittgenstein wrote as follows about the argument from St Augustine which we discussed above:

> Augustine, we might say, does describe a system of communication; only not everything that we call language is this system. And one has to say this in many cases where the question arises: 'Is this an appropriate description or not?' The answer is: 'Yes, it is appropriate, but only for this narrowly circumscribed region, not for the whole of what you were claiming to describe. It is as if someone were to say: 'A game consists in moving objects about on a surface according to certain rules ...' – and we replied: 'You seem to be thinking of board games, but there are others. You can make your definition correct by expressly restricting it to those games'.

If speaking and thinking are more than referring to or classifying or describing the reality around us (as games are more than board games), then the question arises whether there are not more kinds of concepts than classification concepts which somehow reflect the structural divisions of reality. And if a philosopher is to inquire about the nature of concepts, does he not deal with more than the ways in which we classify the reality we experience? In order to get clear on the nature of concepts and of conceptual inquiry, we will need a more adequate model for explaining language than the names model.

## 3.8 WORDS AS TOOLS

In the previous section we distinguished between two linguistic models often used to explain the relation between words, things and concepts: the model of *names* in which words are regarded as names for things or for classes of things and the model of *tools* in which words are regarded as tools used by us to perform speech acts in relation to things. We tried to show in what respects the first of these models is inadequate. What shall we say now of the second?

The tools model can readily be explained with the aid of an important distinction made by various philosophers: the distinction between *speech* and *language*. Gilbert Ryle explains the distinction as follows[7]. A language, such as French, for example, is a supply of words, constructions, intonations, set expressions, etc. Speech, on the other hand, is an activity, or rather a variety of activities, performed in saying things in French, in English, or in some other language. A supply of language components is not a number of activities but the fairly constant means by which these activities are performed, much as a supply of coins is not a transaction or a number of transactions of buying, borrowing, investing, etc., but the constant supply of means by which such transactions are made. One might see the relation between language and speech as more or less analogous to that between capital and trade. Wittgenstein would have compared this distinction to that between the tools in my tool box and the things I do with those tools (hammering, sawing, planing, etc.).[8]

A language, then, is a supply of words, constructions, etc., out of which *sentences* can be formed according to the grammatical rules of that language. The sentences of a language can be used to perform various speech acts. In fact, we could define a sentence as the minimum unit of language needed to perform a complete speech act: to utter a sentence is to perform a locution on the basis of which a set of illocutions could be asserted and various per-illocutionary responses could be evoked. Such speech acts are forms of speech. They are not units of language (as are words, sentences etc.) but acts performed with units of language. Thus, there are English or French sentences, composed of English or French words. But there are no English or French speech acts such as statements, promises, predictions, etc., even though these speech acts are performed with English or French sentences. In fact the same speech act could be performed equally well with the sentences of some other language. Speech acts, then, are forms of speech and speech is the whole body of acts performed with a language. Speech stands to language as trade stands to capital.

In the light of this distinction we could say that *concepts* are related to *words* as speech is to language. Concepts are not words. They are thought forms or mental skills which we exercise by means of words. Words are, as it were, the tools by means of which such conceptual skills are exercised. We could say, therefore, that someone has mastered a *concept* if he is able to use the relevant *word*, or expression, or construction etc. correctly.

> It will be a *sufficient* condition for James's having the concept of *so-and-so* that he should have mastered the intelligent use (including the use in made-up sentences) of a word for *so-and-so* in some language.

Thus: if somebody knows how to use the English word 'red', he has
a concept of red; if he knows how to use the first-person pronoun, he
has a concept of *self*; if he knows how to use the negative
construction in some language, he has a concept of negation.[9]

Conceptual skills are, however, not only exercised verbally. For
instance, if a child learns to exercise the concept 'red', he is able to
perform a whole complex of interrelated skills: he can *select and bring
together* red blocks, crayons, ribbons, etc.; he can *distinguish* red objects
from ones of different colours; he can *call* red objects 'red'; he can *say
from memory* whether or not an object no longer before him is red; he
can *point* to red objects in response to a (verbal) demand for red objects;
and so on. Some of these skills are verbal, whereas others are clearly not
verbal. Even if the child has mastered only the non-verbal skills in this
complex, we could nonetheless say that he has mastered the *concept*
'red'. If, for example, someone suffering from aphasia (an inability to
speak, as a result of brain damage) is able to distinguish red objects from
non-red ones, etc., we would say that he has mastered the *concept* 'red',
even though he cannot use the *word* 'red'. In brief: concepts are not only
verbal skills. They are, more generally, *forms of thought* or, as Geach
calls them, 'mental capacities'. Nevertheless, words remain the
indispensable tools both for learning and for exercising most of our
conceptual skills. Without language, our ability to acquire and exercise
conceptual skills would be severely restricted.

Concepts are *mental* skills (such as being able to distinguish between
differing objects, being able to apply rules, being able to recognise
differences and similarities between things, being able to make
promises, being able to judge and assess situations, etc.) and not
primarily *physical* skills (such as swimming, cycling, or skating).
Physical skills are distinct from but can never be separated from mental
skills. To exercise a physical skill is to engage in some physical or bodily
activity which presupposes, at the same time, the exercise of a number
of mental or conceptual skills. If, for example, someone does breast-
stroke swimming correctly, he will repeat the *same* series of bodily
movements over and over again. As such, breast-stroke swimming is the
application of a rule ('repeat: legs up, kick,  close; legs up, kick close ...')
which in turn presupposes that the swimmer has the mental capacity to
recognise that what he is doing is the same set of bodily movements as
the preceding one.

Conceptual skills are acquired; we are not born with them. The most fundamental concepts are learnt on our mother's knee or in the nursery school. There is the example of the mother of a mentally retarded baby who spent weeks sitting beside her child and looking into its eyes until, one day, the baby became aware of being looked at and thus became conscious of being an individual, distinct from other individuals. The baby was able to distinguish itself from its surroundings and thus for the first time learned the concept of 'I' or 'self'. Most of us acquire such fundamental concepts fairly early in life, without any special teaching effort on the part of our mothers. Other concepts are deliberately taught to us, if not at home then in the nursery school. Look at the games used to teach nursery-school pupils a number of fundamental conceptual skills (see over). Card *a* is used to teach children the concept of *identity*. They have mastered this concept when they are able to see which thing is identical to (the same as) another. Card *b* is used to teach children to apply a *rule* by repeating a given pattern ('complete the necklaces'). The application of a rule presupposes a mastery of the concept of identity, since each further application must be an application of *the same* rule: in the example of the necklaces we must be able to repeat *the same* pattern. Card *c* is an exercise in *classification* concepts. Children have to learn to see which things are related to others by having some characteristics in common. Card *d* is concerned with the concept of *quantity*, which we master when we are able to distinguish fewer from more.

Our learning of conceptual skills is never completed. Throughout life we are constantly learning new concepts and adjusting or discarding old ones. Let us illustrate this process by learning a new concept – the concept '*enclo*'. 'Enclo' is a classification concept, like 'red'. Classification concepts are skills in *distinguishing* objects that belong to the same class from ones that fall outside that class – for instance, distinguishing red objects from non-red ones, or enclos from non-enclos. Enclos are typewriter characters such as e, b, 6, %, $, 0, 8, 9, etc. Non-enclos are typewriter characters such as r, v, 1, x, £, n, 3, etc. Which of the following characters are enclos, and which are not: p, n , &, 4, –, ¾, H, A, d, z, a, L, +, 2, f, v, :, 7, (, g, Q, etc? (For those who, in spite of our examples, are still unable to apply the concept 'enclo', we could give the following tip: an enclo is a typewriter character containing an enclosed space.)

Let us now take another lok at our two models for explaining the nature of concepts. According to the names model, *concepts* are mental representations of the structural divisions of reality (either inherent to reality, or imposed on reality by us during perception), whereas *words*

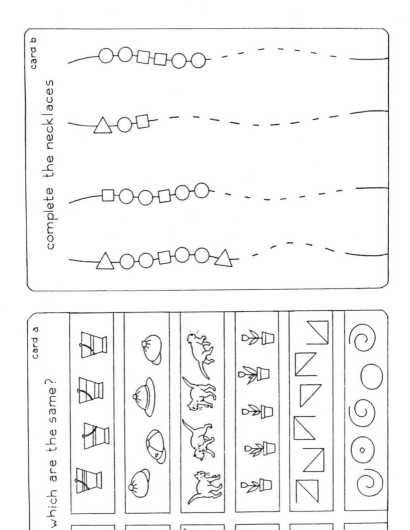

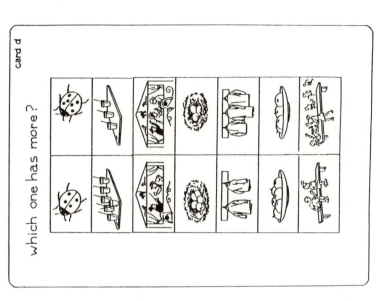

card d

which one has more?

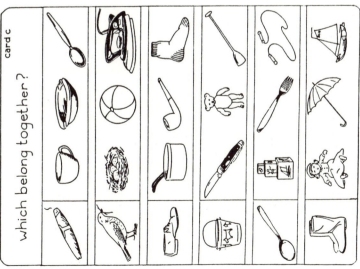

card c

which belong together?

are names for such concepts. According to the tools model, concepts are mental skills and hence also verbal skills, whereas words are instruments used in exercising these skills. With Plato's help we can now draw these two models closer together.

According to Plato, words are instruments for dividing things into classes and for teaching the truth. We have, therefore, mastered concepts (interpreted as skills) if we are able to classify things and to impart the truth. If we formulate the names model in the terminology of the tools model, we may thus define concepts as skills in using words to classify things and to impart the truth. According to Aristotle, words cannot be true or false. In order to impart the truth we have to be able to make a true factual assertion for which we require various kinds of words: names, predicates and connective words. In arguing that a word is an instrument for classification *and* for imparting the truth, Plato is confusing two quite different things: classification *words* and factual *assertions* (for which we require more than classification words alone). Generalising this point we could argue that in performing a speech act we have to exercise a whole complex of conceptual skills, and not only the ability to classify things. In this regard Geach states: [10] 'I thus accept the psychology of the old logic-books, to the extent of recognising the possession of concepts as pre-supposed to acts of judgement, and regarding a judgement as the exercise of a number of concepts.'

In brief: in order to perform speech acts we have to master very many kinds of conceptual skills and therefore we need very many *kinds* of verbal tools for exercising these concepts. Far more than can be accounted for on the basis of the model of names! It would be impossible to enumerate the infinite variety of kinds of concepts we employ in thinking and speaking. Let us try, however, with the help of Aristotle's distinction between names (or referential signs), predicates and connective words to give some examples of the conceptual skills involved in performing a speech act and to show how various words are used to exercise these conceptual skills.

As we argued in chapter 2, our speech acts are always related to the factual context in which they are performed. The factual context is *constitutive* for the various illocutions asserted in a speech act. Hence, when performing a speech act we need to be able to *distinguish* various features in the world from each other and to *indicate* to our hearers to which of these our speech act is related. For this purpose we need to use referential words in the sentences with which we perform our speech acts. Thus, when we say things we usually say them *about* something or *of* something: we say of the cat that it is black, of Santa Claus that he is kind, of the sunset that it is magnificent, and of Peter's efforts that they are worthy of praise. Such speech acts are often performed with sentences having a subject-predicate form: 'The cat (subject) is black (predicate)', in which the subject-term ('the cat') is used *referentially*. The speaker uses it, one might say, to isolate one 'segment' or 'element' from the totality of things about which it is possible to say something, and to indicate that this is what he wishes to deal with in his speech act. Such a reference fails if the hearer cannot make out from it precisely what 'segment' is meant (for example, if he does not know which cat is meant). The speaker will then have to specify his subject term more closely ('I mean the neighbour's cat') until the reference comes across clearly to his hearer.

This referential function is fulfilled by (*a*) *names* ('Peter', 'London', 'Britain' etc.) (*b*) *pronouns* ('I', 'you', 'he', 'this', etc) and (*c*) *identifying expressions and phrases* ('the man in the moon', 'my book', 'some people', 'all people', 'most people', 'one man', etc.) Such identifying expressions and phrases usually consist of a descriptive term ('tree', 'man', etc.) or a descriptive phrase ('man in the moon', 'black cat'), and a term that indicates which of the entities to which this description is applicable is meant (e.g. 'one', 'the', 'some', 'all', 'most', 'my', etc.).

The value of the names model is that it draws our attention to this referential use of words. However, as we have argued in section 3.7 in order to say something about the things to which we refer, we need words with other uses as well.

When performing speech acts with sentences having a subject-predicate form, the speaker uses the predicate term to say something about that which he isolates from all else and indicates for his hearer by means of the subject term. What is said depends on the illocutionary load of the speech act. Thus the predicate term is often used to convey the illocutionary load of the speech act. We can, therefore, divide words that are used predicatively according to the illocutionary load of the speech acts in which they are used. Some predicates are used to convey a *descriptive* illocutionary load because they ascribe factual characteristics to something (e.g. 'the cat *is black*'; 'Nelson's column *is in Trafalgar Square*', etc.), such descriptive predicates are often *dispositional*, that is, they say of that to which they are ascribed that it has a dispositional characteristic (tendency) to behave in certain ways under certain circumstances (for example, 'the cat is sly'). Some predicates are used to convey an *expressive* and/or *prescriptive* illocutionary load. For example: 'Your party was delightful' (primarily expressive); 'Peter's achievement is *worthy of praise*' (primarily prescriptive).

It should be noted that the same word can sometimes be used referentially as key term in an identifying expression (for example, 'the *cat* is black') and sometimes as a descriptive predicate (for example, 'that animal is a *cat*'). This does not alter the fact that the same word is used here to exercise two *different* (though related) conceptual skills: identifying reference and descriptive predication.

Some words are used neither referentially nor predicatively. These include logical terms ('or', 'and', 'if...then', 'is', 'not', 'therefore', etc.) that convey relations between the various elements in a speech act or between different speech acts. The so-called copula 'is' conveys the link between the subject and the predicate in 'the cat is black', whereas the term 'if...then' is used to convey the relation between two speech acts (for example, 'If the cat's away, then the mice will play'). 'Not' is used to deny the illocutionary load asserted in a speech act (for example, 'The cat is not sly').

In brief, in order to perform any speech act whatsoever, we should master at least the following conceptual skills: the various illocutionary skills (constatives, various kinds of expressives, commissives and prescriptives); the ability to distinguish those features of reality to which our speech act is related from those to which it is not related; various logical skills in relating the different aspects of a speech act or various speech acts to each other; denying illocutions which have been asserted, and so on. Furthermore, since illocutionary skills are *social* skills which can only be performed in the relation between people, we need the ability to refer our hearers to those aspects of reality to which our speech acts are related, and to convey to them the illocutionary load of and the logical relations within and between our speech acts.

Although this list of conceptual skills is far from exhaustive, it is sufficient to show (1) how the performance of a speech act comprises the exercise of a complex set of conceptual skills, and (2) how each of the different words in the sentence with which a speech act is performed are used to exercise different conceptual skills comprised in the speech act.

In conclusion we might add that the view on the relation between words and concepts argued for in this section implies a different theory about linguistic meaning from that implied by the names model. The meaning of a word (or other element of language) is not the concept (or thing or class of things) to which that word (or linguistic element) *refers* but the concept which is *exercised* with that word (or element of language) in the speech acts performed with sentences containing that word (or linguistic element). Thus two words are *synonymous* to the extent that they can be used to exercise the same concept (or concepts) in speech acts. A word is *ambiguous* when it could be used to exercise various concepts and when, in a specific speech act, it is not clear which concept is being exercised with that word.

We can summarise and compare the two linguistic models we have been discussing, as shown in Table I.

Table I

| *The Names Model* | *The Tools Model* |
| --- | --- |
| *Concepts:* Mental representations corresponding to the structural divisions in reality. According to *realism* these divisions are inherent in reality. According to *conceptualism* these divisions are applied by us when perceiving reality. | *Concepts:* Forms of thought or mental skills which we usually exercise verbally. A great variety, not to be limited to classification skills which we exercise when dividing reality into classes. |
| *Words:* Names for concepts and hence also for the structural divisions of reality to which our concepts correspond. | *Words:* Tools which we use to exercise a large variety of conceptual skills. |
| *Reality:* That of which the structural divisions are reflected in our concepts. Words (as names for concepts) can be used to refer to these structural divisions or to classify things according to these divisions. | *Reality:* The factual context within which we exercise our conceptual skills and which is partly constitutive for the exercise of these conceptual skills. |
| *The Meaning of a Word:* the concepts (or thing or class of things) for which that word stands, or to which it refers. | *The Meaning of a Word:* the conceptual skill exercised with that word in the speech acts performed with sentences containing that word. |

## 3.9 CONCEPTS AS FORMS OF LIFE

Concepts, then, are forms of thought or mental skills which we usually exercise with words. The exercise of concepts is an inherent part of all our dealings with each other in the world, and hence an essential feature of human life. 'To imagine a language means to imagine a form of life.' [11] What are the implications of this for the nature of concepts? Concepts are forms of thinking and speaking, which in turn are forms of life. But in what sense, exactly, are thinking and speaking forms of life? This is fairly clear with regard to the illocutionary, logical, referential and other conceptual skills involved in performing speech acts, since speech acts are the elementary forms of our personal intercourse with each other in the world. The question is, however, whether this applies to all our concepts. Thus, for example, identifying, distinguishing and classifying objects are also conceptual skills; but we do not only exercise these verbally nor only in our communication with each other. In what way are they, then, to be regarded as forms of life? What do we do when we classify things, and in what sorts of situations in life do we exercise our skill at classification?

Classification is the division of entities into classes according to the characteristics which they have in common. Entities with the same characteristics belong to the same class, whereas entities with different characteristics belong to different classes. In this way we could divide different people into the same class if they are similar with regard to sex, or age, or profession, or marital status, or eye colour, or race, or nationality or any conceivable combination of these or other characteristics. Thus, the same set of entities may be classified in an infinite variety of ways, depending on the characteristic (or set of characteristics) we adopt as a basis for the classification. We may classify in such a manner that any two random entities fall in the same class. Any two random entities always have some characteristic in common (if only the characteristic that we are now thinking of them!). We could also classify in such a way that any two random entities fall in different classes, because there will always be one or more characteristics that they do not have in common, since they would otherwise not be two *distinct* entities.

Classification has three important features: First, the similarities and differences between things are given to us in experience. We do not produce them ourselves. When carrying out a population survey, we will have to find out how many people share which characteristics; we cannot merely think this up for ourselves.

Secondly: which characteristics are to serve as the basis for classification, is a matter of *choice* on the part of the classifier − a choice made on pragmatic grounds in the light of the classifier's aims, interests, concerns, etc. Thus we might divide the same group of people in widely different ways, according to the various ends our classification is to serve. Consider, for instance, the different classifications of persons in a population register, a police register, a medical aid fund register, a school register, a church register, a textbook on cultural anthropology, and so on.

Thirdly: the division of entities into classes is possible only if we are able (have developed the skill) to recognise the similarities and differences on which our classification is founded. As we have argued in the previous section, this ability is not inborn but acquired like all other conceptual skills, if not at our mother's knee, or in some game in nursery school, then in some other way in our dealings with the surrounding world.

It is characteristic of classification concepts that they have a content (or connotation) and a field of application (or denotation). The *connotation* of a classification concept is the set of characteristics which an entity must have if it is to belong to the class of entities to which the concept applies. The *denotation* is the set of entities having these characteristics and hence belonging to the class. Foir this reason there is a close connection between *classifying* entities, *describing* them and *referring* to them. In fact, we could use the same words to do all three things. We can use a classification word to *refer* to those entities which belong to its denotation, and to *describe* entities as having those characteristics which belong to its connotation. Thus we can *classify* some plants as trees, or use the word 'tree' to *refer* to members of the class of trees, or to *describe* something as a 'perennial plant having a self-supporting, woody stem or trunk and growing to a considerable height and size' (Oxford Dictionary). Since theories of language based on the names model tend to reduce all concepts to classification concepts, they can only account for these three uses of words: classifying or 'separating things according to their natures' (Plato, *Cratylus*, 388B), describing (making true statements about things) and referring.

Classification is an activity which we perform *deliberately* in a large variety of situations − for example in botany, zoology and population surveys. In some ways more important, however, is the *intuitive* or unconscious classification in which we bring order to our experience. Thus all perception involves a classificatory organisation of the data perceived. In this regard Kant is correct in maintaining that our perception and cognition of the world around us is not merely a passive registration of sensory impressions but an active ordering of such sensory data. If we wish to get a hold on the chaos of sensory impressions we receive in perception, we must first *recognise* the similarities and differences between the things we perceive, and secondly classify such things according to these similarities and differences. In perception we do not merely register chaotic sensory impressions, nor do we perceive random objects. We only perceive objects that have recognisable characteristics in common or that differ in recognisable ways: for example, people, chairs, tables, houses, trees. This ordering is performed intuitively. It may well be that animals perceive the world in quite different ways, because they order their experiences differently from the way we humans do.

The three features of classification set out above, play their part in our perception as well: (1) the characteristics which things have in common or in respect of which they differ, must be given; (2) we select (or intuitively apply) certain similarities as principles of order; and (3) we must have acquired the ability to apply these relevant principles of order. The conceptual skills that play a role in our perception must therefore also be acquired. We are not born with them.

We become accustomed to ordering our perception in a certain manner, so that we often find it hard even to imagine some other system of ordering, let alone to apply it ourselves. Psychologists call this tendency 'mental set'. It arises in the following way:

First, we order our surroundings according to those characteristics of things which are *of interest to us*. Thus houses are classified quite differently by architects, sanitary inspectors, housing commissions, electricians, house agents, insurance agents, and fire brigades; and animals are classified quite differently by zoologists, furriers, butchers, hunters, circus owners, stock breeders, etc. These examples show that different concerns or interests lead to different classifications of the same set of objects.

Secondly, every classification is *one-sided*: only certain similarities are taken into account, whereas others are ignored. When putting things in the same class we take note only of those similarities in terms of which we group them together and ignore their differences and further similarities as irrelevant.

If we are accustomed to a certain form of classification we become sensitive to (observant of) the relevant similarities and insensitive to (unobservant of) the similarities and differences that are ignored. The latter are no longer noticed in our observation. For instance, because we are accustomed to classifying typewriter characters as *symbols* and not as *shapes*, we no longer observe their forms and take no notice of similarities and differences in these forms (as in the example of the open and closed typewriter characters discussed in section 3.8). For this reason the psychologists Bruner and Goodman state that 'subjects can be conditioned to see and hear things in much the same way as they can be conditioned to perform such overt acts as knee jerking, eye blinking or salivating.'[12]

Briefly: we perceive *selectively*. We are observant of the similarities and differences that are *important* to us, and we therefore learn to apply especially those principles of order that take account of these similarities and differences. For this reason we often find it difficult to exercise other classification concepts than those we are accustomed to.

Language is an important conditioning factor in this connection. When perceiving things, we automatically classify them. For the most important classes we form class words or descriptive terms, for example, 'tree', 'man', 'table', 'dog', 'water'. Such words are used as instruments of classification. By means of them we exercise classification concepts. But since we acquire a certain vocabulary, we have words only for the exercise of *certain* concepts and find it hard to apply other concepts, since we lack the instruments to do so. 'General words tend to *fossilise* our conception of the ever-changing, infinitely various world of things to make us conceive the world as being composed of static *types* rather than of different things, some of which are similar enough to each other to be given the same name.'[13]

Our words and concepts, therefore, determine each other mutually. On the one hand our cultural interests and concerns determine what classification concepts we need to exercise, and thus what classification words we require. On the other hand the words we have (in the language we have learnt) determine what concepts we can exercise and, therefore, what classifications we can make in practice. This, in turn, reinforces our cultural concerns and interests.

Cultural anthropology offers many examples of how a person's vocabulary reflects his cultural and social environments. Paul Henle[14] cites the following examples from the work of Sapir and Whorf to show that languages often differ widely in vocabulary and that this difference

is usually related to various differences in the environment of the
language users. Thus, Whorf has found that Eskimo languages have a
variety of words for different kinds of snow where English has only one.
Aztec is even poorer in this respect, using the same word-stem for cold,
ice and snow. According to Sapir the complete vocabulary of a language
would be a complex inventory of all the ideas, interests and occupations
that take up the attention of the community. Thus, in the
language of the Nootka Indians who live along the north west coast of
the USA, marine animals are distinguished with precise detail. In the
vocabulary of some desert tribes detailed distinctions are made between
berries and other edible food plants. The Paiute Indians speak a
language which permits the most detailed description of topographical
features of the country, since they need to give each other complex
directions for the location of water holes. Sapir points out that this does
not only hold for the physical environment, but even more clearly for
the social and cultural environment. Status systems in various cultures,
however complex, and differentiations due to occupations, are all
reflected in the vocabulary of the languages used.

Briefly, then: (1) Which classification concepts we exercise is
determined by (and determines) what is important and of interest to us
in our social, cultural, and physical environment. (2) Our classification
words therefore reflect the conceptual skills we apply and hence also
our social, cultural and physical concerns and interests. (3)
Classification concepts are therefore ways of orienting ourselves in the
world. They, too, like our illocutionary skills, are forms of life that
constitute our lives as human beings on earth. In this way, to imagine a
language means to imagine a form of life.

The way in which we organise our experience through classification
is determined by practical considerations related to our social, cultural,
and physical circumstances. Where these circumstances differ for
various people or where changes occur in the circumstances of the same
people, this leads to differences and changes in the way they organise
their experience by classification. Our circumstances are not invariable;
nor, therefore, are our conceptual forms of life.

The psychological phenomenon of 'mental set', reinforced by the fact
that our thinking is determined by our *language*, often makes it very
hard for us to depart from established patterns of thinking. There is a
strong temptation to view our conceptual organisation of our
environment as an absolute expression of 'the essence' of things. *These*
classification concepts are then held to be 'true' reflections of the

essential natures of things, and all alternative forms of classification are considered false. Platonic conceptual realism, which we discussed in section 3.7, is a good example of this. In this view the philosopher's task becomes the discovery of the essential nature of things, that is, the one and only true conceptual organisation of our experience.

The Swedish Academy honoured Carl von Linneaus (1707 – 1778) for discovering, through his classification of insects, 'the essential nature of insects'. In contrast to this conceptual realism of *essences*, Charles Darwin wrote as follows in the final chapter of his book *On the Origin of Species*:[15]

> When the views advanced by me in this volume ... are generally admitted ... there will be a considerable revolution in natural history. Systematists will be able to pursue their labours as at present; but they will not be incessantly haunted by the shadowy doubt whether this or that form be a true species. This, I feel sure and I speak after experience, will be no slight relief. The endless disputes whether or not some fifty species of British brambles are good species will cease. Systematists will have only to decide (not that this will be easy) whether any form be sufficiently constant and distinct from other forms, to be capable of definition; and if definable, whether the differences be sufficiently important to deserve a specific name.

In brief, then, we must be wary of all attempts to find an 'essential nature' of things. These attempts usually follow from some form of conceptual realism in which the classification concepts of some culture (or some language) are considered absolute. Against this sort of view we should always remember that our concepts are forms of life, and that forms of life are never static or unchangeable.

We have attempted to show that our classification concepts are contingent, that is, relative to our physical and cultural environment. Changes in this environment require changes in the conceptual skills exercised by us. Classification concepts are thus subject to cultural changes. The question is whether this holds for all concepts: are there any concepts that remain the same even when our culture changes?

According to some philosophers (among them Kant and Strawson) there are in fact *fundamental* concepts which are not contingent (culturally relative). These concepts are necessary elements in all human thought. Without them all thought becomes impossible. Concepts of colour, for example, are contingent: the spectrum is divided differently in different cultures, and words for colours differ from those used in European languages. 'Motor car', 'television', 'double-decker bus', 'pop music', etc., are even more contingent. Concepts such as these are by no means fundamental to all thought in all cultures. But 'identity', 'cause', 'negation', 'knowing', 'believing', 'good', 'bad', 'existence', etc., are somehow essential to thought. We can conceive of no culture (no human thought or action) in which these conceptual skills play no part. Kant's transcendental philosophy was an attempt to find a minimal conceptual structure (*Bewusstsein überhaupt*) that is fundamental to all human thought as such.

In this regard Strawson writes as follows:[16]

> The aim of analytical philosophy is the aim of making clear a network of conceptual connections, grosser and finer, of which, as human beings engaged with the world and each other, we may have a practical mastery without having a clear theoretical understanding. And an important part of this enterprise can be described as that of making clear the basic general structure of our thought and experience.

But how do Kant and Strawson know which concepts are fundamental? Because these concepts are found in all cultures? It is surely impossible in practice to examine *all* cultures in order to ascertain that. Is it, then, because we can *conceive of* no culture where these conceptual skills are not exercised? Could that not as readily be explained as a consequence of our limited imaginative capacities (also as a result of mental set)? In response to philosophers such as Strawson, Ayer writes:[17] 'There is, however, a danger in following Kant too closely. It consists in succumbing to a kind of *a priori* anthropology, in assuming that certain fundamental features of our own conceptual system are necessities of language, which is the modern equivalent for necessities of thought'.

In a sense, I think that Kant and Strawson are right. There are certain concepts which are indeed fundamental to all cultures and to all human thought, simply because the exercise of these concepts belong to the usual *definition* of 'culture' and of 'human thought'. Thus, for example, we would not call the coexistence of people a *culture*, if these people were not able to perform the basic forms of illocutions (constatives, expressives, commissives and prescriptives) and were therefore also unable to live according to agreed rules. And what sort of *human thought* would it be if someone did not master the concept of identity and was therefore unable to see whether two things were or were not the same and hence also unable to distinguish himself from his environment?

In brief, then: (1) Concepts are forms of thought and therefore forms of life. (2) Some concepts are basic to all culture and to all human thought since they belong to the definition of human thought and culture. (3) Many concepts are, however, subject to cultural change.

# 4 Theology and Conceptual Inquiry

## 4.10 CONCEPTUAL INQUIRY AND THE NAMES MODEL

THE sort of questions philosophers ask about concepts depends upon the view they take of the nature of concepts. Thus defenders of a names model would ask quite different questions about concepts than those asked by defenders of the tools model. How do these various forms of conceptual inquiry differ and how are they related?

In section 3.7 we argued that the names model implies the view that concepts are in some sense or other mental representations of the essential structures of reality. On this view, conceptual inquiry becomes the search for real definitions, that is, definitions which state the essential nature of things. According to Plato, the Socratic questions 'What is justice?' 'What is piety?', 'What is knowledge?', 'What is perception?', 'What is the soul?', etc., are questions about the transcendent ideas of which these things are copies. According to Aristotle, a real definition states the essence of a thing, that is, the form which makes that thing what it is. If I were to ask, 'What is man?' I would be looking for the essential characteristic (form) that makes something human and without which it would not be human. It is questionable, however, whether this is more than a roundabout way of asking for the connotation of the word 'man', that is, for those characteristics which something must have if we are to use the word 'man' to refer to it. As we argued in the previous chapter, this is a matter of changeable linguistic convention, and is in no way tied to a supposed essential structure in the things themselves. On the other hand, Socrates, Plato and Aristotle were concerned with more than merely the connotation of words, and we would do no justice to this 'more' by explaining it away as being the result of a mistaken conceptual realism.

The difficulty with an inquiry concerning the essential nature of things, is that it is by no means clear what is actually being sought.

Socratic questions with the form 'what is *x*?' are the vaguest questions we can ask about something, because they gave no indication of the sort of answer required. 'Where is *x*?' and 'When is *x*?' are questions which demand specific sorts of answers. But 'What is *x*?' is quite indeterminate in this respect. Richard Robinson[18] explains this point with the following example: the situation in which I ask 'What is potassium?' may be such that I want to know what the word 'potassium' means, or whether potassium is an element, or to what class of elements it belongs, or what its atomic weight is, etc. Instead of formulating the question vaguely and relying on the context to make clear what I want to know, I should rather formulate it more precisely, for instance 'What does this word mean?' or "Is potassium an element?' Thus it may very well be that an inquiry concerning the essential nature of things does not involve one illegitimate question, but rather a number of important and legitimate questions which are not clearly distinguished from each other. In this way the various answers that can be given to a request for the essential nature of something, are not necessarily alternative answers to the same question. Thus 'Man is a rational animal', 'Man is the most gifted creature on earth', 'Man is a featherless biped', 'Man is the most highly developed primate', 'Man is a person', 'Man is the image of God' etc., could plausibly be interpreted as answers to different questions, rather than as alternative answers to one unambiguous question 'What is (the essential nature of) man?'

In brief: if concepts are in some sense or other mental representations of the essential nature of things, then conceptual inquiry becomes the search for real definitions stating the essential nature of the things defined. This search for real definitions could be rejected as being merely the misguided result of conceptual realism. It could, however, more fruitfully be interpreted as a confused attempt to pursue various important questions at the same time without clearly distinguishing between them. The following are some of the most important questions concerning *x* (or the word '*x*') which are often involved when philosophers ask 'What is (the essential nature of) *x*?'

### 1. What kind of entities are referred to with the descriptive word '*x*'?

We have suggested that the question about the essential nature of something (that which makes something what it is) can be interpreted in this way. This may be either a request for a lexical definition (to what kind of entities do speakers of English usually refer with the word '*x*'?)

or a request for a stipulation (to what kind of entities should we refer with the word '*x*'?). In neither case, however, does the question call for information about the thing *x*. At best, information will be given on our referential use of the word '*x*', and hence on the procedure to follow if we are to distinguish *x* from non-*x*.

With most class words, this procedure is usually straightforward. However, we often run into border-line cases where for various reasons it is not easy to decide whether the word applies or not. This could be due to the fact that in the given circumstances the procedure to distinguish *x* from non-*x* is difficult (if not impossible) to apply in practice, as for example when the forensic scientist has to decide whether a blood stain or piece of charred flesh is human or not, or when a palaeontologist has to decide whether some fossilised bones are human or not. Sometimes, however, the problem involved is a moral and not a pragmatic one. It is not that we are unable in practice to distinguish *x* from non-*x*. It is rather that we are not agreed about when we should *treat* something as an *x* or not. Thus the Spaniards who first went to America were not sure whether the Indians were human beings or animals. Their problem was a moral one (should we treat Indians as human beings?) and not merely a problem regarding the use of words. Similarly the question 'At what stage of its development is a human foetus to be regarded as a human person, so that an abortion at that stage would count as murder?' is a moral issue and not merely a technical difficulty in applying a classification term.

This last point has to do with what we argued in section 3.9. There we showed how our classification concepts are fundamentally determined by our cultural and practical needs and interests. In this way profound moral issues can be involved in deciding where to draw the limits of our classifications. Hence the question 'What is *x*?' could be interpreted as a request for a decision regarding the limits of the class of *x*'s, and this is a decision which could involve moral, cultural, religious and practical issues. It could also be a request for information about the decided limits of the class of *x*'s or (which amounts to the same) for information about the connotation and denotation of the classification word '*x*'.

## 2. *What are the factual characteristics of x?*

This question presupposes that we are able to (and agree about how to) distinguish *x* from non-*x*. We know what the word '*x*' is used to refer to, and would like to acquire some factual information about the thing $x$ thus referred to. To be able to distinguish $x$ from non-$x$ the hearer must, of course, know something about the factual characteristics of $x$, but he need not know everything about it. People were able to recognise a fire – to know to what kind of entity the word 'fire' referred – before it was known that fire consisted of oxidising gases and not of phlogiston. People also could distinguish the kind of animal referred to by the word 'whale' before it was known that whales are mammals and not fish. Thus the question 'What is (the nature of) fire?' may be either a request for an explanation of the referential use of the word 'fire' (What do you mean by 'fire'?), or a question demanding factual information about the phenomenon of fire ('does it consist of phlogiston or of something else?').

### 3. What is the key to the explanation of x?

When the question 'What is (the essence of) $x$?' is meant as a request for factual information about the thing $x$, this is usually in those situations where we are looking for some key element in a complex phenomenon or system of thought in the light of which the whole can be explained. For example, the question as to the essence of the Biblical message is a question about one aspect (or a limited number of aspects) of this message from which all other aspects may be derived. The question as to the essence of religion is a request for one aspect of religion in the light of which all religious phenomena can be understood. The question as to the essence of man could (in the context of psychology, for example) be a request for one aspect of human existence (for example, his sex life, or his economic circumstances, or his early youth, or his genes, in the light of which all psychological phenomena about man could be explained. Thus the question as to the essence of $x$ is often a request for a key that will give us access to a complex phenomenon. It is clear that this is a very important kind of question. It is also clear that this question relates to the factual nature of a phenomenon, not to the meaning of a word.

There are two points about this question that must be borne in mind: (1) We can look for a key element in the factual structure of a phenomenon only if we are agreed on what phenomenon we are examining. One can ask a question about the factual structure of $x$ only if there is agreement on the referential use of the word '$x$'. If the word is too vague we shall first have to agree (stipulatively) on a sufficiently precise denotation, before we can fruitfully inquire into the factual nature of the phenomena that fall within the limits of that denotation. Thus we can ask for a key element in religious phenomena only if we have first reached agreement on what phenomena we should or should not include among religious phenomena. (2) We cannot take it for granted that such key elements can be found in all complex phenomena. An axiomatic system in mathematics does have such a key element: the axioms are the key elements from which the rest of the system may be deduced. Since not all systems of thought are axiomatic, it cannot be assumed that there is one element (or a limited number of elements) from which the rest may be deduced. Attempts to impose such unity on a system often succeed merely in impoverishing the system. Most of the heresies in the history of theology arose from attempts to reduce the entire Christian faith to one of its aspects. Furthermore, attempts to find the essence (key element) of religion often lead to the negation of the diversity of religious phenomena. The question as to the key element in a complex phenomenon is important, but it is often a dangerous question because it may lead to an impoverishing reductionism.

## 4. What is the key to the meaning of x?

The word 'meaning' is ambiguous. Sometimes it is used with reference to words, phrases, expressions, or other elements of language. In section 3.8 we argued that the meaning of a word (or other linguistic element) is the conceptual skill exercised with that word in the speech acts performed with sentences containing it. Sometimes the word 'meaning' is also used with reference to things, events, actions, etc. In this context the word 'meaning' has to do with the value, significance, or purpose of something. When in section 1.1 we distinguished questions of meaning from factual and conceptual questions, we were dealing with meaning in this latter sense. We will deal extensively with the nature of such questions about the meaning of things, events, etc., in chapters 9 and 10.

Questions about the essential nature of $x$ could sometimes be interpreted as requests for a key to the meaning (or significance or value or purpose) of $x$. 'What makes $x$ to be what it is?' means as much as 'What determines that $x$ has the meaning it has?' Thus 'What is (the essence of) man?' could be taken to mean: What determines the meaning of human existence? The fact that man is created in the image of God? Or that he is a seeker after Nirvana? Or that he is a rational being? Or that he is the most highly developed animal? Or something else? 'What is (the essence of) reality?' could be taken as a request for that which determines the significance or meaning of all things or of reality as a whole. Does the meaning of all things derive from the fact that they are created by God, or are manifestations of Reason or of the (Hegelian) Spirit or of Platonic Ideas, or from something else? What is it that determines whether things are real or meaningful? Questions about the meaning of $x$ are clearly questions about $x$ and not about the referential use of the word '$x$'. Nevertheless, we have to be clear about the referential use of the word '$x$' before we can ask questions about the meaning of the $x$ referred to.

### 5. *What are the presuppositions and implications of the concept '$x$'?*

Questions about the essential nature of $x$ can often also be interpreted as questions about the concept '$x$' and not merely about the referential use of the word '$x$' nor about the explanation or the meaning of the phenomenon $x$. Thus Plato used to ask indeterminate 'What-is-$x$?' questions which in theory he interpreted as questions about the transcendent ideas. From the way he describes Socrates dealing with these questions, it is clear, however, that they could also be interpreted as questions about the logical presuppositions and implications of concepts. Thus, for example, in reply to the question 'What is knowing?', which Plato makes Socrates ask, Theaetetus suggest: 'Knowing is the same as observing. I therefore know something when I observe it.' Socrates then proceeds to test this hypothesis by considering its implications. If the implications are absurd, the hypothesis must be untenable. This is why Socrates asks the methodic question: 'If we used the concept $x$ in the same way as the concept $y$, what would be the implications?' In his examination of Theaetetus's hypothesis, that knowing is the same as observing, Socrates comes to the conclusion that this hypothesis has an absurd implication: I know nothing about an object if my eyes are shut and I can no longer see it. Similarly, in the *Euthyphro* Socrates asks Euthyphro "What is piety?", to which the latter replies with the suggestion that acts are pious if the gods approve them. Socrates examines the implications of this suggestion to see whether 'pious' has the same implications as the concept 'approved by the gods'. He arrives at the conclusion that they cannot be equivalent, for if they are, it would be a meaningless tautology to say that the gods approve actions *because* they are pious! In brief, Plato demonstrates that 'Supposing $x$ were equal to $y$, what would the implications be?' is a very useful question to ask when analysing concepts. In this sense Husserl was right when he said that philosophy was an exercise in phantasy. We need phantasy in order to suppose that $x$ is equal to $y$, and also to consider the consequences of this supposition, and to test it in the light of various conceivable situations.

These examples are enough to show that an inquiry concerning the essential nature of $x$ can be interpreted in various ways. It deals in fact not with one unambiguous question but with a variety of questions lumped together under one formula. Thus the question 'What is (the essential nature of) $x$?' could be interpreted as a request for (1) a *definition* of (the referential use of) the word '$x$', or (2) a key to *explain* the phenomenon $x$, or (3) a key to determine the *meaning* of the phenomenon $x$, or (4) an explanation of the logic of the *concept* '$x$'. These are all important questions, but they should be clearly distinguished since the procedure for dealing with them is different in each case.

That these questions are often confused is clear from the fact that the history of philosophy is often interpreted in different ways depending upon which of these questions are considered the most truly philosophical. Thus the history of philosophy is sometimes interpreted as the history of the search for a key to the meaning of human existence or of history or of the universe as a whole, and sometimes as the history of conceptual inquiry. In this way the same philosophical texts are interpreted as answers to quite different questions. Plato's theory of ideas is sometimes viewed as an idealistic theory of reality: reality is ideal and the observable universe is only meaningful to the extent that it reflects this ideal reality. On the other hand, this same theory can also be interpreted as an attempt to solve the conceptual problem of universals: general words are names for general things, that is, the ideas which we remember from our pre-existence in the realm of ideas.

Similarly Descartes' philosophy could be interpreted as a rationalistic view about the meaning of human existence. The meaning of human existence depends upon the fact that man is a rational mind: *cogito ergo sum*. If we look at Descartes' argument in his *Meditations*, however, it is clear that his primary aim is to examine the concept of 'certainty' in an attempt to find a criterion for distinguishing between certain knowledge and uncertain opinion. According to Descartes, certain knowledge is found only in indubitable propositions and in conclusions that follow deductively from such indubitable propositions. 'I doubt' is an indubitable proposition, because it is verified the moment I try to doubt it. 'I doubt' implies 'I think', since doubt is a form of thought. 'I think', in turn, implies (as a necessary presupposition) 'I exist'. If I did not exist, I could not think. Therefore: *cogito ergo sum.*

Kant's transcendental critique of human knowledge could be interpreted as an expression of a rationalist view of reality. According to him the world of human experience is constituted by the rational forms of human thought and perception. Our rational knowledge constitutes the world. Hegel developed this view into an absolute idealism according to which reality is constituted not by our common thought forms, but by the Absolute Spirit or Reason. All things are meaningful because they are rational and they are rational because they are constituted by Reason. Although Kant's transcendental critique does express a rationalist view of reality, it was not developed by Kant for this purpose. Kant was rather interested in an epistemological inquiry concerning the limits of human knowledge, by trying to find the transcendental conditions (that is, the conditions of possibility) for human knowledge.

These examples are enough to show that the works of various philosophers could be read with different questions in mind, either as exercises in conceptual inquiry or as attempts to find keys to the meaning of reality or human existence. Often the primary purpose of these works is to perform a piece of conceptual inquiry, but in doing this some view on the meaning of reality or of human existence is manifested. In a parallel way the gardens at Versailles were designed as gardens for people to walk in and to enjoy, although at the same time they express the rationalist view of reality held at the court of Louis XIV. Similarly the so-called English gardens which were in vogue in the eighteenth and nineteenth centuries, express a romantic view of the world, even though they were not designed to express such views, but simply to be enjoyed and used as gardens.

In brief: if we accept the names model, and view words as names for concepts and concepts as mental representations of the essential nature of reality, then the task of philosophy becomes the search for the essential nature of things. In this sort of inquiry various questions tend to get confused so that the works of philosophers can be interpreted in different ways, depending on which of these questions are considered to be most important. In order to gain clarity about the nature of conceptual inquiry as such, apart from all the other sorts of questionings with which it could be confused, it is necessary to start from another view about the nature of concepts.

## 4.11 CONCEPTUAL INQUIRY AND THE TOOLS MODEL

In section 3.8 we argued that the tools model of language implies the view that concepts are forms of thought or mental skills which we usually exercise verbally in our relation with each other and with the world. When a philosopher concerns himself with the nature of human thought, he is therefore inquiring into the nature of concepts. What is the nature of this sort of inquiry?

Four different metaphors are often used to explain the nature of this sort of conceptual inquiry.[19] Thus Russell described philosophy as a kind of *analysis*, Ryle preferred the metaphor of *geography*, Wittgenstein sometimes considered philosophy as a kind of *therapy* and Strawson describes philosophical questions as similar to *grammatical* questions. We could add a fifth metaphor to this list, because in some ways conceptual inquiry can also be compared to the work of a law scholar trying to *codify common law*. All these metaphors have their limitations, yet each one highlights some or other important feature of the sort of conceptual inquiry pursued by philosophers. Let us examine these metaphors in turn.

### 1. Conceptual analysis

Analysis is what we do when we break things down into their elements and then examine how these elements relate to each other. In this regard, elements are the simplest building blocks out of which a complex structure is composed. Different kinds of analysis concentrate on different kinds of elements: in physics, the elements are electrons, atoms, etc.; in syntax, morphemes; in phonetics, the phonemes; whereas in philosophy, concepts are the elementary building blocks examined by the conceptual analyst.

The metaphor of analysis is inadequate in various respects. In the first place, it may create the impression that philosophy is primarily concerned with the analysis of separate concepts, rather than with the logical relations and logical conflicts between concepts. Thus Ryle declares [20] that he has neither any special objection to nor any special liking for the fashion of describing as 'analysis' the sort or sorts of conceptual examination performed by philosophers. But it is misleading to view this examination as a sort of garage inspection of one conceptual vehicle at a time. On the contrary, it is always a traffic inspector's examination of a conceptual traffic bloc, involving at least two streams of vehicles, hailing from theories, or points of view, or platitudes which are at cross-purposes with one another.

Secondly, the use of this metaphor may also lead to a reduction of all concepts to *homogeneous* elements (as in Russell's logical atomism). It might cause us to lose sight of the complex diversity of concepts and the multiplicity of the relations between them.

Thirdly, the metaphor of analysis is too general to give an indication of the kinds of elements involved, or of the kinds of relations between these elements. Nevertheless, such a *general* metaphor does have the merit of not excluding certain possibilities in advance. We may well, therefore, speak of philosophical inquiry concerning concepts as *analysis*, provided that we get clear about the nature of this kind of analysis, and in particular about the nature of the elements and relations with which this kind of analysis is concerned.

## 2. Conceptual geography

The geographical analogy often used by Ryle is illuminating because on many points conceptual inquiry does resemble the work of a cartographer.

Thus for example, a map represents a *whole* region (not merely isolated points in that region). The relations between the various points are indicated, and there is also an indication of the different kinds of points involved. Similarly conceptual inquiry is also an attempt to 'map' all kinds of concepts. Different kinds of concepts have to be distinguished, and the complex relations between them, within the total field of human thought (and life), must be traced.

Secondly, a map is an *abstraction* from our ordinary observation of the world, enabling us to gain a survey of and insight in our field of observation. This abstraction may be performed in various ways, depending on our concerns and the purposes for which we need the map. Thus one finds survey maps and detailed maps, and various kinds of maps in which different geographical features are singled out (for example political maps, topographical maps, weather charts, road maps, etc.). In 'mapping' concepts, too, we may work in more detail or more generally, or we may focus on the mapping of certain kinds (families) of concepts, for example moral concepts, epistemological concepts, psychological concepts, mathematical concepts, theological concepts, etc. In doing so, we must be especially wary of the hazards of all abstraction: although different conceptual areas may be distinguished, they cannot be understood in isolation from each other, for *in life* itself they are interrelated. For example, theological concepts cannot be isolated with impunity from their relations with moral concepts, epistemological concepts, psychological concepts, and so on.

Along with these similarities there is, however, an important difference between cartography and conceptual inquiry: concepts are not points to be observed; they are skills to be practised. For this reason the relations between concepts are quite different from the relations between points on a map. The nature of the relations between concepts cannot, therefore, be accounted for adequately in geographical language.

## 3. Conceptual therapy

In our thinking we are often confronted with seemingly insoluble problems. An apparently valid argument may lead us to unacceptable conclusions. Sometimes we are confronted with questions for which there are no answers, or only absurd answers. Sometimes we cannot see how something that we know to be the case, can indeed be so. In such situations, as Wittgenstein put it, we feel like a prisoner caught in his own conceptual net. It is the task of philosophy to free us from this kind of captivity. 'What is your aim in philosophy? – To shew the fly the way out of the fly-bottle.'[21] Wittgenstein also compares this captivity with an illness and the philosopher's task with a therapy that might cure our minds. 'The philosopher's treatment of a question is like the treatment of an illness.'[22] According to Wittgenstein, the cause of the illness lies in *language*. The conceptual forms built into our language, cast a spell on us. The philosopher, therefore, has the task of freeing us from this enchantment: 'Philosophy is a battle against the bewitchment of our intelligence by means of language.'[23]

There are various ways in which language may cast a spell on us. First, we may be misled by an analogy, for example the analogy between words and names, or between time and a stream. These analogies raise insoluble problems, because they make us ask questions (or say things) about words or about time that are absurd because they can actually be asked or said only of names or of streams. The philosopher's task is to break down the barriers of our captivity, or at least to make us critically aware of the limitations of such analogies.

Secondly, we may confuse the 'surface grammar' of a language with its 'depth grammar'. For example, because 'That is good' has the same superficial grammatical form as 'That is red', we tend to think that goodness is a descriptive characteristic of things just like redness. This causes us to ask questions about the nature of this supposed characteristic 'goodness', about the way in which we can observe it, etc.; whereas the question is surely whether 'good' is in fact used to refer to a descriptive characteristic of something.

Both these examples demonstrate what we may call (with Gilbert Ryle) category mistakes: we interpret a concept as being part of a conceptual category in which that concept does not belong. Time is not a remarkable kind of stream, and 'good' does not indicate some remarkable kind of observable (or unobservable) characteristic of things, and words have quite different and many more functions than names. The philosopher's task, then, is to examine concepts in order to ascertain within what forms of life, or 'language games', or categories they belong, and by this means to free us from the category mistakes which hold us captive.

It is true that philosophy does have this therapeutic task with regard to thought. Yet philosophy has a more positive *constructive* task as well, and this is not fully accounted for in the metaphor of the therapist.

### 4. Conceptual grammar

Wittgenstein's distinction between surface grammar and depth grammar suggests a similarity between conceptual inquiry and the study of the grammar of a language: the philosopher's task is to examine the depth grammar of our thinking. P.F. Strawson develops this analogy with reference to the following example.[24] When the first book describing Castillian grammar was presented to Queen Isabella of Castille, her response was to ask of what use it was to fluent speakers of Castillian since it told them nothing that they did not know already. Although in a sense it was true that they knew the grammar of their language, there was another sense in which they did not know it. Thus Isabella would have been at a loss if asked to describe the system of rules by which grammatically correct sentences could be distinguished from sequences of words which were not sentences at all or were not grammatically correct sentences. Her practice in constructing Castillian sentences showed that she and her courtiers effortlessly observed such a system of rules. But from this it by no means follows that they could effortlessly or with an effort say what these rules were. The ability to do something, in this case speak grammatically, is very different from and does not necessarily involve the ability to say how it is done.

This example illustrates various features of conceptual inquiry. First of all, people apply grammatical rules, even if they cannot always state the rules. People had a command of grammar long before any book of grammar had been written. Similarly, we master conceptual skills, even though we cannot always state the rules that constitute these conceptual skills. People are capable of logical argument even if they have never heard of logic.

Secondly, conceptual inquiry, like grammar, is concerned with things we already know! Philosophical theorising is therefore an attempt to account explicitly for a practice which we already master implicitly or intuitively. According to Plato, philosophy is *anamnesis* or recollection: the philosopher tries to recall the ideas that he observed in his pre-existence. If we were to demythologise Plato, we could argue that his view of philosophy describes the philosopher as someone who tries to recall the conceptual skills which he learnt at his mother's knee and still commands intuitively. We acquire conceptual skills as we learn the words with which those skills are exercised. We learn to think with concepts as we learn to speak with words.

Thirdly, Isabella's question may well be asked also of conceptual inquiry: what is the use of inquiring after things that we know already? In this regard we may make two points about conceptual inquiry. First, conceptual inquiry provides some insight into the structure of our thinking, enabling us to think critically and reflectively rather than merely intuitively. Secondly, we learn to diagnose our fallacies (errors in the exercise of conceptual skills) and thus to solve the logical puzzles arising from such fallacies. In this case conceptual inquiry has both a *constructive* and a *therapeutic* function.

## 5. Conceptual codification

In the light of our discussion so far, we could also compare conceptual inquiry to the work of a law scholar trying to codify common law. Common law is a body of norms and customs which people in a given community observe intuitively, without accounting for them explicitly. In this respect, the common law of a community is similar to the implicit rules according to which we practise our grammatical skills and our conceptual skills. The law scholar codifying common law is actually doing two things. First, he is trying to give a systematic *description* of the common law in a society; secondly, he does not, in his codifying description, leave unaltered that which he is codifying; he also tries to *improve* it by systematising it. Hence, he is involved in both *description* and *prescription*. The same applies to conceptual inquiry. Our conceptual skills are both *descriptively* systematised and systematically *improved*, since various conceptual skills are related to each other, in a consistent manner.

In section 3.9 we argued that some concepts are fundamental in the sense that the ability to exercise them is part of what we mean by human thought and culture. Many concepts are, however, relative to our particular cultures, and subject to change as our culture changes. Hence the philosopher who pursues conceptual inquiry does not merely describe the conceptual skills exercised by people, nor does he merely try systematically to improve these concepts by relating them to each other in a consistent way. He is also reflecting in a critical way on the cultural process to which our conceptual skills are subject.

In brief: (1) Conceptual inquiry is a critical reflection on the conceptual skills that we command intuitively, with the purpose of tracing the systematic relations between them. (2) In this way the whole complex of conceptual skills inbedded in our forms of life is recorded descriptively and improved systematically. (3) Thus the process of cultural change is guided critically in so far as it determines our forms of thought. This gives us insight into our own forms of thought as they actually are and as they are determined by cultural changes so that we are alerted to possible fallacies in the exercise of our conceptual skills and are thus enabled to eliminate the logical dilemmas arising from such fallacies.

## 4.12 THEOLOGY AND CONCEPTUAL INQUIRY

In section 1.2 we stated that systematic theology is itself a form of conceptual inquiry. Now that we have examined the nature of conceptual inquiry, we are in a better position to explain in what sense this is the case.

In this connection, the definition Karl Barth gives of dogmatics is illuminating. 'As a theological discipline dogmatics is the scientific self-examination of the Christian church with respect to the content of its distinctive talk about God.'[25] According to this definition, dogmatics is a reflective, meta-inquiry in which the church examines the content of its own distinctive way of talking about God, both when expressing its faith in liturgy and when confessing its faith in doctrine.

There are various aspects to this sort of reflection on the content of our talk about God. First of all, the theologian can be interested in this 'content' in the sense of wanting to know exactly *what* the church says and said in the course of history when it was talking about God. This would be the task of an *historical theology*, and much of dogmatics is in fact a matter of historical theology. Secondly, the theologian could be interested in testing this content in the light of its norm: does what the church says and said about God correspond to the Biblical witness about Him? This would be the task of a *Biblical theology*, and much of what is done in dogmatics is in fact a matter of biblical theology. Thirdly, an inquiry into the content of our talk about God also involves a reflection on the fundamental concepts exercised in the church's talk about God. What are the fundamental concepts of the Christian faith? What do they presuppose and imply? What are the logical relations between them? And how are they related to the concepts we exercise in other contexts? These questions are the task of *systematic theology*, and much of what is done in dogmatics is a matter of systematic theology.

Systematic theology is therefore a form of conceptual inquiry since the sort of questions dealt with in systematic theology are conceptual questions. Let us illustrate this with two classical examples of problems in systematic theology.

In his *De Principiis*, Origen argues that

> in the beginning God created by an act of His will as large a number of intelligent beings as He could control. For we must maintain that even the power of God is finite, and we must not, under the pretext of praising Him, lose sight of His limitations. For if the divine power were infinite, of necessity it could not even understand itself, since the infinite is by nature incomprehensible. He made therefore just as many as He could grasp and keep in hand and subject to His providence. In much the same way He prepared just as much matter as He could reduce to order.

If, therefore, we were to suppose that God is infinite, this would imply that He cannot comprehend Himself. Comprehending means grasping, and this implies setting limits to. It would therefore be contradictory to say that anyone comprehended the infinite. God, then, is a finite God and hence able to comprehend Himself. This again has *implications* for the theory of creation: God created a universe He could control. The limitations of the creation are therefore determined by God's own limitations.

The *problem* examined here by Origen is a *conceptual* one: what are the *implications* of the concepts 'finite' and 'infinite' when applied to God? His solution to this problem is dubious, to say the least, but if we are to refute his view (that God is finite) we have to offer a different analysis of the concepts 'finite' and 'infinite'. Thus both the defence and the refutation of Origen's views are tasks for conceptual inquiry.

In his *De Trinitate* Augustine grapples with the question of the relationship between Jesus and God the Father. Is Jesus identical with the Father? Or is Jesus someone else (the Son), *distinct from* the Father? As a methodic point of departure, Augustine inquires whether everything said of Jesus in the Bible can also be said of God the Father, and arrives at the conclusion that some of the things said about the Father and the Son in the Bible are said in such terms as to suggest an essential unity and equivalence of Father and Son, whereas other things are said in such a way as to suggest that the Son is less than the Father, for example in his taking on the form of a servant.

Why cannot we say that the Father adopts the form of a servant? Augustine's answer to this is that it would be contrary to God's *immutability*. But what are the implications of the concept 'immutability' in relation to God? Alas, the Bible provides no systematic answer to this question. We must therefore examine various conceivable interpretations of this concept and test each interpretation (as Socrates did) in the light of its implications. If its implications do not square with what is said of God in the Bible, the interpretation is false. In this way systematic theology can try to arrive at a consistent doctrine of God.

These examples are enough to show how systematic theology is a form of conceptual inquiry in which the theologian tries to map the logical geography of the fundamental concepts of the Christian faith and in this way to determine their logical relations consistently.

In his definition of dogmatics quoted above, Karl Barth says that the way the church talks about God is *distinctive*. In a way, of course, this is correct, since the church confesses a distinctive God. Hence the ultimate standard by which to test what the church says about God, remains the Biblical witness. On the other hand, although what the church says about God is distinctive, the concepts with which the church says this are not distinctive. The distinctive Christian faith concerning God is expressed in ordinary everyday concepts, because, as we argued in section 1.2, the Christian faith is not divorced from our everyday life of which these concepts form a part. Hence it is necessary for the systematic theologian to inquire into the way faith is related to the most basic conceptual forms of ordinary life – for example, evaluative concepts, epistemological concepts and ontological concepts, and also into the way these concepts behave when they are exercised in the context of faith. In Parts Two, Three and Four we will pursue this inquiry.

# PART TWO

## AXIOLOGICAL CONCEPTS

# 5 Introduction

## 5.13 AXIOLOGICAL QUESTIONS

THE philosophical theory of values or *axiology* (axios = valuable) is concerned with a number of fundamental questions about values such as goodness, beauty, justice, etc. It is very important that we should formulate these questions carefully, otherwise we may have difficulties in trying to answer them. Much of the thinking in this field in our western tradition has been influenced by Plato's way of stating the questions, which was defective in two important respects.

Plato asked: 'What are (values such as) goodness, beauty, justice etc.?' In the context of his view that words are names referring to entities, this question suggests that values such as goodness, beauty, justice, etc. are *entities*. Thus the axiological problem becomes: What kind of entities are values? Where and how do these entities exist? Plato's theory of ideas provided the answer: values are universal ideas existing in a transcendent realm of ideas. The concrete entities which we perceive around us are reflections of these ideas. Hence, Plato's question is founded on the assumption that values are entities, and his way of stating it did not allow him to question this assumption.

Nouns such as 'goodness', 'justice', etc. occur mainly in the vocabulary of philosophers. They are less often used by ordinary people. Yet everybody speaks of good or bad deeds, correct and faulty decisions, beautiful and ugly things, proper and improper behaviour, just and unjust policies, and so on. Maybe philosophers, who prefer to use the nouns 'goodness', 'beauty', 'justice', etc., instead of the more customary adjectives 'good', 'beautiful', 'just', etc., are thinking, as Plato did, in terms of *entities*. Perhaps we should rather formulate our axiological questions in terms of evaluative adjectives instead of following Plato by starting with nouns.

Plato's question is also defective in another way, since it is formulated as a 'what-is-x?' question. In section 4.10 we argued that 'what-is-x?' questions are the vaguest and most ambiguous questions conceivable. Above all, there are two important *kinds* of questions that we cannot distinguish if we formulate our questions in the Platonic style: evaluative questions and meta-evaluative questions. Both kinds of questions can be formulated in terms of evaluative adjectives but are difficult to formulate in terms of Platonic nouns.

*Evaluative questions* are those which are asked in *normative ethics* (What acts are good?), *normative esthetics* (What things are beautiful? or: What things are works of art?), and in *normative politics* (What social structures are just?). The answers to these questions are *value judgements* in which we speak of acts, things, situations, structures, etc., as good, beautiful, just, etc.

Meta-evaluative questions precede evaluative ones: they are questions *about* the evaluative questions. For example: What kind of questions are evaluation questions? What kind of speech acts are the value judgements they evoke? What, precisely, do we do when we speak of acts, things, etc., as good, beautiful, just etc.?

It is clear that meta-evaluative questions *precede* evaluative ones: before we can examine what value judgements are valid in ethics or esthetics or politics we have to ask ourselves what kind of speech act a value judgement actually is. In dealing with axiological concepts, we shall concern ourselves mainly with these meta-evaluative questions: What kind of speech act is a value judgement? What kind of arguments can we use to defend or criticise a value judgement? What kinds of value judgement are distinguishable?

In chapter 6 we shall consider naturalism and intuitionism. In terms of these views value judgements are *constative* speech acts, in which it is asserted that something has a certain evaluative characteristic (it is good, bad, beautiful, ugly, incorrect, etc.). In chapter 7 we shall deal with emotivism, in terms of which value judgements are *expressive* speech acts, in which the speaker expresses his feeling or attitude toward an object, situation, or act. In chapter 8 we shall discuss prescriptivism, according to which a value judgement is a *prescriptive* speech act in which the speaker demands or requests a certain attitude from his hearer towards an object, situation, or act. In chapter 9 we shall attempt to show that speech acts in which we state the *meaning* (or significance) of an object, situation or event, are also evaluative: there is a connection between our judgement on the value of something and our judgements on the meaning of something. In chapter 10 we shall examine the nature of a *view of life*, because our justification of value judgements and of judgements on meaning ultimately implies an appeal to the context of a view of life. Ultimate questions are questions regarding a view of life. Can these questions be answered rationally? Or are all answers to such ultimate questions arbitrary and irrational?

# 6 Value Judgements as Constative Speech Acts

## 6.14  VALUES AND CHARACTERISTICS

ARE value judgements constative speech acts? Those who answer this question affirmatively have noted an important respect in which value judgements, like statements of fact, differ from expressions of feelings or taste or attitude.

Statements of fact are *constative* speech acts in which a speaker states facts regarding an object or situation or event, etc., for instance by stating what the factual characteristics of an object or situation are. Conflicting constatives are irreconcilable: if Peter claims that something is red and John claims it is not red, both cannot be right, because they contradict each other. Since both cannot be right, we need some means of determining who is right and who is not. Contradiction calls for discussion; and in practice we argue about the correctness and incorrectness of conflicting factual assertions.

Conflicting *expressive* speech acts are not irreconcilable in the same sense: if a story elicits Peter's appreciation whilst boring John, the expressions of their respective attitudes are not contradictory. It is quite possible that Peter might like a story that bores John to tears; no discussion is needed to determine who is right and who wrong. After all, there is no accounting for tastes.

In this respect *value judgements* are similar to constative speech acts and different from expressive speech acts. Contradictory value judgements, too, are irreconcilable. If Peter considers something good, whereas John insists that it is bad, both cannot be right. As in the case of constatives, we need some way of determining whose value judgement is right and whose wrong. In respect of value judgements, too, contradiction calls for discussion.

Are we to conclude from this similarity between value judgements and constative speech acts that value judgements are in fact constative speech acts? In a constative speech act we state the *factual characteristics* of something; in a value judgement we say what *value* it has. If value judgements are constative speech acts, the value of something is therefore a kind of factual characteristic of it. But what kind of factual characteristic could the value of something be? Those who regard value judgements as constative speech acts, give different answers to this question. Perhaps we might best understand the nature of the problem in this regard by considering the differences between the value of a thing and its *colour*.

Colours have two characteristics: on the one hand they are *directly perceived*. After all, I know whether something is red by looking at it. The difference between yellow and red can likewise be directly perceived. Secondly, colours are *simple* characteristics in the sense that they cannot be defined in terms of other characteristics. We can only explain to someone what colours red and yellow are by showing him red or yellow objects and not by defining the words 'red' and 'yellow' in terms of other characteristics of things.

The *Pocket Oxford Dictionary* gives the following definitions:

> *Red*: of a colour varying from crimson to orange seen in blood, sunset
> clouds, rubies, glowing coals, fox's hair, etc.
> *Reed*: tall straight stalk of kinds of water or marsh plant.
> *Yellow*: of the colour of buttercups, or primroses, or lemons, or gold.
> *Yeoman*: man owning and farming small estate.

The dictionary defines the concepts 'reed' and 'yeoman' by giving their meanings in terms of other concepts, without referring to examples. The concepts 'red' and 'yellow', however, are defined ostensively by referring to examples of red or yellow objects (blood, rubies, lemons, gold, etc., or a specific place in the spectrum). This procedure is followed because the concepts 'red' and 'yellow' are simple: their meanings cannot be analysed in terms of the meanings of other (simpler) concepts.

It is clear that if the value of something is to be a factual characteristic, it must be a quite different kind of characteristic from its colour. 'Good' is not a simple, directly perceived characteristic like 'yellow'. After all, I do not perceive that my Morris is a *good car* in the same way that I perceive it to be a *red car*. Likewise, the difference between a good and a bad car is not perceptible in the same way as the difference between a red and a yellow car. Furthermore, I cannot explain the meaning of the concept 'good' in the same way as I can explain the meaning of the concept 'yellow', that is, by pointing to examples. Let us take a closer look at this last point.

I can explain the meaning of *yellow* to someone by saying that it is a simple characteristic observable in buttercups, primroses, lemons, gold, and in Steven Swaggerer's car. But I cannot explain the meaning of the term 'good' by saying that it is a simple characteristic observable in Morris cars, in Picasso's paintings, in humility, in paying one's debts, and in Sister Martha Charity. The yellow objects have an observable characteristic in common. Morris cars, Picasso's paintings, humility, paying one's debts, and Sister Martha Charity have no observable common characteristic; we do not call them all 'good' by virtue of the fact that they all have an observable characteristic in common.

Suppose I tried to explain the meaning of the term *yellow* to someone by showing him a number of yellow objects and he admitted that all those objects had a common characteristic, but insisted that they were all red. If he persisted in calling all yellow objects that I showed him 'red', I would decide that he was either colour blind or that we were using words differently: I would be using the word 'yellow' in the same sense as he would be using 'red'.

Now let us suppose I tried to explain to someone the meaning of the term *good* by referring to humility, settling one's debts, Morris cars, Picasso's paintings, and Sister Martha. Suppose this person regarded humility as a sign of weakness and piling up debts as a safeguard against inflation, was a Fiat enthusiast and a misogynist, and loved realistic art. He might reply that all my examples did have something in common, that is, that they were all bad. In this case I would not conclude, as in our previous example, that either of us had defective powers of perception, nor that our disagreement was simply a matter of terminology. The disagreement between two people who call the same things good and bad, respectively, is much more fundamental than between two people who call the same thing red and yellow, respectively.

If values are factual characteristics, they are obviously characteristics of a kind differing from colours. Both *intuitionism* and *naturalism* hold values to be factual characteristics. They disagree, however, on the question of what *kind* of factual characteristic the value of something is. According to *intuitionism* values, like colours, are simple characteristics but not perceptible to our ordinary senses. According to *naturalism* the value of something is sensorily perceptible, just like its colour. Values differ from colour, however, in that they are not simple. Let us examine these two points of view more closely.

## 6.15 INTUITIONISM

In summer one can reach the summit of the Zugspitze, the highest
point in the Bavarian Alps, by cableway from the Tyrolean village of
Ehrwald. A splendid view unfolds before one on a clear day. According
to the Michelin guide-book 'The panorama to the south reveals the
glacier summits of the High Tauern . . ., the Tyrolean Alps . . ., the
Ortler and the Bernina, towering over the forward bastions of the
Kaisergebirge, the Dachstein and the Karwendel . . . To the north are
the hazy Bavarian lowlands with the shimmering waters of the
Ammersee and the Starnberger See.' Truly a *beautiful* sight!

What is the nature of the *beauty* that one ascribes to this mountainous
landscape, and how do we perceive that it is a beautiful landscape?
According to intuitionism, beauty (like goodness) is a *non-natural
characteristic* of the landscape, that is, a characteristic that is *objective,
simple* and *non-empirical*.

Intuitionism is opposed to any form of *subjectivism* in values: in
making value judgements, we provide objective information on things;
we do not merely express our subjective experience of or feeling toward
things. The beauty of the panorama described above is held to be an
*objective characteristic* of the scene, not to be reduced to the feelings or
experience of those enjoying it from the summit of the Zugspitze.
Similarly, good and evil, proper and improper, are objective
characteristics of things.

There is much to be seen from the summit of the Zugspitze: the
colour of the sky and the clouds, the expanse of snow, the shapes of the
rock formations, the nature of the vegetation. All these are empirically
observable features of the landscape. But the beauty of the scene is
different from and more than all these empirically observable
characteristics. The beauty of something is neither reducible to, nor
inferable from, its empirically observable characteristics. According to
intuitionism this holds for all values: values, like colours, are *simple
characteristics of things*, that is, characteristics that are not reducible to a
combination of other characteristics. (In section 6.16 we shall see that
the naturalists differ from the intuitionists on this point.)

The empirical characteristics of something are empirically
observable. The value of something, however, is *not empirically
observable*. According to intuitionism we know only intuitively whether
something is good or bad, beautiful or ugly, proper or improper.

The concept *intuition* raises a number of problems. The intuitionists hold that intuition is a special kind of perception that we exercise by means of an extra sense, over and above our other, ordinary senses (sight, hearing, taste, etc.). It is, however, difficult to imagine such an extraordinary sense. All our ordinary senses are coupled with specific organs in our bodies: I see with my eyes, hear with my ears, etc. But with what organ do I have intuitions? What are we to say to people who deny that they have intuitions? Do they suffer from some deficiency? But what kind of deficiency would this be, unrelated as it is to a physical abnormality such as occurs in a case of deafness or blindness?

Let us leave these problems aside and agree, for the sake of the argument with the intuitionists, that there are people who do have such an extraordinary sense by which they perceive intuitively whether something is good, beautiful, proper, etc. This would not mean an end to all the intuitionists' problems. Their crucial problem remains: can they substantiate, by appealing to intuition, their claim that the value of something is an *objective* characteristic of that thing?

Discussions about objective characteristics occur in the context of a distinction between the characteristics that an object has *in reality* (objectively) and those it *appears* to me to have (subjectively). We draw this distinction because our direct perceptions often produce varying results when there is no reason to assume that the observed object has really changed, or because a standard test often shows flaws in our observations. For instance, a sheet of paper that used to look white might look red under a red light without having been painted red. If I put my hands in two basins of water, the water in one basin might feel warmer than that in the other, whereas a thermometer might show no difference in temperature. To account for situations of this kind we draw a distinction between the *real* colour of the paper and the colours it *seems* to me to have under different conditions, or between the real temperature of the water and its apparent temperature.

Meaningful discussion on the question of what characteristics something really (objectively) has, is possible only if we have some criterion or test by which we can distinguish between real and apparent characteristics. We therefore need to have *different* procedures by which to ascertain how something *seems* and how it really *is*. Thus every observation I make of something provides a useful criterion for ascertaining what that object seems like to me in the situation in which I am observing it. But not all observations are adequate criteria for ascertaining what something really is like. Our observations of an object often differ from person to person and from one situation to another.

Therefore, if we wish to ascertain whether an object really has some characteristic, we need an 'objective' test that would produce the same results in different situations and for different people.

For instance, if I wish to ascertain what colour an object *really* has, I shall have to find out what that object looks like to a normal (not colour-blind) observer under certain standard conditions (for example ordinary daylight). A sheet of paper really *is* white if by ordinary daylight it looks white to a non-colour-blind observer, even if now (by the light of my red lamp) it seems red to me. If today, by ordinary daylight, that sheet of paper looks white to a normal observer and tomorrow, under the same conditions, looks red to him, we might conclude that it has changed colour (someone must have painted it). If, however, it looks white to me (by ordinary daylight) and later (by the light of my red lamp) looks red to me, we would say that it has not actually but only apparently changed colour. If it looks red to John and brown to Peter under the same conditions we shall have to conclude that one of them is colour-blind. We shall have to appeal to the normal observer under standard conditions to ascertin whether the sheet of paper is *really red* or *really brown*.

Objective tests for real characteristics thus involve an appeal to standard observers making their observations under standard conditions. Sometimes, however, such standard conditions are accompanied by indirect confirmation through other senses. The water in basin *A* may *feel* warmer than that in basin *B* but *has* the same temperature when I can *see* that a thermometer shows the same temperature as I dip it into the two basins in turn. What we *see* on the thermometer is more constant for everybody than what we *feel* with our hands.

From these examples it becomes clear that a discussion on the objective characteristics that something *really has* and not merely *seems to have* to individual observers is founded on the premise that not all direct observations provide a test for real objective characteristics. Only a *standardised* observation is fit to serve as an objective test, since only a standardised observation will remain constant (because it is standardised), regardless of who appeals to it.

According to intuitionism values are objective (non-natural) characteristics. It is only through intuition, however, that we know what value something has. From our analysis of the concept 'objective characteristic' it is clear, however, that the intuitionists cannot appeal to every intuition in order to ascertain what value something has. If we have a difference of opinion on the value of something we must be able to appeal to a *standardised* intuition in order to clear up our differences. Not any random intuition will serve this purpose.

On what grounds can we distinguish between standardised intuitions and other intuitions? In standardised empirical observations an appeal is made, as pointed out above, to observations made with some other sense, which produces more constant results for everybody, or to a standard (normal) observer. The first of these two possibilities is ruled out for the intuitionist: according to the intuitionist our intuition with regard to the value of something cannot be verified by any other sense, since it is *only* through intuition that we know the value of something, not through perception by any other sense. The intuitionist will therefore have to appeal to a standard (normal) intuiter: the true (objective) value of something will then be the value discovered intuitively in it by the standard intuiter. The problem is, how do we determine who is the standard intuiter? The intuitionist has no satisfactory answer to this question. His definition of the standard intuiter would either be circular or imply an infinite regress.

A circular definition of the standard (that is, not colour-blind) observer would be, for example, that the standard observer is a person who observes in the standard manner. In other words, a person is not colour-blind if he perceives colours in the standard manner, and the standard manner of perceiving colours is that of a person who is not colour-blind. It is not necessary, however, to give such a circular definition of the standard (not colour-blind) *observer*, because a standard observer is someone whose eyes do not show the physical abnormalities characteristic for the eyes of a colour-blind person. In principle such physical abnormalities can be observed under a microscope. But it is not possible to give such a definition of the standard (that is, not value-blind) *intuiter*, since 'value blindness' cannot be detected under a microscope. The standard intuiter can therefore be defined only as the intuiter who intuits in the standard manner, and that is a circular definition. *In principle* the intuitionist cannot distinguish empirically between the standard and the non-standard intuiter: after all, the standard intuiter is a *good* intuiter, and *goodness* can be observed only by intuition, not by observation. The intuitionist would have to say that we know *by intuition* who the standard intuiter is, but how are we to know if we are intuiting *this* correctly? By further intuition? And are we to test this further intuition by even further intuition? Such an answer would lead to infinite regress and is also absurd.

Briefly: intuitionism seeks, on the one hand, to uphold the objectivity of values by regarding them as objective characteristics of things; on the other hand intuitionism holds that we can ascertain only by intuition whether something has these objective (non-natural) characteristics. Since all discussion on objective characteristics implies an appeal to objective criteria, and since the intuitionist cannot provide such criteria, he cannot achieve his aim; if intuition is our only test for the value of something, and if there are no standard intuitions, then the value of something is what it seems to me *subjectively*, not what it is *objectively*. The intuitionist, therefore, cannot account for the objectivity of values nor for the fact that we can and do argue about the value of things.


6.16 NATURALISM


The naturalists agree with the intuitionists that the value of something is an *objective characteristic* of that thing. They do not agree, however, that values are non-natural characteristics. According to them values are *consequential characteristics*. What is meant by 'consequential characteristics'? R.M. Hare uses the following example to explain this term.[1]

Suppose we visit a gallery and look at two paintings (*A* and *B*) painted by the same artist in the same period. Suppose that either *A* is a replica of *B*, or *B* of *A*, and that we do not know which of the two is the original. Once we have compared the two pictures, it would not be absurd to say that they are exactly alike, except for the fact that *A* was signed by the artist and *B* was not. But it would be absurd to say that they are exactly alike, except that *A* was rectangular and *B* was not. For *A* to be rectangular and *B* not, *entails* that various other characteristics must also differ, such as the size of at least one of the angles. The term 'rectangular' clearly *means* 'rectilinear and having all its angles of a certain size, namely, 90 degrees'. If both *A* and *B* have the characteristics that they are rectilinear and that the angle of their corners is 90 degrees, this would entail that both had to be rectangular. In this sense rectangularity is a consequential characteristic, in the sense that it is consequential to (or entailed by) a number of other characteristics, such as rectilinearity and that the angle of all corners is 90 degrees. That a painting is 'signed', on the other hand, is not a consequential characteristic because it is not entailed by other characteristics.

The *intuitionists* hold that the value of something is not a consequential characteristic like 'rectangularity'. According to them value is a characteristic which, like 'being signed', is not entailed by other characteristics. Therefore the goodness of something is not entailed by the fact that it has characteristics *x*, *y* and *z*, as the rectangularity of a picture is entailed by the fact that it is rectilinear and has angles of 90 degrees. Yet it would be absurd to say that pictures A and B are exactly the same, except that A is a good painting and B is not. There must be some other difference between them, if one is to be good and the other not good. If I had two Morris cars it would make sense to say that the one was good and the other not, if they were exactly the same in all respects except that the brakes of one were reliable and the other's not. But it would certainly be absurd to say that one is good and the other bad if they were the same in *all* other respects (including the reliability of their brakes).

Hence, *intuitionism* errs in denying that there is a relationship between the value of something and its empirical characteristics. It is, after all, absurd to say that two things differ in value but not in respect of their empirical characteristics. There must be an empirical difference between two things for us to evaluate them differently. *Naturalism*, by holding value to be a consequential characteristic, does try to account for the relationship between the value of something and its empirical characteristics. According to naturalism, the relationship between the goodness of my Morris and the reliability of its brakes is equivalent to the relationship between the rectangularity of a painting and the fact that the angle of all its corners is 90 degrees. Naturalism has two advantages over intuitionism: it avoids the problems that arise from an appeal to intuition, and it attempts to explain the relationship between the value of something and its empirical characteristics. The question is, however, whether the naturalists lay the right kind of connection between the value of something and its empirical characteristics.

If it is true that there is a relationship of entailment between the value of something and its empirical characteristics, as the naturalists maintain, the following three consequences arise: 1. 'The painting is rectangular' *means the same as* 'the painting is rectilinear and all its angles are 90 degrees'. 'Rectangularity' can therefore be *defined* in terms of the empirical characteristics which entail it. Therefore, if the value of something is not a simple characteristic, as the intuitionists maintain, but a consequential characteristic, as the naturalists do, then the value of something is the equivalent of one or more of its empirical characteristics; then 'This Morris is good' *means the same* as 'This Morris is cheap on fuel, accelerates rapidly, costs little to maintain, has reliable brakes and steering, etc.' (2) That a painting is rectangular can be deduced from the fact that it is rectilinear and that all its angles are 90 degrees. Therefore, if the value of something is one of its consequential characteristics, it can be deduced from the empirical characteristics of that thing. Whether something is good, bad, correct, incorrect or proper could then be deduced from its empirical characteristics. (3) If we disagree on whether or not a painting is rectangular we can always resolve our disagreement by using empirical methods to ascertain whether or not the painting has the characteristics which entail its 'rectangularity'. We need merely ascertain whether the painting is rectilinear and whether all its angles are 90 degrees. Therefore, if the value of something were a consequential characteristic of that thing, we could resolve our disagreement on its value by ascertaining whether or not that thing had the empirical characteristics which entail its value. If we agreed on the empirical characteristics of a thing, we could not (logically) disagree about the value of that thing.

Let us examine whether values are consequential characteristics of things in these three respects.

### 1. Are values definable in terms of empirical characteristics?

Can we say that every value term (good, correct, proper, etc.) is equivalent in meaning to some or other empirical or descriptive term or set of such terms? There are various ways of showing that this is not the case. Bernard Mayo demonstrates this as follows.[2]

> If $x$ means the same as $y$, then it will be self-contradictory to say that something is $x$ but not $y$; if it is not self-contradictory to say so, then $x$ cannot mean the same as $y$. Now even if it is true that what is good is always pleasant and *vice versa*, yet it is certainly not self-contradictory, in the normal usage of words, to say that something good is unpleasant, or something unpleasant good; therefore good and pleasant cannot mean the same, as they must if one defines the other. And the same argument holds against all other possible definitions of good in terms of something else.

Thus, any attempt to *equate* the value of something with one or more of its empirical characteristics is fallacious, since it is not contradictory to say that something has the empirical characteristic(s) but not the value. 'Morris cars that give 40 miles to the gallon are bad' is not a contradictory statement in the way 'pictures that are rectilinear and of which all angles are 90 degrees are not rectangular' is contradictory.

## 2. Can value judgements be inferred from statements of empirical fact?

If a logical inference is to be valid, its conclusions may not state anything that is not included in its premises. But if the value of something is not equal to any set of its empirical characteristics, then a statement of the value of something is not equivalent to any set of statements on its empirical characteristics. A statement of the value of something cannot, therefore, be deduced from any set of statements about its empirical characteristics. From the empirical fact that children often contract measles, it cannot be concluded that it is good for them to contract measles. From the empirical fact that people slaughter animals in order to eat meat we cannot conclude that it is good (or bad) for them to do so. From the empirical fact that my Morris gives 40 miles to the gallon I cannot conclude that it is a good Morris. From the empirical fact that this picture is rectilinear and has angles of 90 degrees I can, however, conclude that it is rectangular.

However, the following inferences *are* valid:

(1) John's horse draws a heavy cart (empirical statement).
   It is bad when horses draw heavy carts (value judgement).
   Therefore: it is bad that John's horse is drawing such a heavy cart (evaluative conclusion).
(2) My Morris has a fuel consumption of 40 mpg (empirical statement).
   Morris cars that give 40 mpg are good (value judgement).
   Therefore: my Morris is good (evaluative conclusion).

These two arguments have evaluative conclusions, but their premises do not consist solely of empirical statements; they also include value judgements. They are valid as arguments because both their premises and their conclusions contain value judgements. Hence value judgements can be inferred from a number of premises *only* if the premises include a value judgement, not if the premises consist only of statements of empirical fact.

## 3. Can disputes about the value of something be resolved merely by reaching agreement about its empirical characteristics?

A dispute about the conclusion of an argument can be resolved if that argument is logically valid, and if agreement can be reached on the acceptability of the premises. But if the conclusion is a value judgement, then the premises cannot consist merely of a number of empirical statements; they must also include a value judgement. Therefore agreement on the empirical statements in the premises is not sufficient to resolve a dispute on the evaluative conclusion. There must also be agreement on the evaluation contained in the premises. A dispute on whether my Morris is a good car cannot be resolved merely by reaching agreement on the empirical fact that it gives 40 miles to the gallon. We must also agree on the evaluative judgement that it is good if Morris cars give 40 miles to the gallon. If I am the owner of a Morris and you are the manager of a petrol company that would like to see higher fuel consumption in all cars we might agree at once on the fact that my car has a fuel consumption of 40 mpg but nonetheless differ on whether or not this is a good characteristic.

Briefly: a dispute about whether or not something has some consequential characteristic can be resolved by reaching agreement on whether or not it has the empirical characteristics which entail the consequential characteristic. A dispute about whether or not a picture is rectangular can therefore be resolved by finding out whether that picture is rectilinear and has angles of 90 degrees. But a dispute about the value of something cannot be resolved simply by reaching agreement on its empirical characteristics. Therefore the value of something is not a consequential characteristic entailed by the empirical characteristics of that thing, as maintained by the naturalists.

Are value judgements a kind of constative speech act in which it is asserted what evaluative characteristics something has? From our analysis it is clear that two significant attempts to answer this question affirmatively, namely intuitionism and naturalism, are in error: values are neither non-natural characteristics nor consequential characteristics. It is apparent, however, that there is in fact a relationship between the value of something and its empirical characteristics and therefore also between value judgements and statements of empirical fact. But this relationship cannot be an inferential one, by which a value judgement must necessarily follow from a statement of empirical fact.

Our examination of intuitionism and naturalism confronts us with two questions: (1) If value judgements are not constative assertions, what are they? and (2) If the value of something is not implied by its characteristics, how can these nevertheless be relevant to the justification of value judgements?

# 7 Value Judgements as Expressive Speech Acts

## 7.17 THE EMOTIVE THEORY

IF a value judgement is not a kind of constative speech act, that is, if I do not ascribe an objective characteristic to something in saying that it is good (or bad, correct or false, proper or improper, etc.), what am I doing when I evaluate something? One possible answer to this question is the answer given by the emotive theory of value, the theory that holds that in saying something is good (or bad, correct or false, etc.) one does not say anything about the object but simply expresses (or reveals) one's feelings about the object. One of the classic examples of this view is A.J. Ayer's[3] argument that a value term adds nothing to the factual content of an assertion.

> Thus if I say to someone, 'You acted wrongly in stealing that money', I am not stating anything more than if I had simply said, 'You stole that money.' In adding that this action is wrong I am not making any further statement about it. I am simply evincing my moral disapproval of it. It is as if I had said, 'You stole that money,' in a peculiar tone of horror, or written it with the addition of some special exclamation marks. The tone, or the exclamation marks, adds nothing to the literal meaning of the sentence. It merely serves to show that the expression of it is attended by certain feelings in the speaker.

The function of a value term is therefore purely *emotive*. It is used to express feelings about certain objects, but not to make any factual assertion about them.

Value judgements are *intentional*, that is, they are always evaluations *of an object*. If value judgements are to be interpreted as expressions of feeling, they must therefore be expressions of intentional feelings, that is, feelings *about an object*. It is clear that Ayer's argument is not concerned with physical sensations such as pain, itching, fatigue, etc.

Such feelings are not intentional: I merely feel pain, not pain about an object. Ayer has in mind only *emotive reactions* (hence the name *emotive theory*), such as joy about something, satisfaction with something, surprise at something, horror of something, fear of something, and so on. All such emotive reactions are reactions to an object and therefore intentional in the required sense. All such emotive reactions are either positive or negative, that is, we either have positive feelings (joy, satisfaction, etc.) or negative feelings (horror, fear, boredom, fright, etc.) about things. Value judgements, too, are two-valued, that is, positive or negative. In this respect our evaluations are like expressions of feeling (emotive reactions). Emotivism holds that a positive value judgement about something is an expression of a positive emotive response and a negative value judgement an expression of a negative emotive response to it.

Expressions of feeling must be distinguished from *manifestations* of feeling. We can speak of *expressions* of feeling when *the speaker* expresses his feelings through his words or actions: for instance, Peter expresses his joy by saying that he is pleased or by shouting 'Hurrah!' and the king of Nineveh expresses his feeling of guilt by rising from his throne, laying his robe from him, covering himself with sackcloth and sitting in ashes (Jonah 3:6). We can speak of *manifestations* of feeling when the feeling is manifested in its physical symptoms. For instance, Peter's embarrassment may be manifested in his blushes, Ann's sorrow in her tears, and John's fatigue in his stumbling. With *manifestations* the relevant feelings are shown in their symptoms or in their physical consequences. With *expressions* the person concerned reveals his emotions to others. It is therefore only in *expressions* of feeling that we have to do with an *action of the person* concerned. Since evaluative utterances are acts performed by the speaker they can only be expressions, not manifestations in the sense defined above.

The emotive theory of values therefore holds that evaluative judgements are not constative speech acts about an object but expressive speech acts in which the speaker expresses his positive or negative emotive reactions to an object or situation or state of afffairs.

## 7.18 FEELINGS AND ATTITUDES

If I express an emotive reaction to something in saying that it is good, as the emotivists maintain, what emotive reaction am I in fact expressing?

In the argument cited above, Ayer speaks of an expression of 'moral *disapproval*'. The emotivist maintains, therefore, that (1), when I call something *bad* or *wrong* I am expressing my *disapproval* of it, and (2) when I call something *good* or *right* I am expressing my *approval* of it. Let us concede that value judgements are expressions of approval or disapproval. The question however, is whether these are expressions of *feeling*. Are approval and disapproval feelings (that is, emotive reactions)? R.M. Hare points out[4] that it is unexceptionable to say that the sentence '*A* is good' is used to express approval of *A*, but it is misleading to think that this approval is a peculiar warm feeling inside us. If the Minister of Local Government gets his underlings to write me a letter approving my town plan, I could hardly conclude that he feels emotionally involved with what I am doing.

It thus seems hardly plausible to describe approval or disapproval as *feelings*. Nevertheless, we do often approve of those things that give us pleasure (or that elicit from us some or other favourable emotive reaction), and find pleasure (or experience some other favourable emotive reaction), in things that we approve of. At a football match I might, for instance, *applaud* a movement of which I approve *and* which is pleasing to watch. In this instance my applause is *both* an expression of approval *and* an expression of pleasure. It also often happens that our value judgements are *both* expressions of approval or disapproval *and* expressions of a favourable or unfavourable emotive reaction. Approval (or disapproval) does not always, however, involve a favourable (or unfavourable) emotive reaction. There are often no feelings involved at all.

Briefly: in a value judgement a speaker always expresses his approval or disapproval of an object of evaluation. Even if approval and disapproval often involve emotive reactions they cannot be reduced to emotive reactions. They are more than that.

C.L. Stevenson has made an attempt to refine the emotive theory in this respect.[5] He maintains that value judgements are not expressions of feeling but expressions of *attitude*. People who differ in their evaluation of something differ in their attitude to it. But Stevenson fails to provide an analysis of the concept 'attitude'. Before we can comment on his suggestion that value judgements be seen as expressions of attitude we have to provide such an analysis.

'Attitude' may mean a physical posture adopted by someone, for instance the posture adopted by a person who is ready to attack, to defend, to embrace, etc. This physical connotation is used metaphorically in *all* cases where someone is intent upon, or is prepared for, a particular act or pattern of behaviour. An attitude may also mean a disposition to a certain pattern of behaviour towards someone or something, as distinct from a posture of the body, as in the sense mentioned above. We shall use the word 'attitude' in the second sense, viz. a disposition to a pattern of behaviour towards someone or something. Such attitudes are *dispositional, intentional*, and *two-valued*.

(1)   An attitude is a *disposition* to act in a certain manner and/or to show a certain emotive reaction to someone or something. Thus an attitude such as obedience is a disposition to action, and an attitude such as jealousy is a disposition to an emotive reaction which shows itself in an act or pattern of behaviour. Not all attitudes involve emotive reactions. They are often merely a disposition to certain behaviour, without any emotion being involved. But attitudes that involve emotive reactions are always also dispositions to action, because a person's emotive reactions are apparent in his behaviour. Jealousy, for instance, shows itself in the way a person acts towards those of whom he is jealous.

(2)   Attitudes are by definition intentional: my attitude is always *to* someone or something. Dispositions such as *humility, pride* and *trust*, for example, are attitudes only in as much as I am humble *before* a certain person or group, proud *of* a specific person or thing, put my trust *in* a certain person. An unrelated disposition to a certain line of action is in itself no attitude: if I state that John is proud of his son (or humble towards his employer), I make a statement on his *attitude* to his son (or his employer). If, however, I say that Napoleon was a proud (or Gandhi a humble) man, I refer to Napoleon's (or Gandhi's) *disposition* to a certain line of action. In themselves such dispositions are not attitudes, since they do not relate to a specific object.

(3)   An attitude may be defined as a disposition to intentional action and (emotive) reaction. As such, attitudes are *two-valued*. That is, they are either *pro-attitudes* (dispositions to feel and to act for something in some or other way), or *con-attitudes* (dispositions to feel and to act against something in some or other way).

A large variety of pro-attitudes is possible because we can be for something in different ways: we can vote for it, or concur with it, or recommend it, or praise it, or applaud it, or be pleased with it, or compliment it, or profess our support for it, or we can promote, or aid it, or encourage it, or work for it, or pursue it, or continue it; or we can be charmed with it, or appreciate it, or like it, or admire it, or be in agreement with it, or prefer it, or hope for it; or we can desire it, or long for it, or set our hearts on it; or we can disapprove of opposition to it, or be sad or angry when it is thwarted. One could mention many more pro-attitudes.

A large variety of con-attitudes is also possible, because we can be against something in different ways: we can vote against it, or thwart it, or hinder it, or delay it, or be on the defence against it, or combat it; or we can refute it, or doubt it, or ridicule it, or insult it, or attack it, or be rude to it; or we can be averse to it, or hate it, or despise it, or abhor it, or blame it, or be angry about it, or be bored with it; or we can hope for (or be pleased with) its frustration, or regret or be angry at its promotion. Here, again, one could list numerous examples.

It is also possible to adopt a *neutral* attitude to someone or something. It is possible, for example, that we do not find someone or something important enough to be for or against him or it. In such a case we show no (specific) attitude. We might also be for it in some respects and against it in others. If such pro's and cons neutralise each other we remain on the fence. It is perhaps simpler not to speak of neutral attitudes (as distinct from pro and con-attitudes) in this regard, since either the absence of an attitude or a combination of pro and con-attitudes is involved here. Attitudes are therefore mainly two-valued: either pro, or con.

In the light of this analysis we may concede to Stevenson that approval and disapproval are attitudes rather than emotive reactions. 'Approval' may therefore be taken to mean 'having some or other pro-attitude to someone or something', wheareas 'disapproval' is having a con-attitude.

Stevenson maintains that a value judgement is not (necessarily) an expression of feeling. It is rather an expression of someone's (pro or con) attitude to something. But as expressions of attitude, value judgements are *vague*: they merely indicate whether the speaker's attitude is pro or con, without specifying what kind of pro or con-attitude he has. If someone says, for example '$x$ is good', he expresses his pro-attitude to $x$ but does so vaguely, without specifying whether he is ecstatic about $x$, is pleased with $x$, is satisfied with $x$, is prepared to stand up for $x$, etc. The specific nature of someone's attitude is not clear *from what he says* in making a value judgement, but from the *context* in which he makes it, or from his behaviour or emotive reaction in that context.

Briefly: in its most plausible form, the emotive theory of value maintains that value judgements are not constative speech acts in which a speaker ascribes a factual characteristic to an object, but expressive speech acts in which the speaker expresses his pro or con-attitude to that object.


## 7.19 EVALUATION AND CONTRADICTION


In Section 6.14 we noted an important difference between expressive speech acts, on the one hand, and constative ones, on the other. Opposed constatives contradict each other: if Peter asserts that something is red and John asserts that it is not red, they cannot both be correct. We therefore need some way of ascertaining which of them is right. Contradiction calls for discussion. Opposed expressives, on the other hand, are not irreconcilable: when Peter expresses his boredom at hearing a story and John expresses his pleasure with it, they do not contradict each other. No discussion is needed to ascertain who is right and who wrong; after all, it is quite possible that Peter might be bored with something that pleases John.

This difference between constatives and expressives may be explained with reference to the fact that expressives, as distinct from constatives, are always *self-referring*: everyone can express only his own feeling or attitude. Peter's expressive and John's expressive express the feelings or attitudes of *different* persons and therefore cannot contradict each other, even if they express mutually differing feelings or attitudes. Peter's (constative) description of an object and John's (constative) description of that object, on the other hand, relate to the *same* object, therefore they cannot be conflicting without being contradictory. Conflicting constatives do not, of course, contradict each other when they relate to different objects: if Peter claims that the pen is red and John maintains that the pencil is not red, they might well both be right.

The question is whether value judgements are in this respect similar to constative or to expressive speech acts. All *objectivist* theories of value (for example intuitionism and naturalism) hold that conflicting value judgements clearly contradict each other, because we in fact find it necessary to discuss the rights and wrongs of our value judgements. From this fact these theories conclude that value judgements are constative speech acts. We have seen, however, that they cannot prove that we argue about the value of something *in the same way* that we argue about the descriptive characteristics of something. From this failure on the part of the objectivist theories, the *subjectivist* theories (for example, emotivism) conclude that value judgements are clearly not constative speech acts but in fact expressions of attitude or of the speaker's feeling about something. Ayer admits that this view implies that we cannot argue about the value of things. If someone maintains that thrift is a virtue whereas his friend considers it a vice, they do not contradict each other. One is simply expressing his approval and the other his disapproval of thrift, and there is no reason why one cannot disapprove of thrift while the other approves of it. From this viewpoint, Ayer states, it is clearly impossible to contradict one another on the value of something.[6]

This is indeed an extraordinary point of view! If differing value judgements are all equally acceptable, because they do not contradict each other, there is no sense in arguing about the question whether something is good or bad. All ethics is therefore founded on a fallacy! S.E. Toulmin[7] shows the absurdity of this consequence of emotivism. He argues as follows. Supposing I ask two people 'What is the right course for me to follow: *A* or *B*?' Suppose one person answers that *A* is the right course and not *B*, whereas the other answers that *B* is the right course, not *A*. I would regard their answers as conflicting. Both cannot be correct. If both were correct, I would be morally obliged to do the impossible, namely to follow two courses of action that exclude each other. But if my two advisers are merely expressing their feelings on *A* and *B*, both answers could be correct: it is quite possible that they might feel different about the two possibilities confronting me. Subjectivism holds that the value judgements of different people can never contradict each other. Such a point of view must be especially absurd to those who are in the position of having to choose.

Briefly: (1) subjectivism is right in denying (and objectivism wrong in maintaining) that (*a*) value judgements are constative speech acts and that (*b*) discussion about the value of something is similar to a discussion about the (correct) description of something; and (2) the subjectivist is wrong in denying (and the objectivist quite right in maintaining) that (*a*) conflicting value judgements about something contradict each other and that (*b*) it is therefore necessary to be able to argue about the acceptability of a value judgement, as we in fact do.

We must now try to find an analysis of evaluation which can explain the way we argue about the rights and wrongs of our judgements on good and evil, and which takes account of the valid elements in both the objectivist and the subjectivist theories of value.

# 8 Value Judgements as Prescriptive Speech Acts

## 8.20 EMOTIVE INFLUENCE

WHAT kind of speech acts are value judgements? In the preceding
chapters we examined two answers to this question, namely the views
that value judgements are constative speech acts and that they are
expressive speech acts. We conclude that value judgements could *not be
constative speech acts* because the value of something cannot be reduced
to or derived from its factual characteristics. Yet value judgements have
important constative implications, because the factual characteristics of
something are essential for determining its value. But value judgements
are *not purely expressive speech acts* either, since it does make sense to
discuss the value of something, whereas it is senseless to dispute about
how we feel. Yet value judgements have important expressive
implications: every value judgement is also an expression of an attitude
for or against something.

In the previous chapter A.J. Ayer and C.L. Stevenson were
mentioned as philosophers who interpret value judgements as
expressive utterances. It would, however, be a one-sided representation
of their view to say that according to them value judgements have *only*
an expressive function. They have added something further.

In his *Language, Truth and Logic*[8] Ayer writes that ethical value terms
serve not only to express feelings; they are also intended to arouse
feelings and thus to stimulate actions. Some value terms are even used
in such a way that the sentences in which they occur have the effect of
commands. The sentence 'You must speak the truth' expresses both a
certain kind of moral feeling in respect of speaking the truth and the
command 'Speak the truth!' The sentence 'You ought to speak the
truth' also contains the command 'Speak the truth!' although the
commanding tone is less strong here. In the sentence 'It is good to speak
the truth' the command is little more than a suggestion. The meaning of
various ethical value terms is therefore bound up with the various
feelings they usually express as well as the various responses one seeks
to evoke through them.

C.L. Stevenson[9] goes even further than Ayer. According to him, the *most important* function of value judgements is to create an influence. Value judgements do not describe people's interests; they endeavour to change or strengthen such interests. Value judgements recommend an interest in an object. They do not state that this interest is already there. For example, in telling someone that he ought not to commit theft one is attempting to persuade him to disapprove of theft. One's ethical judgement has a quasi-imperative character in which, with the aid of suggestion and the tone of one's voice, one is able to influence and modify the interests of one's hearers. If one eventually fails to persuade one's hearer to disapprove of theft one will feel that one has not succeeded in convincing him that theft is bad.

Briefly: according to Ayer and Stevenson value judgements have, in addition to their expressive function, also a function as means of influencing people. In value judgements we do not only express our feeling or our attitude; we also try to evoke or bring about this feeling or attitude in our hearers. The problem with this view is that it makes it difficult to distinguish between evaluative judgements and propagandistic utterances through which we attempt to manipulate our hearers causally. Stevenson's attempts to distinguish between value judgements and propaganda (see his *Ethics and Language*, chapter XII) are by no means convincing.

Furthermore, Ayer's and Stevenson's analysis is founded on a serious confusion. On the one hand both of them suggest that value judgements are a kind of prescriptive utterance. Ayer says that they have the effect of a command, and Stevenson ascribes to them a kind of imperative ('quasi-imperative') character. On the other hand both of them see these prescriptives as a means of causally influencing the hearer. In these views they lose sight of the important distinction between a *prescriptive speech act* in which I tell someone that he ought to do something, and an attempt on my part to influence my hearer *causally* (perhaps by force or manipulation or propaganda) to do what I tell him.

There are three important differences between prescriptives and causal influence. (1) Prescriptives are *illocutions*, whereas attempts to influence someone (through words) to act are *per-illocutions*. (2) In section 2.4 we saw that all prescriptives presuppose the freedom of the hearer to do or refrain from what is requested of him in the prescriptive. All attempts to influence or manipulate someone causally are, however, aimed at taking this freedom from him. (3) In principle the validity of a prescriptive is always open for discussion. Propaganda and manipulation, however, preclude discussion. In the previous chapter we saw that it is essential to value judgements that they should be open for discussion. We must have the option to discuss the question of which value judgements are or are not acceptable. Reducing value judgements to a means of propaganda, however, makes discussion impossible.

The question is whether, following the example of Ayer and Stevenson, we can interpret value judgements as *prescriptive speech acts* without reducing them to a means of causally influencing our hearers.

## 8.21 GENERAL PRESCRIPTIVES

If value judgements are prescriptive speech acts, what kind of prescriptive speech acts are they? One could hardly call my utterance that a Morris is a good car a *command*. Nor is it a *supplication*. In what way, then, could we interpret it as a prescriptive speech act?

Evaluative terms such as 'good' and 'bad' have a gerundive character: '*x* is good' means the same as '*x* is worthy of approval' or 'one should approve of *x*'. The value judgement '*x* is good' therefore *prescribes* a pro-attitude (and '*x* is bad' a con-attitude) towards *x*. In this sense value judgements are prescriptive speech acts.

Speech acts in which a gerundive predicate (good, bad, praiseworthy, deplorable, etc.) are ascribed to something, assert *general* prescriptives: the asserted prescriptive applies to everyone and not only to the hearer. In this respect value judgements differ from, for example, commands, requests and supplications, in which the prescriptive applies only to the addressee. '*X* is good (worthy of approval)' is therefore equivalent to '*x* deserves the approval of *everybody*' or '*one* should have a pro-attitude to *x*'. Obviously the speaker does not claim that everybody in fact has a pro-attitude to *x*. Such an utterance is not a constative assertion but a prescriptive: *x* deserves the approval of everybody − even if not everybody does in fact approve of *x*.

If value judgements are thus interpreted as *general prescriptives* two important consequences follow:

(1)  General prescriptives apply to everyone − including the speaker. If I say: '*x* is good (worthy of approval)' it is implied that *x* deserves *my approval too*. In saying '*x* is worthy of approval' the speaker demands from himself, too, a pro-attitude towards *x* and at the same time meets

this demand by expressing, by undeniable implication, a pro-attitude to
*x*. Emotivism is therefore justified in drawing our attention to the
expressive element in all value judgements. If someone says that *x* is
good, or correct, or that it is proper, or ought to be done, he expresses,
by undeniable implication, a pro-attitude to *x*. If someone says that *x* is
bad, or wrong, or improper, or ought not to be done, he expresses, by
undeniable implication, a con-attitude to *x*.

(2) General prescriptives apply to everyone, not only to the speaker.
In this sense they are *more than self-referring*. Opposed general
prescriptives are therefore logically irreconcilable: they contradict each
other, John's expressive, 'I approve of *x*' does not contradict Peter's
expressive 'I disapprove of *x*'. But John's general prescriptive '*x* is
worthy of everyone's approval' contradicts Peter's general prescriptive
'*x* is worthy of everyone's disapproval'. It would be contradictory to
assert simultaneously that everyone ought to approve of *x* and that
everyone ought to disapprove of *x*. Conflicting prescriptives cannot be
observed simultaneously.

Thus, if we interpret value judgements as general prescriptive speech
acts, we can account both for the expressive element which emotivism
sees in our value judgements, and for the fact that value judgements, as
opposed to expressive utterances, are more than self-referring.

Because opposed value judgements contradict each other it is
*necessary* that we should be able to discuss the validity or invalidity of
our value judgements. The question is what aspect of a value judgement
(as a general prescriptive) makes such discussion possible?

## 8.22 NORMS

In section 2.4 we saw that two factual presuppositions are constitutive
of all prescriptives. First, every prescriptive is based on the
presupposition that the hearer is free (and therefore able) to do or
decline to do what is requested of him. 'Ought' implies freedom.
Second, every prescriptive is based on the presupposition that there is
an (often unspoken) 'convention' or 'agreement' subscribed to by both
the speaker and his hearer and obliging the hearer to do what is
requested of him. The 'agreement' does not *force* the hearer; that would
be in conflict with the first presupposition of every prescriptive. Yet the
'agreement' does *oblige* the hearer in the sense that he would be

acting contrary to the 'agreement' if he did not do what is requested of him. If a sergeant commands a private to peel potatoes, his command is based on the presupposition (1) that the soldier is able to peel potatoes, and (2) that the rules of the army apply to the soldier and would be broken by him if he did not obey the command. If a penitent sinner prays for God's forgiveness his supplication is based on the presupposition that God is capable of forgiving him and that God would be unfaithful to His covenant if He rejected this supplication.

A prescriptive fails if these presuppositions prove to be wrong. It is therefore always possible to argue about the validity of a prescriptive, because we can examine whether its constituting presuppositions are true or untrue. For instance, the private could refuse to obey the command to peel potatoes on the grounds (1) that he is unable to peel potatoes, or (2) that he is not in the army and is therefore not subject to army rules, or (3) that he is subject to these rules but that in terms of these rules he is not obliged to obey the sergeant now because he is doing a job given to him by the captain. Thus, a discussion on the validity of a prescriptive is concerned, above all, with three questions: (1) Is the hearer able to do what is requested of him? (2) Does the hearer accept the 'agreement' or 'convention' on which the prescriptive is founded? (3) Does the 'agreement' or 'convention' oblige the hearer to carry out the prescribed action in the given situation?

As (general) prescriptives, value judgements are in a certain sense *vague*. The command of the sergeant to the private to peel potatoes is specific and clear. The private is told precisely what to do. There is therefore no difficulty about the question whether or not he is able to do what he is told to do. But if the sergeant were to say to the private 'peeling potatoes is good', he would be prescribing a pro-attitude to potato peeling without specifying the concrete content of the required pro-attitude. The question whether or not the private is able to peel potatoes is then no longer relevant, because he would comply with the general prescriptive by showing, in every way *possible to him*, a positive attitude to potato peeling – for instance by encouraging others to do it, by applauding them when they are doing it, or simply by concurring in the sergeant's judgement. Thus, as general prescriptives, value judgements prescribe that everyone should adopt the pro or con-attitude *which is possible to him*, towards the evaluated object. It is therefore impossible for a value judgement to fail as a prescriptive on the grounds that the hearer is unable to obey it. The first factual presupposition of a prescriptive can never be untrue in the case of value judgements, and consequently a discussion about the validity of a value judgement is not concerned with the truth of this presupposition but concentrates, rather, on the second presupposition, namely that there is an 'agreement' that obliges the hearer to a pro or con-attitude towards the evaluated object.

In the case of value judgements the assumed 'agreements' or 'conventions' are *evaluative norms*. The terms 'agreement' and 'convention' must here be construed as functional and not as genetic metaphors: they clarify the way in which norms *function* rather than their *origin*. In a group or community or society certain norms are often explicitly agreed upon and even recorded in writing. The administration of justice, for instance, is concerned mainly with determining whether or not people's actions are in accordance with the norms laid down in the statutes. But we do not always make an agreement with our hearers about which norms to accept before we express a value judgement. Usually we simply *assume* that our hearer accepts certain norms, whether or not these are agreed to in our society. This assumption underlies every value judgement.

For instance, if I tell someone 'Jack's yellow Morris is good (worthy of approval)', my value judgement is founded on the assumption that my hearer accepts the 'agreement' that we shall approve of (and deem worthy of approval) all cars with the following seven characteristics: (1) low fuel consumption; (2) reliable brakes and steering; (3) sturdy, rust-resistant bodywork; (4) spacious interior; (5) rapid acceleration; (6) low purchase price; (7) low maintenance cost. I take it that these norms are fairly generally accepted in our society. But to my knowledge they have never been explicitly agreed upon and recorded in writing, nor have they been explicitly agreed upon between me and those to whom I commend Jack's yellow car. Nonetheless, if my hearer accepts these norms, which I have assumed, he is *obliged* to accept my (general) prescriptive and to have a pro-attitude towards Jack's yellow car in so far as this car has the seven characteristics stated in the norms. But my hearer is *not forced* to obey my general prescriptive. He could always avoid this obligation and reject my value judgement. In doing so, he could advance two kinds of arguments against my value judgement.

(1) He could tell me 'I accept the norm you assume. Therefore I also accept the obligation to approve all cars that have the seven features stated in the norm. Yet I do not accept your general prescriptive, because Jack's car does not comply with the norm. Look at all that rust on the rear mudguard! And a little Morris isn't all that spacious inside.

No, I am not obliged to have a pro-attitude towards Jack's car!' In this case, our discussion about the validity of my value judgement hinges on the question whether or not the evaluated object (the yellow Morris) shows the empirical features required in the norm. The empirical features of something are thus indeed relevant to its evaluation. In this respect naturalism is correct.

(2) But there is another way in which my hearer could avoid the obligation to obey my (general) prescriptive. He could argue as follows. 'I agree with you on the factual characteristics of Jack's car. His car has all seven of the characteristics required in your norm. But I do not accept your norm. Your value judgement is based on the assumed agreement that we approve of all cars that show these seven features. I, however, am not a party to that agreement and therefore I am not obliged to act in accordance with it'. In this case the discussion is not concerned with the empirical features of the car but with the acceptability of the presupposed norm. In chapter 10 we shall examine the way we defend our evaluative norms.

In section 6.16 we suggested that the value judgement 'This $x$ is good (worthy of approval)' may validly be inferred from the following two premises: (1) good $x$'s are those that have the features $a$, $b$, and $c$; and (2) this $x$ has the features $a$, $b$, and $c$. In the first premise a norm is stated, while the second is an assertion that $x$ meets the stated norm. The evaluative conclusion is justified only if *both* premises are justified. Naturalism errs in holding that the justification of the second premise is enough, thus overlooking the role of evaluative norms. If, however, we interpret value judgements not as constative speech acts (inferable from other constative speech acts), but as general prescriptions, we are able to account for the function of norms: like all other prescriptive speech acts, a value judgement is based on a presupposed 'agreement'.

In appealing to an 'agreement' the speaker acknowledges by implication that the agreement is (still) valid. He thereby (re-)*affirms* the agreement. Since we appeal to a norm in making a value judgement, every value judgement also implies a *commissive* in which we commit ourselves *vis-à-vis* our hearer to adopt the attitude prescribed in the value judgement towards all things that meet the agreed norm, now and in future. If someone commends a certain action in some people and condemns it in others, we can accuse him of using double standards. This charge applies all the more if he condemns others for something that he does himself (and therefore, by implication, approves of in himself). If I declare an $x$ commendable and later adopt a con-attitude towards this (or another ) $x$, I may be called to account and am obliged to explain this apparent violation of my commitment. Such an explanation could take either of two forms: (1) I may attempt to show that this $x$ has since changed and thus no longer (as before) has the features stated in the norm to which I am committed. For example, age and wear may have increased the maintenance costs of my car. I remain true to my commitment to approve of all things that meet the norm, but this $x$, alas, no longer meets the norm. (2) It is also possible that I have since changed my mind about which $x$'s are worthy of approval. This $x$ still meets the norm, but I no longer accept the norm. In such a case I have rescinded my (earlier) commitment to approve all $x$'s with these features and have replaced it by another commitment, namely to disapprove all $x$'s with these features.

Briefly: every evaluative utterance implies a *commitment* to adopt the same attitude to things which conform equally to the presupposed norms. If I first approve and later disapprove an $x$, it may be because this $x$ has since changed and no longer conforms to the norms. I am therefore still applying the same norms. I might also change my norms, thus replacing my commitment to measure *all* things in the light of this norm by a commitment to measure *all* things in the light of the new norm. If two things are equal in terms of the characteristics stated in the norm, we cannot maintain that they merit different attitudes. As we pointed out in our discussion of naturalism in section 6.16, we cannot call one thing good and another bad if the two are exactly alike (or have the relevant characteristics in common).

If I commit myself, as in a value judgement, to the agreement that all $x$'s merit the pro (or con) attitude of everyone, including myself, I am by implication adopting a positive stance towards everyone who accepts this agreement and a negative one towards everyone who rejects it. My commitment to the agreement that all $x$'s, past, present and future, merit attitude $y$, thus has the following four implications: (1) I am implying that I have a pro-attitude towards every occasion in the past when I did show attitude $y$ to an $x$ (for example, I am contented, self-satisfied, pleased, prepared to say that my attitude was the correct one, etc.); (2) I am implying that I have a con-attitude towards every time in the past when I did not show attitude $y$ to an $x$ (I feel guilty, am prepared to admit that my attitude was wrong, etc.); (3) I am implying that I have a pro-attitude to others who have attitude $y$ to $x$ (I agree with them, praise them, am prepared to acknowledge that they have the correct attitude, etc.); (4) I am implying that I have a con-attitude to others who do not have attitude *y* to an *x* (I disagree with them, I am prepared to acknowledge that their attitude to *x* is wrong, I accuse them, I am intolerant towards them, I am tolerant towards them, etc.). (I can only tolerate or not tolerate something that I am *opposed to*. Someone cannot be said to tolerate something if he is in favour of it. Tolerance is therefore as much a con-attitude as intolerance!)

## 8.23 THE ILLOCUTIONARY LOAD OF A VALUE JUDGEMENT

Like all our other concrete speech acts, our value judgements have a complex illocutionary load. In the preceding analysis we have attempted to show that this can be accounted for most plausibly by interpreting value judgements as general prescriptive speech acts. From the vague general prescriptive asserted in a value judgement we can infer all other illocutionary elements. Furthermore, we can by this means account for the way in which we discuss the value of things.

We could, therefore, list the various illocutionary components of a value judgement as follows. In making the utterance '*x* is good (worthy of approval)', a speaker does the following:

(1) *Prescriptive element*: he declares that *x* merits a pro-attitude from everybody.

(2) *Expressive element*: he expresses by (undeniable) implication a pro-attitude to *x*.

(3) *Commissive element*: he appeals (and commits himself undeniably) to the 'agreement' (norm) to have a pro-attitude to all *x*'s with certain factual characteristics.

(4) *Constative element*: he implies (undeniably) that this *x* has the characteristics stated in the 'agreement' (norm).

(5) *Further expressive element*: he adopts, by implication, a negative attitude to all instances where others (or he himself in the past) violate this agreement and a positive one to all instances where someone else (or he himself in the past) adheres to the agreement.

One final remark: we often perform a speech act not so much for the illocution *explicitly asserted* in it as for the *implied* illocutions. Thus, for example, I could use the (constative) assertion, 'John, the door is open' for the contextually implied prescriptive. I am not primarily concerned with giving John information; I want to ask him to shut the door. As far

as its formal structure is concerned, however, my speech act remains a
statement of fact, even if used as a request.

In the same way a value judgement may be used under certain
circumstances for the constative or the expressive or the commissive
implied in it and not primarily for the general prescriptive explicitly
asserted in it. As far as its formal structure is concerned, however, my
value judgement would still remain a general prescriptive speech act.
Thus I may applaud a successful movement at a football match by
shouting 'well played'. Here I would be using a value judgement for its
*expressive implication*. Sometimes we use a value judgement merely to
say that something meets the stated (and agreed) criteria (for example
when the teacher of the second grade checks the pupils' sums and marks
them right or wrong). In such a case she is actually concerned primarily
with the *constative implication*. Thus, the form of value judgements (like
that of all gerundive utterances) is characterised by the general
prescriptive, explicitly asserted in them, even when under certain
circumstances they are used for one of the illocutions implied in them.

# 9 The Ascription of Meaning

## 9.24 DESCRIPTIVE STATEMENTS AND THE ASCRIPTION OF MEANING

MANY speech acts are *intentional*, that is, they are speech acts *about* something. In intentional speech acts we often give a *description* of something, that is, we say what characteristics that thing has. Such characteristics are often widely different. Among others we may distinguish three kinds of characteristics: *directly observable* characteristics, *dispositional* characteristics and *impressive* characteristics. I have to take only one glance at a cat to see whether it is black. 'Black' is, in this sense, a directly observable characteristic of the cat. Dispositional characteristics are not directly observable in this sense. I would have to watch the cat over a longer period and under certain circumstances in order to ascertain whether it is treacherous. Dispositions (or tendencies) towards certain kinds of behaviour are only manifested under specific circumstances. As long as the required circumstances are absent, the dispositions cannot be observed. Some things have the disposition (or tendency) to impress the sensitive observer in some way, or to evoke a certain emotion or attitude in those who encounter them. Thus, for example, the panoramic view from the Zugspitze is *impressive* in the sense that it tends to evoke feelings of awe etc. in those enjoying it. In this case we may speak of impressive characteristics. Black, large, in the park, skew, loud, sweet are examples of directly observable characteristics. Dangerous, fragile, intelligent, treacherous are examples of dispositional characteristics. Impressive, fearsome, mysterious, abhorrent, sublime, glorious (the glory of God) are examples of impressive characteristics. All these characteristics are *empirical*: we observe through our senses whether or not something has one of these characteristics. This also applies to impressive characteristics: I need no special sense (intuition) to observe that something has a tendency towards evoking a certain reaction, emotion or attitude in those (including myself) who encounter it.

A descriptive speech act, in which we state what characteristics something has, is always a *constative speech act* in the sense that its form is characterised by the constative illocution explicitly asserted in it. Like all speech acts, however, descriptive speech acts are complex. Besides the explicitly asserted illocution, further illocutions are asserted by implication. A speech act in which I ascribe an impressive characteristic to something is always by implication expressive as well. The speech act 'The view from the Zugspitze is impressive' states that this view tends to make a profound impression on observers (including the speaker) and implies that the speaker is also impressed. In this sense all impressive descriptions are by implication expressive.

Not all intentional speech acts are descriptive. In the preceding chapter we saw that value judgements are intentional but not constative speech acts. They could rather be viewed as general prescriptive speech acts. After all, the value of something is not one of its characteristics but rather a gerundive indication that one should have a positive (or a negative) attitude to it. Value judgements and descriptions are both intentional: they respectively say about something what value and what factual characteristics belong to (or are *properties* of) it. A useful terminological distinction would be to call the factual characteristics of something *constative properties*, and its value a *prescriptive property*. This distinction merits closer scrutiny.

As living human beings we have to *act* in the world. Our actions, however, are always actions within a given situation and this situation determines our *possibilities for action*. In acting, I can do only what is possible in the situation in which I find myself. I cannot realise possibilities for action that are not available to me in my situation. In my present situation (behind my desk) I can read, write, or drowse (because these possibilities are open to me here); but I cannot swim, play football, or drive a car, because those possibilities are *not* open to me in my present situation. If I cross Trafalgar Square I could bump into Nelson's column (the possibility is open to me), but I *cannot* bump into the statue of Eros, because that happens to be in Piccadilly Circus and not in Trafalgar Square. Thus, what we as human beings *can* or *cannot* do in our world is determined by the *factual* nature of the world (as our total acting situation). From this it becomes clear that in a constative, in which we make a statement on the factual nature of the world, we give our hearer an assurance on the way our possibilities for action are determined in the world. In the statement 'Nelson's column stands in Trafalgar Square', I give my hearer an assurance on what he *can* or *cannot* do regarding the column: he can bump into the column in Trafalgar Square but not in Piccadilly Circus (we shall deal with this point in detail in Parts Three and Four). The factual characteristics (or *constative properties*) of something are therefore determinations of what we *can* or *cannot* do with regard to it.

Although my situation determines what I *can* or cannot do, it does not determine what I *ought* or ought not to do. My situation determines my *possibilities for action*; it does not, however, determine which of these possibilities I ought to realise. From the factual description of the situation (and hence the specification of what we *can* or *cannot* do within that situation) we cannot, therefore, deduce prescriptions for what we *ought* or *ought not* to do within that situation. From the fact that Nelson's column stands in Trafalgar Square and that I can bump into it there, it does not follow that I *ought* to bump into it if I find myself in the Square.

Briefly: whereas the *constative properties* of something determine what we *can* or *cannot* do with regard to it, its *prescriptive properties* determine what we *ought* or *ought not to do* with regard to it, or, more generally, what *attitude* we should have toward it. We cannot deduce the prescriptive properties of something from its constative properties. Naturalists mistakenly consider such a deduction possible, because they overlook the difference between constative and prescriptive properties.

In section 4.10 we distinguished between the meaning of words on the one hand, and the meaning of things, events, situations etc. on the other. In this chapter we are dealing with meaning in the latter sense. In this sense we could define the *meaning* of something as the totality of prescriptive properties of that thing. We thus know the meaning of something when we know what attitude we ought to have towards it. We know the *meaning* of a situation when we know what we ought to do in that situation. We know the *meaning* of life when we know what ideals or objectives we ought to pursue in life.

Briefly: a speech act *describes* something to the extent that the speaker uses it to say what constative properties (factual characteristics) something has. A speech act *ascribes meaning* to something to the extent that the speaker uses it to say what prescriptive properties (meaning) something has.

## 9.25 WAYS OF ASCRIBING MEANING

There are various ways in which we could ascribe meaning to things. We can do so directly, in a gerundive speech act. We can also use a *descriptive speech act* to say indirectly what the meaning of something is, or we could use metaphors or parables or analogies to indicate the meaning of things. In this regard one might also refer to what D.D. Evans calls *onlooks*. Let us examine more closely these three ways of stating meaning.

## 1. Meaning ascription in gerundive speech acts

Since all gerundives assert general prescriptives, their primary function is to ascribe meaning to things. They are intended primarily to prescribe what attitude everyone should adopt towards something. In chapter 8 we argued that value judgements ascribe meaning in this sense. We have also seen that value judgements are vague indications of the attitude appropriate to something: a value judgement does not say concretely *what* attitude one should have to something. It merely states whether it should be a pro-attitude (approval) or a con-attitude (disapproval).

To ascribe meaning to something more concretely we might, instead of using the predicates 'good' (worthy of approval) and 'bad' (worthy of disapproval), use gerundive predicates that say more precisely what pro-attitude or con-attitude is appropriate to something. Thus we might say: 'This place is *sacred*' (in the sense that this place ought to be venerated); 'John's achievement is *admirable*'; 'His efforts are *praiseworthy*'; 'The king is *unimpeachable*'; 'His conduct is *reprehensible*'; 'He is an *honourable* person'; 'God is *worthy of worship*'; and so on.

In the following chapter we shall pay attention to a very important group of meaning ascriptions belonging to this category: those in which a *meaning determinant primacy* is ascribed to something. For example: 'God is that than which nothing greater is conceivable' (*aliquid quo maius nihil cogitari potest*) (St Anselm); 'God is that, than which nothing is more excellent or more divine' (St Augustine); 'God is that which concerns man ultimately' (Paul Tillich); 'Nirvana is the highest good'; 'The classless society is the highest ideal'.

## 2. Meaning ascription in descriptive speech acts

Descriptive speech acts are formally *constative*: they state what constative properties something has. Like all other speech acts, however, descriptions are complex. Apart from the constative illocution that they assert explicitly, they imply a number of other illocutions. The question is whether a description cannot by *implication* also ascribe meaning to something. In section 9.24 we saw, however, that the prescriptive properties (meaning) of a thing can never be inferred from its constative properties. To put it more generally (but also less precisely): values cannot be inferred from facts. Does this mean that a description can never (even by implication) ascribe meaning to something? Let us examine this with the help of an example.

The statement 'Nelson's column stands in Trafalgar Square' has a descriptive predicate (' ... stands in Trafalgar Square') with a primarily *constative* function: it states a fact regarding Nelson's column and therefore gives us an assurance concerning our possibilities for action in respect of Nelson's column. *Prima facie* we cannot infer from this statement what we ought to do with regard to Nelson's column, or what attitude is appropriate to it. It would appear that this statement only has a constative function and does not ascribe meaning to that which it describes.

Let us suppose, however, that we are members of a primitive celtic tribe for whom Trafalgar Square is a sacred place, in the sense that everything in it or attached to it ought to be venerated. In that case the speech act 'Nelson's column stands in Trafalgar Square' would not merely state a fact regarding Nelson's column but would also say what attitude is appropriate toward Nelson's column. We would then be dealing with a descriptive speech act which ascribes meaning to that which it describes.

This example may be set out schematically as follows:

(1) 'Nelson's column stands in Trafalgar Square' (descriptive statement with a primarily constative function).
(2) 'All things in or attached to the sacred Trafalgar Square ought to be venerated' (meaning norm for our celtic tribe).
(3) 'Therefore: Nelson's column ought to be venerated' (ascription of meaning inferred from (1) and (2)).

If we presuppose (2), we imply (3) when asserting (1). In addition to its constative function, the descriptive statement (1) implies an ascription of meaning (3) provided it is asserted within a context where a meaning norm (2) is presupposed.

A descriptive statement does not always imply an ascription of meaning. It is only when we assume a *meaning norm* which obliges us to adopt a certain attitude to those things which have certain constative properties, that a speech act which ascribes these constative properties to something by implication ascribes a meaning to it as well. Unlike our imaginary celts, we have no normative 'agreement' in our society to the effect that everything in Trafalgar Square is to be held sacred.

Therefore the meaning Nelson's column has for us is not determined by the fact that it stands in Trafalgar Square. But the descriptive statements 'The president has delusions of grandeur' and 'The professor is authoritarian' do ascribe meaning for us because in our society we do have 'agreements' about how we ought to be disposed towards people with delusions of grandeur or authoritarian personalities. In principle, however, it is always possible that a description does ascribe meaning to things, because it is always possible that the necessary meaning norms might be introduced. Thus one might interpret even the descriptive statement about Nelson's column in such a way that it ascribes meaning.

The speech act 'Nelson's column is sacred' implies *undeniably* that it is appropriate to venerate Nelson's column. We cannot say that Nelson's column is sacred, and yet deny that it is appropriate to venerate it, because we would then be contradicting ourselves. It cannot be denied without contradiction that a gerundive speech act ascribes meaning to something. The speech act 'Nelson's column stands in Trafalgar Square' (performed by a member of our celtic tribe) implies contextually that it is appropriate to venerate Nelson's column as a sacred object. The implication is valid only because the speech act is performed *within the normative context* of the view of life of our celtic tribe, who hold that Trafalgar Square is sacred. One could therefore deny the implication without contradiction. If I said, 'Nelson's column stands in Trafalgar Square but it is not appropriate to venerate it as a sacred object', I would not be contradicting myself; I would merely be rejecting the normative context of the celtic tribe and thus also denying that my speech act ascribes meaning as it would have if it were performed within that context. In the same way the following descriptive statements *contextually* imply ascriptions of meaning. Such contextual implications are valid only within a normative context in which a relevant norm of meaning is assumed, but may also be denied if the normative context is rejected. Thus 'He helped me at the risk of his life and with great effort when I was in trouble' implies that I ought to be grateful to him, 'He is well-disposed towards us' implies that we ought to trust him, 'He is hostile to us' implies that we ought to be hostile to him, and 'Johnny is only a child' implies that we ought not to give him too much responsibility.

In brief, it cannot be denied without contradiction that a gerundive speech act ascribes meaning to something. This can however always be denied in respect of descriptive statements since one could always reject or suspend as irrelevant any assumed normative context in which the descriptive statement is asserted. This makes it possible (for instance in science) to give a value-free description of a state of affairs. We could aim at merely providing a *factual description* of a state of affairs without pronouncing by implication on the way people *ought to* act regarding this state of affairs. Thus a purely *descriptive* exposition is possible because we can *suspend as irrelevant* any possible normative context. But suspending as irrelevant is not the same as rejecting a context. It is always possible to lift the suspension and to determine the meaning of the described situation in the light of the assumed norms. Nevertheless, factual description remains something different from the ascription of meaning and can, if so wished, always be done without implying any ascription of meaning.

From the fact that descriptions can only be used to ascribe meaning when we assume a *normative context* within which they are asserted, it follows that my hearer can grasp what meaning I ascribe to something in my descriptive statement only if he knows within what normative context I am speaking. For example, we can understand what attitude our imaginary celts prescribe and express with regard to Nelson's column in their statement 'Nelson's column stands in Trafalgar Square' only if we know that they assert this within the normative context of their view that the Square is a sacred place. Likewise, if someone said, 'Johnny is only a child', or 'The professor is authoritarian', or 'The paratrooper shoots down the defenceless freedom fighter', his hearer can grasp what attitude he considers appropriate (and expresses) with regard to Johnny, the professor or the paratrooper only if he knows what norms are assumed in the context of the view of life or the ideology within which the speech act is performed.

If we wish to ascribe meaning to something we can do so *less ambiguously* in gerundive speech acts than in descriptive ones because descriptions can ascribe meaning to something only if we assume a normative context. Descriptions ascribe meaning if we assume (often unspoken) normative presuppositions, whereas gerundive speech acts ascribe meaning without our having to assume that our hearer knows what our normative presuppositions are. On the other hand, descriptive speech acts have a great advantage over gerundive ones in this regard, because they can usually express the meaning of something more *concretely*. We shall illustrate this in more detail.

All gerundive predicates such as 'commendable', 'laudable', 'praiseworthy', 'worthy of conservation', 'fit to be burned', etc., have two components: (1) they specify a certain attitude, and (2) they declare this attitude to be appropriate with regard to that to which they are ascribed. We have seen that value judgements are *vague*, because they indicate only whether the meaning of something is positive or negative, without specifying its concrete content. If we wish to use only gerundive utterances to ascribe meaning to something *concretely*, and not as vaguely as in value judgements, we have to give a *full* description or specification of the complex set of attitudes that are appropriate toward that thing. This is usually impossible in practice because attitudes can be very complex. The question is, therefore: how can we ascribe meaning to something concretely (thus specifying what concrete set of attitudes is appropriate toward it) without being compelled to describe these attitudes in full? To avoid this difficulty we use descriptive predicates. In saying 'Johnny is only a child', for instance, we convey that it is appropriate to treat Johnny as a child and we assume that our hearer knows the normative context in which we are speaking and the concrete set of attitudes that are considered appropriate with regard to children within this context. In the utterance, 'Nelson's column stands in Trafalgar Square' one of our celts makes it *concretely* clear to his fellows what attitude is proper with regard to Nelson's column, because they know exactly (without needing exhaustive specification) what attitude is appropriate within the context of their religious practices with regard to things in Trafalgar Square.

Briefly, *gerundive* speech acts ascribe meaning to things *less ambiguously* than descriptive speech acts because their meaning is not dependent upon implicit normative assumptions. *Descriptive* speech acts ascribe meaning to things *more concretely* than gerundive speech acts because they can convey the meaning of something without giving an exhaustive description of the attitudes appropriate toward that thing.

Before ending our discussion about the way we ascribe meaning to things in descriptive speech acts, it may be useful to say something about a group of descriptive speech acts that pose special difficulties in this connection, namely impressive utterances such as 'Yahweh is glorious' and 'This place is holy'. Yahweh's glory consists partly in the fact that He inspires those to whom He reveals Himself, to glorify Him. Yahweh is therefore a glorious God because Israel is inspired to glorify Him. In this sense 'glory' is an impressive predicate. The same applies to holiness. Rudolf Otto[10] defines holiness as a *mysterium tremendum et fascinans*: something is holy if it tends to overawe and fascinate people.

If the Israelite says that Yahweh is glorious, he states that Yahweh inspires him to glorify Him and at the same time he gives expression to this glorification of Yahweh. If someone says that a certain phenomenon is holy he is stating that this phenomenon tends to overawe and fascinate people (including himself), and at the same time he is expressing these attitudes. The question is, however, whether there is not more to it than this. The Israelite would not only glorify Yahweh; he would also feel obliged to glorify Yahweh and to regard it as *blasphemy* if someone else did not do so. The speech acts 'Yahweh is glorious' and 'Yahweh is holy' are thus not only impressive but also prescriptive (ascriptive of meaning). In our example of the sacred Trafalgar Square of our imaginary celtic tribe, we used the word 'sacred' as a prescriptive rather than as an impressive term. We often consider a certain attitude appropriate toward a phenomenon if the phenomenon evokes that attitude in us by its impressiveness, as in the situation where we say that the view from the Zugspitze is sublime. However, this connection between impressiveness and prescriptiveness need not necessarily be there. It often happens that something evokes a certain reaction in us and that we deplore this reaction (in ourselves). It is not uncommon, for example, for a German in uniform to evoke a strong feeling of irritation in a Dutchman, but it is also possible that a Dutchman may deplore this feeling in himself as an irrational prejudice. In that case we have an example of impressiveness with a contrary prescriptiveness. Whether or not someone feels that he *ought* to be irritated at the sight of a German in uniform depends on the prescriptive norms by which this response is judged and not merely on the fact that the German happens to evoke this response. Hence, with regard to impressive acts as well, we must be able to assume a meaning *norm* if we are to deduce prescriptive implications from what is asserted.

## 3. Onlooks

In the speech act 'Nelson's column is (a monument) in Trafalgar Square' our celt does the following: (1) he asserts (constatively) that Nelson's column has *all* the factual characteristics of a monument in Trafalgar Square (the column is literally, not figuratively or only in certain respects, a monument in Trafalgar Square); (2) he asserts (prescriptively) that one should show Nelson's column the attitude that (in the context of the celtic norms) is considered appropriate to all things in Trafalgar Square; (3) in the context of the celtic norms, (1) (the constative) is the ground for (2) (the prescriptive). In other words, if we assume the celtic norms of meaning, Nelson's column must be treated as sacred *because* it stands in Trafalgar Square.

Similarly the speech act 'Johnny is only a child' states, first, that Johnny is a child in all factual respects; secondly, it prescribes that Johnny must be treated as a child. The similarity in factual characteristics is, by contextual implication, the ground for the similarity in meaning. Johnny must be treated as a child *because* he is in fact a child.

Often, however, we wish to convey a *similarity in meaning* in this kind of speech act (Johnny ought to be treated as a child) without being prepared to admit a complete *factual similarity* (Johnny is not a child in all factual respects). Our speech act still ascribes meaning but there is something odd about its constative content. In such cases we often say, 'I look on *x* as *y*', and not '*x* is *y*'. Let us follow D.D. Evans[11] and speak of *onlooks* in such cases.

In this regard we may distinguish between *analogical* and *parabolic* onlooks.

(a) *Analogical onlooks.* In the speech act 'I look on (the 35-year-old) Johnny as a child' the following is done. (1) It is asserted (prescriptive) that one should have the attitude to Johnny that (in the context of the speaker's norms) is appropriate to children; (2) it is asserted (constative) that Johnny is a child in certain factual respects (for example, his behaviour, his emotional development) but not in others (his age); Johnny is not literally a child but there is a *factual analogy* (partial similarity) between Johnny and children; (3) in the context of the speaker's norms (2) (the constative) is the ground for (1) (the prescriptive). In other words, if we assume the speaker's meaning norms, the respects in which Johnny is in fact like a child are the *relevant* respects on the basis of which it is appropriate to treat him as a child.

Compare the following further examples: 'I look on the earth as the home of mankind (because human beings live on earth)';

'I look on James as a brother (because he treats me in a brotherly fashion)';

'I look on the priest as my shepherd (because I can go to him for guidance in the problems of life)';

'I look on students as parasites (because they sponge on society for their keep instead of working for it)'; and

'I look on other people as tools (because I can use them to achieve my own aims)'.

These examples raise the following points. (1) The *degree* of factual similarity suggested in the different analogical onlooks varies greatly. There is, for instance, a much higher degree of factual similarity between Johnny and a child than between students and parasites. Although all analogical onlooks assert that it is appropriate to treat *x* as *y* (prescriptive), they do not all assert the same degree of factual similarity between *x* and *y* (constative). (2) The factual similarity remains important nevertheless, because (within the normative context) it is the *ground* for the correspondence in appropriate attitudes. It is only within the context of the norms assumed by the speaker that the factual similarity between *x* and *y* (Johnny and a child, students and parasites, the priest and a shepherd etc.) is relevant to the correspondence in appropriate attitudes.

(b) *Parabolic onlooks.* Analogical onlooks ascribe meaning to things and have a *reduced* constative function. In parabolic onlooks (parables) this constative function is reduced even further. In parabolic onlooks a metaphor is used to convey the attitude that is appropriate to something. For instance, the attitude we ought to have towards God is suggested in Luke 14 by way of the parable of the beggars whom a man invited off the street to share his banquet when his invited guests would not come. We ought to have the same attitude (gratitude and wonder, etc.) to God that the poor beggars presumably had to the rich man. The point of this parable is solely to indicate what attitude we ought to have to God, not to state a factual similarity between God and a rich man who prepares a sumptuous banquet. We accept that this attitude is proper to God on the grounds that we are told so by Jesus, not on the grounds of a factual similarity between God and the man in the parable. In this regard one might also consider the comparison St Paul draws between the church and the body of Christ.

Briefly: (1) in *analogical* onlooks one is not only told what attitude is appropriate to something, but also that something is similar to something else in some factual respects. *Parabolic* onlooks are concerned only with suggesting an appropriate attitude, not with asserting a factual similarity. (2) In *Analogical* onlooks the relevant attitude (within the assumed normative context) is appropriate on the ground of the factual similarity. In *parabolic* onlooks the relevant attitude is appropriate on other grounds, for instance on the ground of the speaker's authority (that of Jesus, in our example).

# 10 Views of Life

## 10.26 NORMS AND VIEWS OF LIFE

IN section 8.22 we saw that all prescriptive speech acts are based upon
the assumption of an (often unspoken) 'agreement' or 'convention',
subscribed to by both speaker and hearer and obliging the hearer to do
what the speaker asks of him. In value judgements and ascriptions of
meaning, such an 'agreement' takes the form of an evaluative norm or
meaning norm. Thus my value judgement that Steven's Morris is good
could be based on the assumption that my hearer concurs with the
normative 'agreement' that all cars with a low fuel consumption
(including Steven's Morris) are good (worthy of approval).

My prescriptive fails if my hearer does not accept the assumed
agreement. My value judgement on Steven's car therefore fails if my
hearer does not accept the norm to which I am appealing. If I wish to
sustain my value judgement under such circumstances I shall first have
to ask my hearer to accept the assumed norm. I shall have to do more
than *assume* a normative 'agreement'; I shall explicitly have to *make* this
'agreement' with him. But a request to someone to accept a normative
'agreement' is also a *prescriptive* utterance, which in turn is founded on
an assumed agreement. In the same way that I would have to justify my
value judgement (or ascription of meaning) by appealing to a normative
'agreement', I have to defend my normative 'agreement' by appealing to
a further normative 'agreement'. Every norm is founded on a higher
norm. My request to my hearer to concur with the normative
'agreement' that we should approve of all cars with a low fuel
consumption is founded on the further normative 'agreement' that we
ought to approve of all forms of energy conservation (including cars
with a low fuel consumption). This higher norm, in turn, is founded on
the even higher norm or *ideal* of ensuring that mankind will in future
have adequate sources of energy to keep the earth fit for human
habitation.

Briefly: all value judgements and ascriptions of meaning are founded
on assumed norms. Such norms are founded on higher norms or ideals;
so that we justify our value judgement by appealing to norms, and such

norms are, in turn, justified by pointing out that they are consistent with higher norms and ideals to which we ascribe. As reasonable people we determine and evaluate our acts and attitudes with regard to things and situations that we meet in life by referring to our norms and ideals. More generally, we might say that everyone determines and judges his whole *way of life* in the light of the total set of norms and ideals that he accepts and allows to direct his life.

Apart from our norms and ideals there is a further factor that determines our attitude to life, namely our expectations regarding the future. My buying a raincoat today arises not only from my ideal to be dry tomorrow but quite as much from my expectation of rain tomorrow. There is in fact a very close link between our actions, our ideals and our expectations. For example, if we know what someone's ideals and expectations are, we can predict his actions. If we know that someone is expecting rain and would like to keep dry, we shall find it understandable that he carries a raincoat or an umbrella. If we know someone's actions and expectations, we can draw conclusions about his ideals. If someone expects rain and carries a raincoat we can assume that he prefers to keep dry. Similarly, we can infer someone's expectations from his ideals and his actions. (Someone who likes to keep dry and who puts on a raincoat is almost certainly expecting rain.).

There is a further link between our ideals and our expectations: there is no sense in pursuing an ideal if we do not think that this ideal is realisable. In fact, if we lose faith in the realisability of our ideals we feel powerless and lose the urge to pursue such ideals.

In the short term our expectations are usually inductive, that is, we found our factual expectations for the foreseeable future on the order that we have perceived about us in the past. Science plays an important role in this, since the scientist tries to determine by scientific methods what expectations for the future we may reasonably have on the grounds of our past and present experience. Such prognoses become less reliable when they relate to expectations in the longer term. Futurology is little more than guess-work. On our final eschatological expectations, science has no grip whatsoever. In the final analysis such expectations are as much dependent on our view of life as the ideals that we pursue. The eschatological utopia someone *expects* is closely related to his view of life and is as inaccessible to inductive verification as the utopia he *pursues* as an ideal.

In the light of the foregoing we might define a *view of life* as *the total set of norms, ideals and eschatological expectations in terms of which someone directs and assesses his way of life.* Our norms and ideals are always justified by reference to such a view of life. In the final analysis, questions such as 'What ought I to do?', 'What ought I to pursue?', 'What is the meaning of the things and situations I encounter?' are posed and answered within the framework of a view of life, because such questions can be answered only in the light of the norms that we accept. To the extent that every person asks such questions, every person has a view of life.

## 10.27 BASIC CONVICTIONS

A view of life can have an integrating effect on one's way of life only if it is consistent within itself. If a view of life contains contradictory norms it cannot provide unambiguous answers to the question of what things and situations are commendable and what acts and attitudes are good. Contradictory ideals cannot be pursued.

As a rule, the unity and consistency of one's view of life are determined by some *basic conviction* on which it is based. A classic attempt to express such a basic conviction is St Anselm's statement in the *Proslogion* that God is that, than which nothing greater can be conceived (*aliquid quo nihil maius cogitari potest*). St Augustine, again, calls God 'that, than which nothing is more excellent or more divine', or also: 'that which exceeds all else in worth' (*De Doctrina Christiana* I. 7,7). Other examples of basic convictions are to be found in the Buddhist conviction that Nirvana is the highest aim of life, in the Marxist's conviction that the classless society is the ultimate goal of all history, in the pantheist's conviction that Nature is the true reality and all other things merely its parts, in the humanist's conviction that Mankind and its advancement are the objective to which all else must be subservient, etc.

Although these and similar convictions differ in many ways, they are all attempts to do the following in some way or other: first, they all define a certain *x* (an object, or metaphysical entity, or ideal, or person, or something else) as distinct from all other entities. That *x* is unique in the sense that the attitude appropriate to it differs from attitudes appropriate to any other reality. Secondly, the attitude we ought to adopt to any other thing or situation or event, etc., is ultimately determined by its relation to *x*. The meaning of all things is therefore determined by their relation to *x*. Briefly: in the conviction fundamental to a view of life, a certain $x$ is deemed to be unique because it is the primary determinant of meaning for all other things. The classical views of life that have played and still play a role in history and human culture, are similar to the extent that all of them offer an answer to the same basic question: what is the primary determinant of meaning? They differ from each other, however, in the answers they give to this question. To some the primary determinant of meaning is the God of the Bible, to others Nirvana, or Allah, or the Absolute, or Ideas, or Nature, or Mankind, or Reason, etc. There are also individuals or groups who, in practice if not in theory, claim for themselves the status of primary determinant of meaning.

Most classical views of life had or have doctrinal experts or dogmaticians who attempt to give a systematic formulation to the fundamental doctrines of these views of life. In such a systematic doctrinal scheme the following is done: first, the way in which the primary determinant of meaning within such a view of life differs from everything else, must be explained. Here dogmatics should also explain how the attitude which is appropriate to the primary determinant of meaning differs from that appropriate to all else. How, for example, does the love, trust, obedience etc. which is appropriate to God differ from that which we owe to anything or anybody else? From this it is clear how close a relationship there is between dogmatics and ethics.

A vital logical principle in ethics is the universalisability of norms (see section 8.22). In terms of this principle two things that are *equal in fact* must also be treated equally. For example, if two people perform the same act, we cannot approve of one's actions and condemn the other's, unless it can be shown that there are relevant factual differences between the two cases. But then we would be dealing with acts that *differ* in fact. This principle implies also that something to which a unique attitude is appropriate, would also have to be unique in factual respects. If, for instance, God were not completely different in factual respects from all else, there would be no grounds for treating Him in a completely different way from all else. Therefore dogmatics has to explain not only how we ought to behave in a unique way towards God, but also how God differs in fact from all else. In short, dogmatics has to explain in what way we are to understand God's transcendence. In Part IV we shall deal with this question in more detail.

Apart from explaining the unique character of the primary determinant of meaning, the doctrinal system of a view of life must also explain the nature of the relationship between this primary determinant of meaning and all else, as well as the way in which the meaning of all else is to be determined by this relationship. In this sense Christian dogmatics must explain how our entire lives and the world in which we live relate to God, the Creator, Redeemer and Consummator of all things. It must also show in what way this relationship determines the meaning of our lives and, linked with that, what attitudes we ought to adopt towards the reality in which we find ourselves. Here again the close link between dogmatics and ethics becomes apparent.

Briefly: the doctrinal system in which someone tries to account for his way of life will have to contain an answer to the following questions: Who or what is the primary determinant of meaning? In what way is he or it distinct from all else and what does this entail for the way we are to behave towards him or it? In what way are all things related to this primary determinant of meaning and what implications does this have for the meaning of our lives and our world, for the ideals and norms by which our lives are to be directed and the eschatological expectations that we may (possibly) have? These are the final and most fundamental questions of life. Any view of life is ultimately an attempt to provide an answer to these questions.

The question is whether every human being tries to find an answer to these ultimate questions. Has everyone a view of life? Everone does have a certain attitude to life or way of life. We have also seen that every human being asks normative questions with regard to his own actions and the things and situations that confront him. This requires every human being to bring about some degree of coherence and consistency in his way of life, but the extent to which people pursue this kind of reflection may differ. Not all people are equally reflective, nor do all reflect to an equal extent on the correctness of their own ways or on the meaning of their lives.

To many people no single entity is a primary determinant of meaning in their lives. They have varying central interests, related, for instance, to their families, their work, a certain social group to which they belong, a certain political or sporting activity, or something else. To such a person none of these things is more important than all others. He may never have considered what is *most* important to him. He may also never have been in a situation in which he had to choose between his interests. To such a person nothing in his life is the primary determinant of meaning. As long as such a person does not experience a crisis in which he is forced to choose between his interests, or is forced by other people with other interests to account for the relative importance of the things by which his attitude to life is determined, he can readily carry on without asking the final questions about a primary determinant of meaning which is more important than all else.

Although everybody brings some degree of consistency or coherence into his *way of life*, this does not mean that everybody makes one entity the primary determinant of meaning. There are those who can serve more than one master, as long as the interests of their masters do not conflict in practice. On the other hand there are many who strive to keep their lives 'whole' by making one master the primary determinant of meaning, although not all of these have a view of life in the sense of a systematic doctrine. Nor can it be said that everyone who has a doctrinal system, consistently directs his life in accordance with it. There are many who build intellectual palaces, yet live in hovels.

Even if there are people who can ignore the ultimate questions of life because the circumstances of their lives have not forced them to answer these questions, and even if there are people who answer them exhaustively for intellectual reasons without realising these answers in their own lives, these ultimate questions remain vitally real. The problem is, however, whether any discussion is possible on which view of life presents the true answers to these ultimate questions of life. Are there true answers to ultimate questions?

## 10.28 THE RATIONALITY OF A VIEW OF LIFE

It is always possible to discuss with someone else whether the way I acted in a certain situation, or my attitude to a certain phenomenon, is right or wrong. In such a discussion I can justify my actions or attitude only by appealing to norms. If my companion went further and asked me to justify my norms I could do so only by appealing to higher norms or ideals. I would have to justify my ideals by showing that they formed part of a complete way of life, and I would have to justify that way of life by pointing out that it accorded with my basic conviction that $x$ is the primary determinant of meaning ($x$ being, for example, the God of the Bible). If my companion pressed me even further and demanded some justification for my holding this God to be the primary determinant of meaning, answering him would become problematic. We would have reached the ultimate criterion, the end of a series of justifications of justifications of justifications. I could advance no grounds to justify my final ground. I could merely *testify* that this was my final ground. In fact, anyone can justify his answer to the *ultimate* questions only by circular argument – by a *petitio principii*. For example: it is only *as a Christian* that someone accepts the gospel as the true answer to ultimate questions, and it is only on the strength of his acceptance of the gospel as the true answer, that he is a Christian. The same applies *mutatis mutandis* to any answer given to the ultimate questions of life.

But what do we say of those who have a different ultimate ground which they hold to be the primary determinant of meaning in their lives? If there are no criteria by which to judge our ultimate criterion – and this seems to be impossible, since the ultimate criterion is indeed the *ultimate* one – there is no possibility of deciding who is right. Does this imply that any answer to a question about the criterion that *finally* determines meaning or about the primary determinant of meaning must be arbitrary and unfounded because it is by definition impossible to advance further grounds? If our ultimate criterion is arbitrary and unfounded, does this imply that all norms that can be justified only by an appeal to the ultimate criterion are likewise arbitrary and unfounded? And are all decisions justified by an appeal to such arbitrary norms equally arbitrary and unfounded? Does this end in total relativism? There are many who accept this kind of relativism. According to them, all our actions and decisions depend upon our whole way of life, which is in turn determined by the social or geographical conditions that have produced us. We might offer a sociological explanation of someone's actions, decisions and value judgements, but we cannot justify them. Ultimately they do have causes, but no grounds.

In *The Language of Morals*[12] R.M. Hare points out that this kind of relativism misuses the terms 'unfounded' and 'arbitrary' when applying them to a decision which is defended with an appeal to norms that in turn are founded upon higher norms, which fit into a total view of life, which is founded upon a basic conviction. Such decisions are neither unfounded nor arbitrary; on the contrary, they are as well-founded as possible. There is simply no way they could be better founded or more soundly defended. If our opponent is not satisfied with such a justification of our decisions because he does not concur with the total view of life in terms of which this justification is offered, Hare sees no possibility of further discussion. Hare maintains that we can justify our actions, attitudes and decisions *within* the framework of a view of life. To speak of founded or unfounded decisions has meaning only within such a framework. For our choice of a view of life, however, no grounds can be advanced; as far as this choice is concerned, Hare maintains, everyone must do as he sees fit.

In the final analysis, when it comes to taking a stand on the acceptability of a total view of life (and thus a basic conviction), Hare fails to avoid relativism. Can we accept this? Is it ultimately of no account what view of life we adopt as a justification for our actions, attitudes and decisions? Is no discussion about such final presuppositions possible between people with different views of life, because they have no common criteria on which to base such a discussion?

Perhaps we might avoid this impasse by distinguishing between two kinds of criteria: (1) criteria that derive from a view of life (criteria internal to a view of life) and (2) criteria that derive from an analysis of the function of views of life as such (external functional criteria).

In the nature of the case, people with different views of life will have no criteria of the first kind in common, except to the extent that their views of life overlap. It is not unusual for differing views of life to overlap to a greater or lesser extent by having certain norms and ideals in common. In this respect, Jews and Christians have a good deal in common and so have Christians and Humanists. There are even basic Christian norms and ideals that are acceptable to a Buddhist. But they would differ regarding the grounds on which they consider such common norms and ideals acceptable. Although differing views of life do overlap, they contradict one another as total views of life. No one can be a Buddhist and a Christian at the same time.

Two statements or systems or theories can, however, contradict each other only if they are of the same order. They must purport to be alternative answers to *the same* questions, or alternative constructions that purport to fulfil *the same* function. The Christian faith and Buddhism are alternative views of life that purport to fulfil the same function by seeking to provide an answer to the same ultimate questions. In order to fulfil this common function they must be subject to common functional criteria. Since these criteria are common they cannot be derived from a particular view of life. The fact that two people differ on the question of which view of life is acceptable implies that they agree: (1) that their respective views of life exclude each other; (2) that their respective views of life seek to fulfil the same function by providing answers to the same questions; thus also (3) on the function of a view of life, and (4) on the common criteria that a doctrinal scheme has to meet in order to fulfil that function.

Someone may therefore reject another's view of life for two kinds of reasons: (1) because it formulates and provides a basis for a way of life that cannot be accepted in terms of one's own basic conviction, thus providing unacceptable alternative answers to the questions to which one's own view of life provides correct answers; and (2) because it cannot be a functional view of life since it does not meet the common criteria for the fulfilment of the function of a view of life. Hence, we may reject a view of life because it is an incorrect alternative or because it is not an alternative at all since it cannot satisfactorily fulfil the function of a view of life.

It is clear that arguments of the first kind are not possible in a discussion between people with different views of life because they appeal to criteria that are not commonly accepted. Arguments of the second kind are possible, however, because they do appeal to common criteria. What, then, are the criteria that any view of life has to meet if it is to fulfil the function of a view of life and to be valid as an alternative view of life? We may apply the following five criteria:

     (1) freedom from contradiction,
     (2) unity,
     (3) relevance,
     (4) universality,
     (5) impressiveness.

## 1. Freedom from contradiction

The first requirement a view of life (as an attempt to formulate and form a basis for a way of life) has to meet is that it must contain no contradictions. A contradictory view of life cannot express a viable way of life. A contradiction, after all, asserts something but at the same time denies what it has asserted, thus asserting nothing. A view of life that contains contradictions cannot, therefore, fulfil its function of asserting what way of life is appropriate. In this connection we distinguished in section 2.6 between true contradictions and paradoxes or apparent contradictions. Parodoxes fulfil an important didactic function because they force us to take account of apparently opposed prescriptives and to do justice to both. In doing so, however, we have the obligation of showing that such paradoxes are only apparently contradictory. We can assert two apparently contradictory prescriptives without prejudice to either only if we are prepared to demonstrate that they merely appear to negate each other.

## 2. Unity

A view of life may be free from contradiction in the sense that it contains no conflicting doctrines and thus no prescriptives that negate each other. It may nonetheless lack unity, because there may be no positive coherence between its various doctrines. In this regard we may consider the difficulty referred to in section 10.27, namely of someone whose life is directed by a variety of interests (his family, his business, his hobby, his sport club), none of which he regards as a primary determinant of meaning.

In practice it may well be possible to serve two (or more) masters in this fashion, but only as long as no situation arises in which the interests of these masters conflict. If that happened, contradictions would arise within such a person's view of life, making it untenable. He who serves two masters always faces the risk of meeting a situation in which he would be forced to choose between his two masters. 'Either he will hate the one and love the other, or he will be devoted to one and despise the other.' (Matt. 6: 24).

Apart from the fact that a view of life without unity carries this risk within it, it cannot fulfil the aim of a view of life, to integrate or keep 'whole' one's way of life. In this sense it cannot be a 'wholesome' view of life.

## 3. Relevance

A view of life has the function of determining and integrating one's way of life. All its various doctrines must therefore have implications for the way we run our lives. If someone's view of life contains tenets that have no implications for our way of life, or that make no clear difference to how we would have to live if we accepted them, such a view of life might be an interesting speculative construction but would lack the existential relevance a view of life needs in order to fulfil its function.

## 4. Universality

Not only must a view of life be existentially relevant: it must also have universal relevance to our way of life, that is, it must determine our actions and our attitudes in *any* situation we meet in life. A view of life becomes untenable if situations arise for which it has no practical implications, or in which the attitudes or actions that seem correct in terms of that view of life prove to be impracticable. From this it becomes clear that a view of life cannot be a static, closed system. In life we are constantly confronted with new situations that make new demands of us. In modern life the demands or challenges that we have to face differ completely from those of the previous century or of the middle ages. A view of life that is not universal enough to enable us constantly to face new challenges in life does not fulfil its function of making life liveable.

## 5. Impressiveness

Any viable view of life must be able to refer to something or someone, which impresses men as being more important (or more determinant of meaning) than anything else. Only in this way can the basic conviction of a view of life (that is, the conviction that $x$ is the primary determinant of meaning) become evident for those who commit themselves to this way of life. Thus Christians, for example, are inspired by the person of Jesus, and it is evident to them that a Christian way of life is the only appropriate one. In this regard Ian T. Ramsey[13] speaks of 'discernment' and 'commitment'. A person's commitment to a certain way of life is dependent upon his discernment that someone or something is the primary determinant of meaning. Ramsey maintains that it is hypocritical to have that discernment without proceeding from it to commitment. Faith without action is dead. On the other hand it is self-misleading to commit oneself to a way of life without founding this commitment on the discernment of something that is more important than anything else.

The appropriateness of a way of life, then, is evident to its adherents because they can refer to something or someone that inspires them to live this way of life.

In the light of a person's view of life, the things, situations and events that he encounters in life also have an evident meaning to him. Intuitionism (see section 6.15) rightly draws our attention to the way in which the value or meaning of things is somehow evident to us. In this regard, however, intuitionism makes two mistakes: first, the value or meaning of things is not *directly* evident, as the intuitionists maintain. It is only *in the light of* someone's view of life, which refers to something or someone that inspires him, that things have an evident value or meaning. Secondly, this capacity for inspiring someone is not a 'non-natural' characteristic, observable only through a special sense (intuition). It is simply an impressive characteristic, as empirical as all other impressive characteristics (see section 9.24). I need no special sense to perceive that something inspires me, nor do I suffer from some sensory deficiency if I fail to be inspired by something that does inspire others.

If someone is not inspired by anyone or anything in this way, he is incapable of committing himself wholeheartedly to a certain way of life. This incapacity may reveal itself in existential lassitude or *taedium vitae*, in which life loses all meaning. If a view of life is not linked with something or someone that inspires people in this way, it cannot have the evident character that would bring people to commit themselves to a life in conformity with it, nor can it then fulfil the function of determining people's way of life.

Freedom from contradiction, unity, relevance, universality and impressiveness are therefore five external criteria to be met by a view of life if it is to function as such. The question, however, is whether these five criteria offer an adequate basis for deciding which way of life is the one and only appropriate one, excluding all others. That they do not offer such a basis is clear from the following considerations.

(*a*) In order to determine which view of life is the *only* correct one it would be necessary to compare all views of life in the light of the criteria mentioned above. In such a comparison we should have to take account not only of the existing, but of all *possible* views of life, and we do not know what views of life might arise in the future.

(*b*) The above-mentioned criteria might be met by more than one view of life. More than one view of life might be free from contradiction, have coherent unity, be existentially relevant, have universal applicability and be able to refer to something or someone that inspires those who deem this view of life valid. In such a case these criteria would not provide an adequate basis for choosing.

(*c*) The demand of universality (fourth criterion) implies that a view of life must be relevant to *every* situation in life. We do not know, however, whether this will always be the case in future. Anyone may trust that his own view of life will remain relevant in the future, but this cannot be demonstrated in advance. It is also impossible to demonstrate what view of life will in future best meet the demand for universal relevance.

(*d*) The fifth criterion (impressiveness) is not really a basis for comparing views of life. What inspires one person and directs his whole way of life may leave another unaffected. If the adherents of two different views of life refer, respectively, to two different persons or phenomena as that which inspires them in their respective ways of life, we have no further *external* criterion for choosing between these two sources of inspiration.

Therefore, even though there are external criteria that any view of life has to meet if it is to be functional as a view of life, these criteria are not an adequate basis for deciding which view is correct, to the exclusion of all others. We are therefore left with the question whether any commitment to a view of life is not arbitrary and irrational. Is it justifiable to base one's entire life on such an arbitrary and irrational commitment? This question prompts three observations.

First, it is unrealistic to ask whether or not people are justified in committing themselves to a view of life. Everyone has to live in some way or other. Whether he wants it so or not, everyone practises a specific way of life and thereby excludes all others. The question is not whether we should adopt a certain way of life, but merely which way of life we are to find acceptable. This question concerns everybody.

Secondly, it is incorrect to call such a commitment to a view of life arbitrary. It is unrealistic to think that we can, so to speak, line up all possible views of life in a neat row and then objectively set about making a choice. We are never detached in making such a choice; everyone of us is already in the position of having been inspired by something or someone – or by a group of things that are all important to him. A commitment to a view of life is never an arbitrary choice between equal possibilities; it involves responding to whatever inspires one as being more important or more determinant of meaning than anything else.

Thirdly, a commitment to a view of life is not irrational in the sense that there can be no discussion about it. On the contrary, the external criteria that we listed form a basis for such a discussion. If opponents challenge someone for accepting a view of life that is contradictory, that has no coherent unity, that is irrelevant or not universally applicable, he cannot ignore such criticism. If we accept Karl Popper's definition of rationality as openness to criticism, every view of life is in principle open to such outside criticism and is therefore a rational matter.

# PART THREE

# EPISTEMOLOGICAL CONCEPTS

# 11 Introduction

## 11.29 EPISTEMOLOGICAL QUESTIONS

### 1. Believing

THE Apostles' Creed starts with the words 'I believe . . . ' What do these words actually mean? Do we claim, in using these words, that we *know* the statements included in this creed to be true? Or that we are of the opinion that they are true? Or is belief something quite different – neither knowledge nor opinion?

A complication arises from the fact that the word 'belief' is ambiguous. We can *believe someone,* that is, *believe that* what he says is true, because we *believe in him.* On the one hand, therefore, we speak of *belief in* someone; on the other hand of the *belief that* a statement is true. To believe *in* someone means trusting him or having faith in him or in his knowledge or his skill or in his good faith. In this sense some people *believe* more strongly *in* one doctor than in another (have more faith in), *believe* more *in* one cure than in another, in one procedure than in another. If someone says that he believes *in* a witch doctor his words express his confidence in the witch doctor's skill in curing people.

Thus the Apostles' Creed declares 'I believe *in* God the Father, etc.' and not 'I believe *that* God is the Father . . . ' Are we to conclude from this that the Creed is solely an expression of trust in God, and not also of the *belief that* certain statements about God are true?

'Believe that . . . ' is also ambiguous. We often use these words parenthetically with constative speech acts (see section 2.6). In doing so, we tell our hearer with what degree of certainty, or conviction, we perform the constative speech act. We may be using these words to show that our certainty about a statement is minimal. 'I believe that *p*' is then roughly equivalent to 'I think that *p*' or 'It seems to me that *p*' or 'I surmise that *p*'. But if we say, 'I firmly believe that *p*' or 'I am convinced that *p*', we intimate that our certainty about the truth of *p* is strong. Through the words 'I believe that' we are therefore saying that we are more or less certain of the truth of a constative speech act. This certainty may range from weak surmise to strong conviction, as represented on the scale in Table II.

## Table II

| uncertain | certain |
|---|---|
| (weak surmise)↑ | ↑(strong conviction) |

'I *believe* that *p*'            'I *firmly believe* that *p*'
'I think that *p*'               'I am convinced that *p*'
'It seems to me that *p*'
'I surmise that *p*'

Is the Apostles' Creed an expression of belief in the sense of confidence or trust in God, or also of belief in the sense of being convinced of the truth of certain statements? If it is also a matter of belief as conviction, what degree of certainty does it suggest? Where along the scale do we have to put this belief? Does the Creed express a weak surmise or firm conviction? Or does this vary from one believer to another? Or could we also speak of *knowing* in a religious context? What is *knowing*, and how does it differ from *believing*?

### 2. Knowledge and acquaintance

There are two kinds of *knowledge*: (1) knowledge of (or *acquaintance* with) things, persons, places, etc., and (2) knowledge of truths (true statements) about things, persons, places etc. We can be *acquainted* with Peter and we can *know that* Peter has red hair. We can be *acquainted* with London and we can *know that* London is the capital of England. We can be *acquainted* with persecution or poverty and we can *know that* St Paul knew persecution and poverty.

We say that we are *acquainted* with something only if we have personal experience of it. In this sense, *acquaintance* is by definition knowing at first hand. From hearsay I can *know truths about* many things, but I cannot get acquainted with those things *themselves*. It is possible to be more or less acquainted with something, depending on whether one has had more or less personal experience of it. As for being acquainted with people, we have to distinguish between having contact with someone and being acquainted with someone: I may have seen someone without getting acquainted with him. I may even meet someone regularly and speak to him, and yet have a very superficial acquaintance with him because he is reticent towards me. Much contact with a person does not necessarily lead to one becoming well acquainted with that person.

Acquaintance with things always leads to *knowledge of truths* about those things. When I am acquainted with someone, I know several things about him on the strength of this acquaintance. It is impossible to be acquainted with something without also knowing something *about* it. The better I am acquainted with something or someone, the more truths I come to know about it or him.

I may get acquainted with something, and through the same experience I may know much about it. I cannot get acquainted with something through hearsay, but I can come to know much about it from hearsay. Not all knowledge of truths is first-hand. In fact, most of the truths we know are known through evidence or reports from others and not through personal experience. Therefore, although I cannot be acquainted with something without knowing some truths about it, I may know truths about it without being acquainted with it.

Briefly: I am *acquainted with* something or someone if I have had personal experience of it or him and therefore know some truths *about* it or him at first-hand; I *know that* certain statements about something are true on the strength of the experience by which I got acquainted with that thing, or on the strength of the testimony given by others.

### 3. Knowing and believing

*Acquaintance with* is readily distinguished from *knowing about* or *knowing that*. What is more difficult, however, is drawing a precise distinction between *knowing that* and *believing that*. Both words may be used parenthetically with constative speech acts. I can say '*I believe that p*' and also '*I know that p*'. In saying 'I believe that *p*' I intimate that I am (more or less strongly) convinced of the truth of *p*. But what do I mean when I say '*I know that p*'? Does this also express my conviction? Is 'I know that *p*' equivalent to 'I am firmly convinced that *p*'? Or is it something different? Or something more?

One way of distinguishing between *knowing that* and *firmly believing that* or *being convinced that* may be to see them as different attitudes towards true statements. We say of true statements that we know or believe them. Are knowing and believing, then, different attitudes we have toward these true statements?

That we cannot distinguish in this fashion between *knowing* and *believing* is apparent from the following example (adapted from one used by Norman Malcolm): at 10 o'clock one morning I say 'I know that the statue of the Earl of Pembroke at the Bodleian library has a marshal's baton in its hand.' At 12 o'clock I pass the statue and remark,

when I see it, 'This morning at 10 o'clock *I knew* that Pembroke had a
baton in his hand.' But suppose I arrived at the Bodleian at 12 o'clock
and found that during the night student pranksters had replaced the
baton with a table leg. I would no longer be able to say 'At 10 o'clock
this morning I *knew* that the statue had a baton in its hand, but it now
appears that I was mistaken.' I would rather say 'At 10 o'clock this
morning *I believed* (was firmly convinced) that the statue had a baton in
its hand, but it now appears that I was mistaken.'

This example deals with two situations. In one situation I say 'This
morning I knew that *p*', and in the other 'This morning I believed (was
firmly convinced) that *p*' The only further difference between the two
situations is that in one instance *p* subsequently proved to be untrue and
in the other instance it proved to be true. There is, however, no
difference between the two situations as regards the attitudes I had
towards *p* at 10 o'clock, nor as regards the degree of certainty or
conviction that I felt towards *p*. In one instance I speak of my attitude to
*p* as 'knowing' and in the other instance I speak of precisely *the same
attitude* as 'believing' (or 'being firmly convinced'). From this example
it is clear that the difference between *belief* (as firm conviction) and
*knowing* is not a difference between two different attitudes adopted
towards *p*.

We may find it more fruitful to regard knowing not as something
*different from* but as something *more than* believing. A view commonly
found in the history of epistemology, is that knowing may be defined as
justified true belief. Thus Plato already discussed this view.

It is clear that 'firmly believing' is implied in 'knowing'. It would,
after all, be contradictory to say 'I know that *p*, but I do not believe that
*p*'. What is involved here is not believing, in the sense of surmising with
uncertainty. Saying 'I know that *p*' implies that I believe with certainty,
(am convinced) that *p*. Believing permits degrees of certainty; knowing,
on the other hand, does not, because knowing implies maximum
certainty.

But 'knowing' is more than merely 'firmly believing' or 'being
convinced'. Someone may firmly believe that *p* without our being able
to say that he *knows* that *p*. In the middle ages most people firmly
believed that the earth was flat. Since this belief was erroneous their
believing was not knowing, even if they did say 'We know that the earth
is flat.' It is always possible to have an untrue belief. But 'untrue
knowing' is a contradiction in terms. In the light of this we can
understand the example of Pembroke's baton. It is possible to say 'This

morning at 10 o'clock I *firmly believed* that Pembroke had a baton in his hand, but it has since become apparent that I was mistaken.' I cannot, however, say without contradiction 'This morning at 10 o'clock I *knew* that the statue had a baton in its hand, but it has since become apparent that I was mistaken.'

But knowing is also more than simply having a true belief. If $p$ is true, and if someone believes that $p$ on the grounds of his wife's intuition or the dream of a friend or his own (inaccurate) recollection of the testimony of a known liar, we shall not say "He knows that $p$.' In the *Theaetetus* (201) Plato points out that orators and lawyers are capable of causing people to believe by means of oratorical tricks. Even if such beliefs were true we would not say that the orators had given the people knowledge. If a true belief is arrived at by invalid means it is not a justified belief and consequently not a form of knowing. In order to know one should not merely believe, one should also be entitled to this belief. One should have 'the right to be sure', as Ayer puts it.[1] The truth of a belief is not sufficient justification for having it. For such a belief to be justified, one must have *sufficient evidence* as grounds for the belief.

Briefly: in terms of this view someone can say 'I know that $p$' only if (1) he firmly believes that $p$, (2) $p$ is true, and (3) he has sufficient grounds for his belief. Knowing, then, is not something different from believing; it is (firm) belief plus something more.

It is debatable, however, whether this traditional view about the relation between believing and knowing is tenable. In order to ascertain whether it is, we have to examine more closely the concepts of believing (being convinced), truth and sufficient evidence.

Taking this traditional view about believing and knowing as our point of departure, we shall deal with the following questions: In chapter 12 we shall examine the nature of believing or being convinced. In chapter 13 we shall deal with the concept of truth. What are the main views about the nature of truth and what are the merits and demerits of each of them? Chapter 14 will be devoted to the question of adequate grounds. What must be the nature of evidence if we are to have the *right* to be sure? In chapter 15 we shall deal with the relation between believing and knowing in the light of our conclusions in chapters 12 – 14. In chapter 16 we shall try to draw conclusions about the nature of religious belief from our analysis of the concepts of believing, knowing, truth, and grounds. Is the Apostles' Creed concerned with surmise, conviction, or knowledge?

# 12 Belief

## 12.30 BELIEVING AND UNDERSTANDING

I MAY or may not understand a statement (constative speech act) made by someone, and I may or may not believe it. What is the difference between understanding or not understanding it on the one hand and believing or not believing it on the other? And how are they related?

I *understand* a speech act if I know what it *means*. In Part One we suggested that the meaning of a speech act lies in its illocutionary load. I understand what someone is saying to the extent that I understand what constatives, expressives, commissives and/or prescriptives he is asserting in his speech act, and how these are related to the factual situation in the world. To the extent that I do not know this, and to the extent that I think he is asserting other illocutions related to other aspects of the world, I misunderstand him.

Whereas *understanding* is related to *meaning*, *believing* has to do with *truth*. I believe what someone says if I accept that what he says is *true*. Only constatives, however, can be true or false. Expressives, commissives and prescriptives can succeed or fail in other ways, but not by being true or false (see section 2.5). Although we may therefore understand or misunderstand the assertion of any illocution, we cannot believe or disbelieve the assertion of any illocution. Only constative assertions can be believed or disbelieved, because only constatives are true or false.

Briefly: as with all other kinds of speech acts, we can understand or misunderstand constative assertions (statements) because they have a meaning. In contrast to all other kinds of speech acts, we can believe or disbelieve constative assertions, because they can be true or false.

It is possible to understand a statement without believing it: I may understand the proposition someone is stating, yet consider his proposition false. In this sense belief is by no means a precondition for understanding. It is, however, neither possible to believe nor to disbelieve a statement unless one understands it; it is only if I understand what proposition someone is stating that I can accept his proposition as true or reject it as false. In this sense understanding is a precondition for both believing and disbelieving. Believing is, however, more than merely understanding. it is understanding *and* accepting as true. But what does that mean: accepting something as true? In this regard a useful approach is found in H.H. Price's essay on 'Some Considerations about Belief'.[2] According to Price, 'believing that *p*' may be analysed into the following three elements:

(1) understanding *p* (Price speaks of 'entertaining *p*', which to him means the same as 'understanding *p*');

(2) having evidence on the grounds of which *p* is more likely than not *p*;

(3) assenting to *p*. According to Price assenting to *p* has two elements: (a) an *emotional* element, that is, a feeling of sureness or confidence regarding *p*. This element may have various degrees: my feeling of certainty may vary from opinion (a low degree of certainty) to absolute conviction (a high degree of certainty); (b) a *volitional* element, that is, preferring *p* to not-*p*, choosing in favour of *p*, or deciding for *p*.

The argument in this paragraph may be summed up as follows:

(1) We *understand* a speech act if we grasp its meaning (illocutionary load).

(2) We can understand a statement without believing it, but we cannot believe it without understanding it. This implies that believing is understanding plus something more.

(3) According to H.H. Price, 'believing that *p*' is the same as 'understanding *p*' *and* 'assenting to *p* on the grounds of the available evidence'.

(4) The question is: what is the relation between my assent to a proposition and my evidence in favour of that proposition?

## 12.31 FEELING OR CHOOSING?

Can it be said that my evidence is the *cause* of my assent? Or is it merely a *reason* that I advance for my *deciding* to assent to the proposition? Is my belief-that-*p* a *condition* brought about in my mind by the considered evidence, or is it a *choice* made on the grounds of the considered evidence? Does the evidence persuade me to believe, or do I choose to believe on the grounds of the evidence?

On this point Price wavers between two possibilities. On the one hand he maintains that 'assenting to *p*' contains an element of feeling, that is, a feeling of certainty or confidence. But feeling is not an act that I can decide to perform or not to perform; it is, rather, a condition btought about in my mind by the evidence I have considered. I *am convinced by* the considered evidence. On the other hand, however, Price finds a volitional element in 'assenting to *p*', that is, choosing for *p* and against not-*p*. In this regard the evidence is not the cause of my choice but the reason on the strength of which I make my choice. Can both these points be maintained? Should we not say rather that believing is either a kind of choosing or a kind of feeling, but that it cannot be both?

According to *Descartes*, believing is in fact something that we can *choose* to do. In his *Meditations IV* he asks himself how it is possible for us to arrive at erroneous judgements, if the faculties we have received from God are perfect. According to Descartes, we receive two perfect faculties from the perfect God: the *faculty of understanding*, and the *faculty of will*. Our faculty of understanding enables us to understand propositions about the world. But understanding is not the same as assent. Our faculty of understanding neither affirms nor denies propositions; it merely presents propositions to our faculty of will for assent or rejection. Since our faculty of understanding neither affirms nor denies propositions, it cannot make erroneous affirmations or denials. Erroneous judgements cannot, therefore, originate in our faculty of understanding. But our faculty of will has a much broader range than our faculty of understanding. Through our will we can freely affirm or deny propositions, even if we do not understand them. Erroneous judgements are a consequence of abuse of the gift of will that we have received from a good God: we assent to propositions that our faculty of understanding has not yet mastered.

The assumption at the root of Descartes' argument is that assent to a proposition (unlike understanding it) is a function of the will. We *decide* freely what propositions we wish to accept as true or reject as false. Erroneous judgements therefore result from ill-considered decisions: we choose to assent to (or reject) propositions before we have considered them carefully enough to have understood them properly.

What does it mean to 'consider' a proposition? In his *Enquiry Concerning Human Understanding* (Section X) David Hume gives the following answer: 'A wise man proportions his belief to the evidence.' In other words, it is characteristic of the wise man that he carefully weighs the evidence for a proposition and the evidence against it, and only then decides whether and with what degree of certainty he will believe that proposition. If there is strong evidence in favour of a proposition and none against it, a wise man will accept that proposition with certainty. If the evidence for a proposition is somewhat stronger than the evidence against it, a wise man will consider the proposition merely probable. If, however, the evidence against a proposition is stronger, a wise man will not assent to that proposition. It is most unwise to believe wildly, without considering the evidence, for this merely leads to superstition or erroneous judgements.

Briefly: according to this view we can *decide* freely whether we shall accept a proposition as true or reject it as false. But if we are wise and wish to avoid superstition and error we shall take such decisions only on the strength of the evidence for or against that proposition.

A different assumption lies at the root of Hume's argument in his *Treatise on Human Nature* (Book I, Part III, Section VII). Here Hume asks himself what the difference is between an idea that I imagine (without believing it) and an idea that I believe. According to Hume, the difference does not lie in the content of the idea but in the way we conceive such ideas, or in the way we 'feel' about such ideas.

> An idea assented to *feels* different from a fictitious idea, that the fancy alone presents to us: and this different feeling I endeavour to explain by calling it a superior *force*, or *vivacity*, or *solidity*, or *firmness*, or *steadiness*. . . . I confess, that it is impossible to explain perfectly this feeling or manner of conception. . . . we can go no further than assert, that it is something *felt* by the mind, which distinguishes the ideas of the judgement from the fictions of the imagination. It gives them more force and influence; makes them appear of greater importance; infixes them in the mind; and renders them the governing principles of all our actions.

In his *Treatise* Hume assumes, therefore, that believing is a kind of *feeling* towards an idea ('something felt by the mind'). This implies, however, that believing is not something we can decide to do. I do not decide to feel about something in a certain way; I simply find myself feeling that way. Feelings or emotions are aroused in us; we do not choose them.

Which of these views is the correct one? To the extent that believing-that-$p$ is equivalent to being-certain-that-$p$ or being-convinced-that-$p$, Hume's argument in the *Treatise* presents the most plausible view. But it is debatable whether being certain or being convinced is a kind of feeling or emotion. We are often certain of something when no emotion is involved. It is true that we sometimes feel strongly about our convictions or our beliefs, but this is mostly the case when our conviction or belief is under attack and therefore insecure. This does not, however, imply that conviction or certainty is a kind of feeling or emotion. It is clear that Hume himself was not too happy with the identification of belief with feeling. He uses the analogy between feeling and believing to illustrate the nature of believing, as being convinced or being certain. Certainty or conviction is like a feeling or an emotion in that it is something I find within myself, not something which I can decide to do. If I happen not to believe something I cannot simply decide to believe it. I may, of course, decide to admit, confess, or declare to someone else that I am certain, but I cannot be certain or uncertain by choice.

Descartes and Hume (in the *Enquiry*) are correct in maintaining that the way from doubt to certainty is through the consideration of evidence. But the consideration of evidence does not lead to a *decision* to be convinced that $p$ or that not-$p$. It leads, rather, to *becoming convinced* by the considered evidence. It is possible to choose whether or not to shut one's eyes deliberately to certain evidence, or to consider such evidence only partially, to treat it seriously, or to allow it to affect one. But it is not possible to choose whether or not to become convinced by the evidence that one does eventually consider. A reasonable man is one who does not ignore the evidence and who, as far as possible, gives serious consideration to all arguments and all evidence. He does not try to shield his convictions by disregarding arguments raised against them. We can, of course, decide to protect our beliefs irrationally by wearing blinkers, even if it is doubtful whether this is wise or intellectually honest. But this freedom is not the freedom to become or not become convinced at will by evidence that we eventually do decide to consider.

Briefly: someone *believes* that $p$, if (1) he understands $p$ and (2) is convinced, by the evidence considered by him, that $p$ is true. Becoming convinced is something that happens to us, not something we can decide to do. And yet we do sometimes think of believing as something we can decide to do and which we can therefore be called upon to justify in the way we are called upon to justify actions. Maybe the term 'belief' is ambiguous, so that we could distinguish between believing as being convinced by the considered evidence and believing as an act of some sort. We shall return to this problem in section 14.42.

## 12.32 BELIEVING AND ACTING

The passage from Hume's *Treatise on Human Nature* discussed above, contains another important note on believing and being convinced. If we are convinced of the truth of a proposition, we understand it and 'feel' certain about it. According to Hume, however, this certainty implies that propositions we believe determine our actions: 'It renders them the governing principle of all our actions.' The question is: how do our beliefs determine our actions?

It is important to draw a clear distinction here between two senses of 'believing' or 'being convinced'. On the one hand we say 'I believe that *p*'; on the other hand we say 'I believe that I must do *x*'. In the first case we refer to my belief that a certain *constative* is true; in the second, to my belief that a certain *prescriptive* applies to me and that I ought to obey it.

In Part Two we argued that ideals and evaluative norms are general *prescriptives*. An ideal is something one *ought* to pursue and an evaluative norm defines a class of things in respect of which one *ought* to have a certain pro or con-attitude. We also argued that the ideals and norms by which a person's attitudes are determined, form part of his view of life. This implies that *prescriptive beliefs* ('I believe that I ought to do *x*') have an important function in the context of one's view of life. The question arises, however, whether this is the only kind of belief that plays a part in one's view of life: do not *constative beliefs* ('I believe that *p*') also play an important part in a view of life?

In brief: does a view of life include only beliefs on how we ought to live, or does it also include factual beliefs? Does a view of life merely contain prescriptives (norms and ideals), or also factual claims? We shall return to these questions in chapters 16 and 19.

It is clear that prescriptive beliefs can indeed be 'the governing principles of all our actions'. When we say that someone is or is not *acting in accordance with his convictions* we (usually) have in mind such prescriptive beliefs. In the passage we have cited from Hume's *Treatise*, however, he was not concerned with prescriptive beliefs, but with beliefs that something does or does not exist in reality – hence with *constative beliefs*. Now the question is whether, and if so, *how*, our constative beliefs can determine our actions. Since epistemology is concerned primarily with constative beliefs (ones that are true or false), we have to consider this question more closely. How do our beliefs on the factual nature of the world determine our actions?

A useful point of departure for dealing with this question is the behaviouristic analysis of belief that R. B. Braithwaite offers in his essay on 'The Nature of Believing'.[3] According to Braithwaite, 'I believe that $p$' presupposes that I understand $p$. In this respect Braithwaite agrees with Descartes, Hume and Price. (Like Price, Braithwaite speaks of 'entertaining $p$' in the sense of 'understanding p'.) But Braithwaite does not agree with Hume's view that the difference between believing and understanding lies in a *feeling* of certainty. According to him it lies, rather, in a disposition to act as if $p$ is true. Braithwaite maintains that 'I believe that $p$' means the conjunction of two propositions: (1) a proposition about my inward experience, 'I understand $p$', and (2) a proposition about my observable behaviour, 'I have a disposition to act as if $p$ is true.'

Note that, according to Braithwaite, believing-that-$p$ is not equivalent to understanding-$p$ plus acting-as-if-$p$. After all, I can believe $p$ at a moment when my actions have no connection with $p$. My belief that the British Museum is in London shows itself only at times when the location of the museum is at issue, or when I want to visit the museum, or when I want to explain to someone how to reach it. But this does not imply that I hold this belief only at those moments, and not also at times when my actions have nothing to do with the museum. 'I believe that $p$' does not, therefore, imply that I act as if $p$, but rather that I have the *disposition* to act as if $p$. Dispositions are connected with actions which are determined by a number of factors. On its own, not one of these factors can cause such an action; it can be caused only by *all* factors together. One factor may lead to the action, but then only if all other factors are present. Therefore believing-that-$p$ is only one of the factors that jointly determine our acting-as-if-$p$. According to Braithwaite these factors include (1) our external circumstances (the given situation, etc.) and (2) our internal circumstances (wishes, needs, etc.). My disposition to act as if $p$ is therefore my tendency to act in a certain way under certain external and internal circumstances.

Braithwaite illustrates the dispositional character of believing with the following example[4]:

My disposition to act as if strawberries gave me indigestion means that, under relevant external circumstances (my being offered strawberries) and my needs being to preserve my health, I shall behave in a manner appropriate to the indigestibility of strawberries, namely, I shall refuse them. Under similar external circumstances, if my need is to have indigestion (e.g., in order to avoid some unpleasant duty), I shall accept the strawberries. And my belief that strawberries are, to me, indigestible, as distinct from my merely entertaining the proposition in thought, consists of such a disposition to action.

In his essay Braithwaite also attempts to answer a number of objections that might be raised against his theory. It could be argued, for instance, that his theory cannot account for cases where our beliefs have little or no effect on our actions, such as beliefs about events in the distant past or about remote astronomical phenomena. If believing-that-*p* differs from understanding-*p* only in that it implies acting-as-if-*p*, the difference falls away when there is no possibility of acting-as-if-*p*.

Braithwaite's answer to this is, firstly, that his theory is not concerned with *actual* actions but with the disposition to act. Whether such a disposition is actualised depends on the circumstances. Braithwaite's theory implies only a difference in *disposition* between believing-that-*p* and understanding-*p*, not a difference in actualised disposition. The difference between believing-that-*p* and understanding-*p* lies in the way someone *would* act *if* certain circumstances occurred. Whether or not such circumstances even do occur is irrelevant here.

The question arises whether Braithwaite can explain cases where the disposition concerned not only remains unactualised but where it is in principle *impossible* to actualise it. Whether he can deal with such cases depends on the kind of impossibility involved. Is it a matter of *logical* impossibility, *empirical* impossibility, or *technical* impossibility?

A situation or action is *logically* impossible if we contradict ourselves when we claim that such a situation exists or that someone performs such an action. For example, it is *logically* impossible for my aunt to be a man, for me to draw a square circle, or to fall upwards if I jump off London Bridge.

A situation or action is *empirically* impossible (or causally impossible) if it is in conflict with a law of nature. For instance, it is *empirically* impossible for me to jump a thousand feet high, to burn water (as one could burn petrol), and to jump off London Bridge without falling.

A situation or action is *technically* impossible if it cannot be brought about or performed with the technical means currently at our disposal. Until quite recently it was *technically* impossible to put a man on the moon or to fly faster than the speed of sound.

According to Braithwaite, believing-that-*p* implies that it must be *logically* possible to act-as-if-*p*. But if it is not logically possible to act-as-if-*p*, this is so because *p* is contradictory. Believing-that-*p* is then impossible: a contradictory 'assertion' negates itself, so that nothing is asserted and there is nothing to believe. According to Braithwaite, technical and empirical (causal) possibilities are not relevant to his theory. Believing-that-*p* implies 'acting-as-if-*p* under circumstances *A*, *B*, *C*,' etc. These circumstances must be logically possible, but they need not be empirically or technically possible. For instance, if one were to die immediately after coming to believe a certain proposition, it would be (empirically) impossible to act in accordance with belief in the proposition. Yet it might well be said 'If he had lived, he would have acted in such and such a way'. And for belief, according to Braithwaite, no more than a proposition of this kind is required. This is why he can say that the existence of causal laws preventing your acting in accordance with your belief has no bearing on this question, because it would always be possible to imagine a world in which they did not hold, and to ask what you would do under these (causally impossible) circumstances.

But what about beliefs about events in the distant past? It is logically impossible to act appropriately in such instances, because the appropriate actions would all have to be in the past and it is logically impossible to go back in time in order to act in the past. 'Going back in time' is, after all, a contradiction in terms.

Braithwaite's answer to this is that all past events have consequences for the future. If I believe that a certain event occurred in the past, it implies that I shall also believe that the consequences of that past event will occur in the present and in future, and in respect of these consequences my actions will be different. Believing that Locke was born in 1632 *seems* like a kind of belief that can have no effect on my actions, but it does imply that I would not buy an autographed letter said to have been written by Locke if there were strong evidence that the letter had been written before 1632. I would also become very sceptical of the scholarship of someone who regarded such a letter as authentic. This belief was, in fact, one of the reasons why Braithwaite attended a congress in Oxford in 1932 at the tercentenary commemoration of Locke's birth. Thus for every historical event which I believe to have happened, I could imagine a possible action that would be performed differently or not at all if I did not believe it.

But what about beliefs about events in the past that are unlikely to have consequences in the present or in the future? How can one act as if they are true? In such cases, Braithwaite maintains, it is still possible to fall back on *verbal* behaviour. My belief that Locke was born in 1632 implies at least my disposition to answer '1632!' if (1) I am questioned about it (external circumstance) and if (2) I wish to answer my questioner truthfully (internal circumstance).

Briefly: if $p$ is not contradictory and it is therefore logically possible to believe that $p$, it is logically possible to conceive of a situation in which my believing or not believing $p$ would have an effect on my actions in that situation. One cannot, therefore, conceive of any cases in which my belief-that-$p$ could have no effect on my action and in which my belief-that-$p$ could therefore imply no disposition to act-as-if-$p$.

Braithwaite also deals with an objection of a totally different nature. According to him, 'I believe that $p$' differs from 'I understand $p$' in that the former is a *prediction* that I shall act as if $p$, if certain internal external circumstances occur. But predictions can never be quite certain. I therefore always have to wait for the relevant circumstance to arise in order to see whether I would indeed act as predicted. This implies that I can never be absolutely certain that I believe that $p$ or am convinced that $p$. Whether I do will only become apparent in the light of my future behaviour. This seems an absurd conclusion: whether or not I believe $p$ or am convinced of $p$ is not a fact about myself of which I *myself* am unsure or that I myself can only discover by observing the way I behave!

Braithwaite's answer is that 'I believe that $p$' is indeed a prediction about my future behaviour, but that I can here and now have sufficient grounds for this prediction and can therefore already be certain without having to wait for the prediction to be realised. According to Braithwaite I can conclude from three different kinds of evidence, which are accessible to me in the present, that I have a certain disposition to act and will therefore act in a certain way under certain future circumstances. Firstly, I can conclude from my past behaviour under circumstances $A$, $B$ and $C$ that I will behave similarly under similar circumstances in future. Secondly, I can carry out a 'mental experiment': I can imagine the hypothetical circumstances $A$, $B$ and $C$ and then ask myself how I would act under those circumstances. Thirdly, beliefs are often coupled with feelings of certainty or conviction, even though they are in themselves dispositions to act and not feelings as Hume maintains. I know directly that I have this feeling of certainty, and from this I can conclude that I shall act as if $p$.

This answer by Braithwaite is most unsatisfactory. That I am now convinced of $p$ remains a mere hypothesis regarding my future behaviour. Whether or not this hypothesis is true will become apparent only if I do act accordingly in future. The grounds that I already have, according to Braithwaite are no more than ways in which I can now arrive at this hypothesis, not methods of verifying the hypothesis. Braithwaite merely posits grounds on which I can *assume* that I believe that $p$ (= will act as if $p$), not methods of ascertaining here and now whether this assumption is true. I shall have to wait and see! On this point, however, Braithwaite's analysis is untenable: I do not conclude from my behaviour that I believe something! *For me*, the question whether I now believe that $p$ is not a hypothetical issue to be decided by observing my own behaviour. This remarkable position is the consequence of Braithwaite's *behaviouristic method*. Let us illustrate this as follows.

If it is not quite clear to me *what* someone is stating, he could explain what he means by telling me what I should do to verify his statement. Thus someone could explain to me the meaning of his statement 'The Eiffel Tower is in Paris' by saying to me 'If you go to Paris – the capital of France – you will see a high steel tower in the middle of the city. This tower is named after a certain Mr Eiffel.' The meaning of my assertion 'The Russian flag is red' can be explained by saying 'If you compare the colour of the Russian flag with the colours of the spectrum, you will find that it corresponds with the lower end of the spectrum.' We can often explain the meaning of a descriptive predicate to someone by telling him what procedure to follow in order to verify whether this predicate is correctly ascribed to something. For example, if I want to ascertain whether I am correct in calling something red, I shall have to check whether that thing has a colour that corresponds with the lower end of the spectrum. My dictionary in fact defines the word 'red' as 'having . . . the colour which appears at the lower or least refracted end of the visible spectrum'.

*Logical positivism* raises this methodological hint to the status of a general methodological principle. (It is debatable whether this hint is valid for all statements and whether it can therefore indeed be raised to the status of a methodological principle. We shall deal with this point in detail in Part Four). *Behaviourism* is an attempt to apply this principle in psychology. To ascertain the meaning of all kinds of psychological terms, the behaviourists say, we have to inquire into the conditions under which such terms could properly be ascribed to someone. Thus, to know what *belief* is, we have to ask ourselves: how do we ascertain whether someone believes that *p*? or: under what circumstances could we correctly describe someone as believing that *p*? The correct answer to this question is: we verify whether someone believes that *p* by observing his behaviour and seeing whether he acts as if *p* (including whether, if asked, he will say 'I believe that *p*'). Behaviourism concludes, then, that 'believing that *p*' means the same as 'having the disposition to act as if *p*.'

This behaviouristic argument holds for questions about the beliefs of a third person. 'He believes that *p*' is a *statement* about someone. In order to verify this statement I would indeed have to observe the person's words and actions. But Braithwaite goes further and asks this behaviouristic question also in respect of 'I believe that *p*'. The question then becomes 'How do I ascertain whether *I* believe that *p*?' (or, under what circumstances can I correctly describe *myself* as believing-that-*p*?). The behaviouristic answer to this question would then be 'When I have the disposition to act as if *p*'. This answer, which is correct with regard to third persons, is absurd for the questioner himself; I never attempt to verify whether I believe that *p* by observing my behaviour!

'He believes that *p*' is a *statement* about someone which can be verified in the light of his actions. It is doubtful, however, whether 'I believe that *p*' is a *statement* about myself (and even more doubtful whether it is a statement that I would have to verify in the light of my own behaviour). Is not 'I believe that *p*' rather an *expressive* (and not a constative) speech act in which I express my belief? What am I expressing when I express my belief, and how does this relate to my future actions? We shall deal with these questions in the next paragraph.

Before proceeding to do so we have to say something about a problem that arises from Braithwaite's analysis and which he does not deal with in his essay. According to Braithwaite, believing-that-*p* is a *disposition* to act-as-if-*p*. In other words, believing-that-*p* is one of a number of factors that *jointly* lead to someone's acting as if *p*. From my knowledge of someone's beliefs I can predict how he will act under certain circumstances only if I also know what other factors determine his actions. For instance, I can predict that someone will decline to eat the strawberries I offer him only if I know that (1) he believes that strawberries give him indigestion and (2) he does not want indigestion. His *wishes* (Braithwaite speaks of *needs*) are therefore as much dispositions to act as are his beliefs. The question is, however, whether Braithwaite as a behaviourist can explain the difference between a wish and a belief. More specifically: what is the difference between the ways in which wishes and beliefs, respectively, determine our actions? By merely saying that they are dispositions to act he has not succeeded in distinguishing between them.

Briefly: Braithwaite demonstrates convincingly that there is a connection between someone's belief that *p* and his actions. But he fails to distinguish between the way someone's belief-that-*p* and the way his wishes ('needs'), are related to his actions. Furthermore, Braithwaite is misled by his behaviourism, so that he fails to take account of the difference between 'I believe that *p*' and 'he believes that *p*'. In order to do justice to this difference we shall have to go beyond behaviourism.

## 12.33 BELIEVING AND EXPECTING

According to Braithwaite the fundamental methodological question in an analysis of the concept 'believing' is: under what circumstances can we correctly say of someone that he believes that *p*? This behaviouristic approach is limited in two respects. On the one hand it leaves room only for the use of the concept 'believing' in *descriptive statements*. Any use of the concept in non-constative contexts is excluded or is reduced to special forms of constative usage. On the other hand this approach is based on an analysis of belief in the case of third persons ('he believes that *p*'), without allowing for the possibility that belief in the first person ('I believe that *p*') may differ. As a result, Braithwaite's method compels him to interpret 'I believe that *p*' in the same way as 'he believes that *p*': both are treated as *constative* assertions.

A methodological question that gives one more scope than the behaviouristic approach is 'What do I do when I say "I believe that *p*", as opposed to "he believes that *p*"?' In this question we are not forced into considering only the constative use of 'believing'. Even if 'He believes that *p*' is a constative assertion about someone, it does not follow that 'I believe that *p*' is a constative assertion about myself.

In the previous paragraph we suggested that 'I believe that *p*' was not a constative but an *expressive*; I use it to express my belief. But what am I actually expressing when I express my belief? This question may take us somewhat further if we consider that the words 'I believe that *p*' are used to express a *constative belief*. If we know what a constative is, we can infer from it what someone is doing when he expresses his belief about that constative.

In chapter 9 we argued that a constative (in which we say what the world is factually like) is used to give our hearer an assurance about the way our possibilities for action are determined in this world. While a prescriptive is used to tell someone how he *ought* to act, a constative serves to give him an assurance on how he *can* act in this world. His belief that the constative is true is therefore an *expectation* on his part that he will indeed be able to act as assured in the constative. In my assertion 'I believe that *p*' I *express my expectation* that my possibilities for action in the world are determined as assured in *p*. In my assertion 'He believes that *p*' I *state* that he expects his possibilities for action in the world to be determined as assured in *p*.

It is clear that a person's ideals and norms (that is, his prescriptive beliefs) determine his actions. My beliefs about what I ought to do determine what I in fact do. Someone's expectations (that is, his constative beliefs) are, however, equally determinant of his actions. My buying a raincoat today is determined not only by my ideal (or wish) of remaining dry tomorrow, but equally by my expectations of rain tomorrow. In section 10.26 we pointed out that there was a close relation between someone's actions, his prescriptive beliefs and his constative beliefs; from any two of these one might infer the third. If a person puts on a raincoat (action) and wishes to stay dry (prescriptive belief), we can be sure that he is expecting rain (constative belief). If someone puts on a raincoat (action) and expects rain (constative belief), he undoubtedly wishes to remain dry (prescriptive belief). If someone expects rain *and* wishes to remain dry we can predict that he will take along a raincoat (or umbrella) when he goes out.

It is clear from this that our actions are never determined by our prescriptive beliefs *alone*, but always by our prescriptive and constative beliefs together. In the light of this observation we can understand what Braithwaite means when he says that someone's beliefs are only one of the factors determining his actions. There are also his wishes and needs. *Aristotle* argued along similar lines in his theory of the *practical syllogism*. According to Aristotle, two factors determine what someone does. These he called the two premises of the practical syllogism. The first is an aim or ideal, or prescription, which the person accepts (we called this a prescriptive belief). The second premise is a factual statement accepted by this person (this we called a constative belief). The conclusion of this practical syllogism is an action.

This link between actions, prescriptive and constative beliefs may also provide some insight into the nature of *prescriptives* (as illocutions).

If someone asserts a prescriptive to me (that is, asks or demands that I do something), I can either assent to or reject his prescriptive. If I reject it, I can advance either of two reasons: (1) I may say that I am unable to carry out his prescriptive; that is, I do not expect (*constative* belief) to be able to do what he is asking; or (2) I may question his right to ask or demand this of me; that is, I lack the *prescriptive* belief that there is an 'agreement' obliging me to do what he is asking or demanding of me. (In this regard, see section 2.5 on prescriptives and section 8.22 on normative 'agreements'). Aristotle would have said: if we question one of the premises of the practical syllogism, the obligation to accept the conclusion (that is, to perform the action) falls away.

Briefly: our *constative beliefs* are expectations held by us with regard to the way our possibilities for action are determined. Such expectations (together with our prescriptive beliefs) are one of the two 'sources' of our actions. In the light of someone's constative and prescriptive beliefs we can explain why he does what he is doing and we can predict what he will do under certain circumstances in the future.

# 13 Truth

## 13.34 INTRODUCTION: THE CONCEPT OF TRUTH

KNOWING-that-*p* implies believing-that-*p*. I cannot say 'I know that *p*' if I do not expect that my possibilities for action are determined in the way assured in *p*. In chapter 11 we argued, however, that knowing is more than merely believing. Apart from his believing-that-*p*, the *truth* of *p* is required before we can say of someone that he knows that *p*. But what is truth?

We are here concerned with truth as a term applicable to *constatives*. In this sense we say that a proposition is *true*, we speak of *truths* in the sense of true propositions, and we are concerned about the *truth* in regard to an event or state of affairs in the sense of a complete set of true propositions regarding that event or state of affairs. Apart from constatives, *prescriptives* are also sometimes said to be *true*. Thus one might say that someone's *prescriptive belief* is true in the sense that it ought to be done or carried out. In the Gospel of St John 3:21 and in the First Epistle of St John 1:6, we read about those who *do the truth*. Apart from true (constative and prescriptive) *speech acts*, we also sometimes speak of true *things* or *people* or *states of affairs*. Thus we sometimes speak of the *true x* in the sense of (1) the *genuine x* or in the sense of (2) the *ideal* or the *perfect x*. According to St John's Gospel 15:1, Jesus calls himself the *true* vine, in the sense of the *perfect* or the *ideal* vine, on which we should grow as branches.

In epistemology we are primarily concerned with propositional truth, that is, the truth of constative beliefs or constative assertions. What are we saying about a proposition when we say that it is true? Various answers have been given to this question in the course of history, all of which are variations of four different theories of truth: the correspondence theory, the coherence theory, the pragmatic theory and the performative theory. Let us try to form a coherent concept of truth in the light of the merits and demerits of each of these theories.

## 13.35 THE CORRESPONDENCE THEORY

The correspondence theory is the most common theory of truth in the history of philosophy. According to this theory a proposition (or constative assertion or constative belief) is true if it *corresponds* to the facts or to reality. But what is meant by 'correspondence'? One way of answering this question is by viewing beliefs as mental images of reality as it is in itself outside the mind. Beliefs *correspond* to reality as an image corresponds to that of which it is an image. Beliefs are true to the extent that they accurately represent the things in themselves of which they are mental images. The difficulty with this view is that it cannot explain how we could ever discover whether our beliefs are true. Things in themselves are in principle inaccessible to me because of the logical impossibility of experiencing how things are when we do not experience them. I cannot take up a vantage point outside of my experience in order to compare my experience with things in themselves.

Maybe we can avoid this difficulty by applying the correspondence theory to the truth of propositions rather than to the truth of beliefs viewed as mental representations. Truth is then not the correspondence between my experience (mental representation) of something and that thing as it is in itself outside my experience. Truth is rather the correspondence between my propositions or constative assertions on the one hand and my experience (or mental representations) on the other. In this way both ends of the relation are accessible to me so that I am in a position to verify the correspondence. Truth is then a correspondence between *propositions* and the *facts* of experience.

This suggestion raises new problems. Are propositions and facts not so unlike each other, that it is impossible for the one to be a representation of the other in the way that a picture can be a representation of the pictured object?

This difficulty could be met by assuming a *structural* similarity between propositions and facts. The structure of a true proposition corresponds with the structure of a fact and in that sense the proposition pictures the fact. This structural correspondence means that for every thing (or relation between things) as element in a fact, there is a corresponding term as element in the proposition 'picturing' that fact.

In this view the conventions of a language determine which words in the sentence are used to correspond with which things or relations in the fact pictured by the sentence. The most plausible version of the correspondence theory in this form is found in Ludwig Wittgenstein's *Tractatus Logico-Philosophicus* (1921), and the most devastating criticism of it is put forward by Wittgenstein himself in his posthumously published *Philosophical Investigations* (1953).

The most important difficulties with this form of the correspondence theory are the following:

(1) It is based on the view that words are signs that correspond with things or relations. In other words, it is based on a names model of language. In chapter 3 we showed why this model is inadequate.

(2) If a proposition is true when it corresponds structurally with a fact, then each true proposition must have a corresponding fact. This raises problems in connection with true *negative* propositions (for example: 'There is no water on the moon') and true hypothetical propositions (for example: 'If the cat's away, the mice will play'). Can there be negative facts and hypothetical facts, with which these true assertions correspond? And how do facts occur negatively or hypothetically? Proponents of the correspondence theory have gone to great lengths to explain the occurrence of such negative and hypothetical facts, but without success.

(3) There may be considerable differences between the grammatical structures of sentences in which the same proposition is asserted in different languages. The structure of a proposition asserted in Hebrew is often markedly different from that of the same proposition asserted in English or Swahili. In which language then, does the structure of true propositions reflect the real structure of the facts? Does a proposition asserted in Hebrew offer a truer representation of the structure of a fact than the same proposition asserted in English? (Is Hebrew really the language spoken in heaven?!) Or should we construct a logical esperanto in which the true structure of the facts is reflected? But how are we to determine what elements the facts contain? Does not this theory imply the fallacy of projecting the grammatical structure of some language (English, Swahili, German, Hebrew, or Esperanto) onto reality? The correspondence theory defines *true* as a relation of *similarity* between propositions and facts. In order to achieve the necessary equivalence between propositions and facts (without which they cannot be similar) the theory has to define the structure of the facts in terms of the structure of propositions. The result is an ontology derived from grammar.

If the correspondence theory is rejected because of the objections set out above, two possible solutions remain to the question of truth (*a*) The truth (of propositions) may still be seen as connected with the *relation* between propositions and facts, but this relation can no longer be seen as one of similarity or picturing. But what relation is it, then? (*b*) The truth (of propositions) may still be seen as a relation of *correspondence*, but not a correspondence with the facts. It becomes a correspondence with something else, which has the necessary equivalence with propositions. This latter solution is the one chosen by the second important theory of truth: the *coherence theory*.

## 13.36 THE COHERENCE THEORY

According to the coherence theory propositions cannot correspond with facts, but they can correspond with *other propositions*, since the necessary equivalence is found in this case. Thus the truth of a proposition lies in its relation to other propositions. There may be, for instance, relations of contradiction, non-contradiction and implication between propositions. According to the coherence theory, a proposition is *true* only if it is coherent (implied by and not in conflict with) all other true propositions.

Proponents of this theory argue that the correspondence theory is merely a muddled version of the coherence theory itself. The *correspondence theory* maintains that the proposition 'The grass is green' is true if it corresponds with (is not conflicting with) the facts (that the grass, like my jersey, is green) and is untrue if it is in conflict with the facts (for example, that the grass is yellow). The *coherence theory* on the other hand, maintains that the proposition 'The grass is green' is true if it is implied by (not in conflict with) those *propositions which are already accepted as true*: 'This is grass', 'It has the same colour as my jersey', 'My jersey is green'; and it is untrue if it is in conflict with the *proposition already accepted as true*: 'The grass is yellow'. What the adherents of the correspondence theory in fact compare with propositions is not some reality beyond our propositions, but other propositions which have already been accepted as true. In actual fact there are propositions that we accept as true without dispute, and propositions that are open to dispute and of which we wish to test the truth. Propositions of the latter kind are tested against the former kind. The so-called *facts* referred to by the correspondence theory are nothing but these propositions which have already been accepted as true and indisputable. The proposition 'He has seen a ghost' is untrue because it is in conflict with views (propositions) on ghosts which we have already accepted as true.

In the course of history two groups of thinkers have defended the coherence theory of truth: the great idealistic system builders (for example, Spinoza, Hegel, Bradley) and some logical positivists. According to the former group, the whole of reality is *one* great, logically coherent system. The philosopher's task is to describe this system. A proposition is true if it is coherent with this all-embracing description; it is false if it is in conflict with this description. According to positivist adherents of the coherence theory all metaphysics is meaningless. Therefore it is also meaningless to speak of facts in themselves outside our factual propositions. Propositions cannot, therefore, be verified by comparing them with 'metaphysical' facts. Consequently, propositions are true if they are coherent with the total set of propositions accepted in science.

It is clear that mathematics functions as a model for this theory. In mathematics the test for the truth or acceptability of a proposition is indeed its coherence with other propositions of the mathematical system and ultimately its coherence with the axioms of the system. Mathematics is always the ideal of the idealistic system builders. Compare, for instance Spinoza's book *Ethica Ordine Geometrico Demonstrata*. Starting from indubitable axioms, a deductive system is construed to account for all reality. In such a system the criterion for truth is indeed coherence with the whole system.

Defenders of the coherence theory are correct in maintaining that we cannot accept as true different, mutually contradictory propositions. If we accept that one proposition is true, it implies (1) that we reject all propositions inconsistent with this one, and (2) that we also accept as true all propositions logically implied by that first proposition.

The coherence theory cannot, however, derive a complete criterion for truth from this kind of coherence. If a proposition is true because it is coherent with other true propositions, the question arises: how are these other propositions true? By being coherent with still further true propositions? If we are to avoid an infinite regress we shall have to appeal to some criterion other than coherence in order to guarantee the truth of the ultimate propositions in the series. Briefly: if a proposition is true because it is implied by a logically coherent system of propositions, the system as a whole must also be true, and this cannot be so through coherence. In fact, it is logically possible that there could be various mutually exclusive systems, all equally coherent within themselves. The question is, then, how we are to choose between such systems.

To avoid this dilemma, adherents of the coherence theory abandon the theory itself. The idealistic system-builders try to prove that the first principles (axioms) of their system are somehow indubitably true. Thus Descartes' attempts to find an indubitable true first principle (*cogito ergo sum*) and to derive from that his entire system, in which he wants to explain everything (God, man and the world). In doing so, he in fact departs from the coherence theory. His first principle is true, not because it is coherent with other propositions in his system but because it cannot be doubted.

The positivist adherents of the coherence theory fall back into historical relativism in their attempts to escape this dilemma. Propositions are true if they are coherent with the system, and the only acceptable system is the current set of scientific theories. This makes truth relative to current scientific opinion. Furthermore, it makes all progress in science impossible. Copernicus could never have revolutionised our scientific view of the world if the Ptolemaic theory prevailing in his time had been his ultimate criterion for truth.

If a proposition is true because it is logically coherent with all other true propositions and if an infinite regress cannot be avoided by falling back on the correspondence theory, the question arises whether there is not some other way of ascertaining the truth of the coherent *system as a whole* (as opposed to other coherent systems). Pragmatism offers a possible answer along these lines.

## 13.37 THE PRAGMATIC THEORY

According to the pragmatic theory of truth a *proposition* is true if it is coherent with a true theory and a *theory* is true if it serves its purpose of being an instrument with which to control our environment. A proposition is true if it forms part of a theory which *works* in practical life. In what sense can a theory be said to 'work'? Proponents of pragmatism, such as C.S. Peirce, William James and John Dewey, differ on this point.

*C.S. Peirce* (the father of pragmatism) refers especially to practice in scientific inquiry. He starts by criticising Descartes' subjectivism.

According to Descartes an idea is true if it is *clara et distincta,* that is, if it seems obvious to *me.* Peirce maintains that truth is not subjective in this way but objective, the same for everybody. True propositions are not those which seem true *to me,* but those which everybody accepts as true. But how are we to deal with the possibility of some people being mistaken so that a proposition could be true even though not everyone accepts it? Peirce's reply is that only those propositions are true which the scientific community accepts as true, that is, which are consistent with those scientific theories which, in the practice of scientific inquiry, yield results which are acceptable to the scientific community as a whole. 'The opinion which is fated to be ultimately agreed to by all who investigate, is what we mean by the truth.' Does not this view make truth relative to prevailing opinion?

While Peirce looked on truth as that which functions satisfactorily in the practice of scientific inquiry, *William James* looked on truth as that which functions satisfactorily in daily life. Unlike Peirce, James did not take scientific theories as paradigm context for true propositions. He took views of life as his examples. James held a view of life to be true if we could satisfactorily live by it, that is, if life in accordance with such a view of life is meaningful. In this way James also attempted to justify belief in the existence of God (that is, the truth of the proposition 'God exists'). 'On pragmatic principles, if the hypothesis of the existence of God works satisfactorily, in the widest sense of the word, it is true.' Whereas Peirce makes truth relative to the prevailing opinion in the scientific community, William James makes truth relative to the individual. Assertions are true if it is meaningful for me to believe them, and others are true for someone else if it is meaningful for him to believe them. Apart from the relativism contained in this view and the problems that arise from it, James's view invites the objection that 'true' cannot mean the same as 'useful to believe', because there may be false propositions which could nonetheless be usefully believed. For instance, under certain circumstances it might be very useful if all drivers believed that other drivers were drunk! This belief would have the useful effect that people would behave much more cautiously on the roads!

Like Peirce, *John Dewey* thought of truth in the context of scientific inquiry. According to him, a scientific investigator proceeds as follows: (1) He starts by doubting or by feeling uncertain. Scientific inquiry always starts with doubt and then attempts to eliminate this doubt. Dewey did not have Descartes' methodic doubt in mind here. On the contrary, he maintained that the investigator does not *decide* to doubt; he simply finds himself doubting (being uncertain). (2) His first step out of this doubt is to formulate his uncertainty or doubt as a *problem*. (3) He then tries to form an idea as a proposed solution to his problem. Such an idea (or hypothesis) is actually a kind of *plan*, by means of which the investigator attempts to overcome his doubt. An idea is not a representation or 'image' of what we believe. It is a plan to help us find our way about in our environment. As such, the idea extends beyond immediate perception. (4) Once the investigator has formed an idea or hypothesis, he tries to test it experimentally. It proves true if it leads to a solution to the formulated problem; in other words, when it *works*. For example, if we are lost in a wood, we can conceive a plan (form an idea) to find our way out of the woods. If this plan (idea) works, and we succeed in finding our way, this idea turns out to be true. It is clear that Dewey, like Peirce and James, makes the *truth* of a theory relative to the purposes for which we employ that theory. The trouble with this view, however, is that our purposes are not always valid. According to Dewey, a theory is valid if it offers a solution to the problems confronting us. The question is, however, whether a theory is true also when it offers a solution to an invalid problem.

Briefly: (1) according to the pragmatic theory of truth a proposition is true if it is coherent with a theory and a theory is true if it works; (2) the various pragmatists have in mind different examples of theories: Peirce thought in particular of empirical hypothesis, James had in mind views of life, and Dewey thought of plans or ideas as proposed solutions to problems; (3) thus truth becomes *relative* to the prevailing scientific opinion (Peirce), the experience of the individual that his life is meaningful (James), or the problems that an investigator poses for himself (Dewey).

## 13.38 THE PERFORMATIVE THEORY

In an essay on 'Facts and Propositions'[5], F. P. Ramsey provides the following example:

> It is evident that 'It is true that Caesar was murdered' means no more than that Caesar was murdered, and 'It is false that Caesar was murdered' means that Caesar was not murdered. They are phrases

which we sometimes use for emphasis or for stylistic reasons, or to indicate the position occupied by the statement in our argument.

The words 'true' and 'false' add no information to the propositions to which they are attached. At the most they add emphasis or stylistic effect. They have the same function as exclamation marks.

Ramsey's argument involves a confusion between assertions about states of affairs (first-order assertions) and assertions about such first-order assertions (second-order assertions). 'Caesar was murdered' is an assertion about Caesar, giving us information about Caesar. 'It is true that Caesar was murdered' is not an assertion about Caesar and indeed does not provide further information about Caesar. It is, however, an assertion about the assertion about Caesar. Ramsey is therefore correct in saying that the second-order assertion gives no further information about the subject of the first-order assertion. The second-order assertion is after all not concerned with the subject of the first-order assertion, but with the first-order assertion as such.

According to P.F. Strawson 'true' and 'false' are terms that occur *only* in second-order assertions, that is, in assertions about other assertions. I might say, for example, 'It is true (false) that $p$' with reference to the proposition $p$ asserted by someone else, or asserted by me in the past. We also use the term 'true' in an attempt to forestall possible objections to what we want to say by conceding the *expected* objection before it is expressed: 'Although it is true that such and such is the case, it is also . . . . ' 'The use of 'true' always glances backwards or forwards to the actual or envisaged making of a statement by someone.'[6] Briefly: we normally use the words 'true' or 'false' only with reference to a specific proposition someone has asserted or is expected to assert.

What are we *stating* about someone's asserted or expected proposition when we state that it is true? According to Strawson we state nothing about it, but we do other things with reference to it. 'What you are saying is true for example, is an expression of agreement. 'What I said is true after all' is a re-affirmation of what I said. It means, 'I still maintain it, in spite of arguments to the contrary'. 'It is true that $p$ ... but ...' is a concession to forestall an expected objection.

In discussing the merits of the Welfare State, I might say: 'It is true that the general health of the community has improved (that $p$), but this is due only to the advance in medical science.' It is not necessary that anyone should have said that $p$, in order for this to be a perfectly proper observation. In making it, I am not talking *about* an actual or possible speech-episode. I am myself asserting that $p$, in a certain way, with a certain purpose. I am anticipatorily conceding, in order to neutralise, a possible objection. I forestall someone's making the statement that $p$ by making it myself, with additions.[7]

Strawson thus maintains that 'true' functions as a sign of affirmation and 'false' as one of denial. '$p$ is true' is equivalent to 'I confirm, concede, or accept an asserted or expected proposition $p$'; '$p$ is false' is equivalent to 'I deny an asserted or expected proposition $p$'.

One might comment as follows on Strawson's view: he is correct in saying that the assertion '$p$ is true' implies that the speaker accepts or concedes $p$. I cannot say without contradiction, '$p$ is true, but I do not accept that $p$'. Strawson is also correct in saying that the assertion 'I accept (concede) that $p$' implies that the speaker maintains that $p$ is true. I cannot say without contradiction, 'I accept (concede) that $p$, but $p$ is not true.' But Strawson is mistaken in regarding '$p$ is true' as equivalent to 'I accept (concede) that $p$'. There is a very important difference between '$p$ is true' and 'I accept that $p$'. It is always possible that one person might accept $p$ whereas another rejects it. My assertion '$p$ is true', however, contradicts your assertion '$p$ is false'. '$p$' cannot be true and false at the same time.

Briefly: (1) Strawson is correct in saying that '$p$ is true' is a second-order assertion with reference to an asserted or expected proposition '$p$'. (2) Strawson is also correct in saying that a speaker's assertion '$p$ is true' affirms or concedes the proposition '$p$'. (3) Nevertheless '$p$ is true' is more than merely an affirmation of $p$, or an expression of one's own belief about $p$. In saying '$p$ is true' we do more than in saying 'I affirm, concede, believe, am convinced, etc., that $p$'. The question is, however, what more do we do?

## 13.39 TRUTH AND THE APPRAISAL OF CONSTATIVES

What is the illocutionary load of the predicate 'true'? In the history of philosophy truth has frequently been associated with goodness and beauty. For example, all three were sometimes considered to be 'eternal values'. Those who tended towards naturalism and attributed a descriptive function to the terms 'beauty' and 'goodness', usually also defended the correspondence theory, in which 'truth' was also given a descriptive function. On the other hand, those who subscribed to an emotive theory of 'goodness' and 'beauty', defended an emotive view of 'truth' as well.

In this regard it is interesting to note that A.J. Ayer in his *Language, Truth and Logic* used virtually the same argument to express his views on 'goodness' and on 'truth'. On 'goodness', Ayer says that

> the presence of an ethical symbol in a proposition adds nothing to its factual content. Thus if I say to someone, 'You acted wrongly in stealing that money', I am not stating anything more than if I had simply said, 'You stole that money'. In adding that this action is wrong I am not making any further statement about it. I am simply evincing my moral disapproval of it. It is as if I had said, 'You stole that money', in a peculiar tone of horror, or written it with the addition of some special exclamation marks. The tone, or the exclamation marks, adds nothing to the literal meaning of the sentence. It merely serves to show that the expression of it is attended by certain feelings in the speaker.[8]

On 'truth' Ayer says virtually the same as about 'goodness', that is, that

> in all sentences of the form '*p* is true', the phrase 'is true' is logically superfluous. When, for example, one says that the proposition 'Queen Anne is dead' is true, all that one is saying is that Queen Anne is dead. And similarly, when one says that the proposition 'Oxford is the capital of England' is false, all that one is saying is that Oxford is not the capital of England. Thus, to say that a proposition is true is just to assert it, and to say that it is false is just to assert its contradictory. And this indicates that the terms 'true' and 'false' connote nothing, but function in the sentence simply as marks of assertion and denial.[9]

Ayer is correct in maintaining that 'truth', like 'goodness', is not a *descriptive* term and adds nothing to the information provided. In this Ayer is in full agreement with Ramsey and Strawson. But that 'true' is not descriptive does not imply that it is superfluous, functioning as a mere sign of assent (thus Ayer and Strawson) or a mark of emphasis (thus Ramsey). Truth (like goodness and beauty) is an *evaluative* term, not a *descriptive* one. Evaluation is not description.

What do we evaluate with the terms 'true' and 'false'? In section 2.5 we argued that the terms 'true' and 'false' are used to judge the success of the *constative* function of our speech acts. Thus we may judge *a statement* to be true if its constative function succeeds and sincere if its expressive function is felicitous. A statement is insincere if the speaker does not have the belief he purports to express in the statement. A statement is false if our possibilities for action are not determined as assured in the statement.

From the above it is clear that there is a close relationship between '*p*', 'I believe that *p*' and '*p* is true'.

(1) '*p*' is a constative in which the speaker gives his hearer an assurance on the way our possibilities for action are determined;

(2) 'I believe that *p*' is an expressive in which the speaker expresses his belief (expectation) that our possibilities for action are indeed determined as assured in *p*;

(3) '*p* is true' is an evaluative judgement in which the speaker pronounces the constative *p* to be successful: the assurance regarding our possibilities for action is successful because we are able to act as assured.

These three assertions presuppose each other in the sense that it would be contradictory to assert one of the three but deny either of the others. On the other hand we cannot infer from the close relationship between these three assertions that they are identical. Strawson and Ayer are therefore mistaken in equating these assertions – although we can understand how they arrived at this equation.

In the light of the above we can take a new look at the traditional theories of truth. The *correspondence theory* errs in viewing the truth of a proposition as a correspondence or similarity between the proposition and a factual state of affairs. It is correct, however, in stating that the truth of a proposition is connected with a relationship between the proposition and a factual state of affairs. A proposition is true if the facts are as stated in the proposition. Here one may compare Aristotle's definition: 'To say of what is that it is not, or of what is not that it is, is false; whereas to say of what is that it is, and of what is not that it is not, is true.' Compare also Tarski's definition: ' "*p*" is true if and only if *p*'. In other words, a constative is true if our possibilities for action are indeed as assured in the constative. But a constative is not some kind of representation or image of a situation, nor, therefore, can it be an accurate or inaccurate representation. It is an *assurance* about what we are able to do. The factual situation (as determinant of our possibilities for action) is therefore a condition for the success of the constative (= assurance)), not something represented or mirrored in the constative.

The *coherence theory* is correct in holding that the constatives we assert (or are prepared or assert) may not contradict each other. Contradictory constatives (assurances) negate each other: one constative takes back what the other has asserted. I cannot, for example, say 'The Eiffel Tower is in Madrid' whilst also saying 'The Eiffel Tower is not in Madrid', because the one constative would deny the assurance I am giving my hearer in the other. In such a case I would be giving no assurance at all, and I would simply fail to assert a constative. I may be trying to confuse my hearer, to be funny, or to give him an example of a contradiction, but I would certainly not be giving him an assurance regarding his possibilities for action. We see, therefore, that a constative that contradicts another constative of mine retracts or is retracted by the other constative. If I do not assert a constative (or if I retract my constative) there is no constative left which could be true or false. If I wish to assert a constative which could be *true* I must first see to it that the constative is asserted and not retracted by the assertion of another constative contradicting it. If I do not retract my constative, however, it does not necessarily follow that it is true. For *truth*, more is needed than coherence with other constatives. My constative must not merely be a constative; it must also be a *true* constative. My possibilities for action must indeed be as assured in the constative.

The *pragmatic theory* errs in defining 'truth' in terms of the pragmatic criteria by which the acceptability or unacceptability of theories (especially in the sciences) are assessed. The acceptability or unacceptability of such theories is relative to the purposes for which we employ them, whereas truth is not relative to purposes which we happen to have. Yet the pragmatists provide an important insight: the truth of a constative becomes apparent if we *can act* in accordance with it. Such action is not, however, the realisation of whatever aims we happen to have; it is the realisation of the possibilities for action assured *in the constative*.

*Ramsey, Strawson* and *Ayer* are correct in pointing out the close links between '$p$', '$p$ is true' and 'I am convinced that $p$'. They err, however, in reducing '$p$ is true' to '$p$' or 'I believe that $p$'.

# 14 Justification

## 14.40 RATIONALISM

IF 'knowledge' is defined as 'justified true belief', what kind of justification is required here? What kind of evidence do we need as a ground for our belief if we are to call this belief *knowledge*? When is our evidence sufficient to give us what Ayer calls 'the right to be sure'?

We would in any event be entitled to be sure that *p* is true if it were impossible to doubt the truth of *p*. Where doubt is impossible we could hardly avoid being sure! Furthermore, we must be sure that *p* is true if *p* is deducible from other indubitable propositions. A belief is, therefore, justified if it is indubitable or deducible from indubitable propositions. This is the crux of the *rationalist* ideal of knowledge, of which the views of Descartes and Hume are classical examples.

What kinds of propositions are indubitably true and therefore acceptable as grounds for a justified belief? According to rationalism three kinds of propositions qualify for this purpose: (1) *a priori propositions* (for example, in mathematics); (2) *self-verifying propositions* (such as Descartes' 'dubito', 'cogito', and 'sum'), and (3) statements about the immediate *data provided by our senses and by introspection* (for example, 'I have an idea of God', 'I receive a red sensory impression', 'I hear a humming sound', and 'I feel pain').

### 1. A priori propositions

Rationalism has often taken mathematics as its ideal and has sought the certainty characteristic for mathematical propositions. These propositions are *necessarily true* in the sense that they cannot be denied without contradiction. If I denied that $2 + 2 = 4$, I would be uttering a contradiction. That $2 + 2 = 4$, follows from the definitions of the symbols $2, +, =$ and $4$, as agreed upon in the rules of mathematics. In this sense mathematical propositions are *analytical*: since their truth follows from the agreed meaning of the terms of which they are composed, we can ascertain their truth simply by analysing the meaning of these terms. From their necessary character it follows that they are true *a priori*: we know beforehand (*a priori*) that they will still be true tomorrow and a hundred years hence (provided that we continue to use their constituent terms in the same sense). The statement 'There is a tree outside my window' is not true *a priori* in this sense. We do not know with certainty that it will still be true tomorrow (or a hundred years hence), because it is always possible that the tree now standing there will have gone by then. Such propositions about experiential facts are therefore true *a posteriori*, that is, we know with absolute certainty only afterwards (*a posteriori*), in the light of our experience, whether they are true. They are therefore also contingent (= dependent), because it depends on the fortuitous circumstances in our experiential world whether or not they are true. Mathematical *a priori* propositions, however, are necessarily true and are therefore not contingent. They are always true, regardless of what happens in the world. We need not first wait to see what will happen in the world tomorrow before we can say that '2 + 2 = 4' will be true tomorrow too.

The *a priori* propositions of mathematics do have a high degree of certainty. Yet they do not provide indubitable grounds for all our knowledge. Two considerations are relevant here. First: we have to bear in mind that the necessity of these propositions is obtained at the cost of their factual content. Their truth is not dependent upon the state of the world; nor do they have anything to say about the state of the world or any direct implications for this state. Our knowledge as knowledge of facts concerning the world is therefore never deducible from these necessary *a priori* propositions. Consequently, these propositions offer us a much too narrow basis for knowledge: no factual knowledge is possible on this basis.

Secondly, *a priori* propositions may be necessarily true, but they are not indubitably true. We can make mistakes in mathematical calculations, and therefore we can in principle always doubt the truth of our mathematical propositions. Doubt is possible as long as there is a possibility of error, and we *can* err, also in mathematics. It follows that the necessary truths of mathematics cannot provide us with an indubitable basis for knowledge.

## 2. Self-verifying propositions

Descartes deliberately sought for indubitable grounds. He therefore began by methodically doubting anything that was open to doubt. He included the *a priori* truths of mathematics because it was conceivable that by the will of God or under the influence of a malicious demon he could make a mistake every time he added 2 to 3 or ascertained how many sides there were to a square. The object of Descartes' methodical doubt was to arrive by a process of elimination at propositions that could not be doubted because not even a malicious demon could mislead us as regards their truth. *Certain* knowledge is possible only on the grounds of such propositions. Descartes held that there were such truths about which doubt was totally impossible. For example, I cannot doubt the fact that I am doubting, nor, therefore, the fact that I think (because doubt is a form of thought). I therefore cannot doubt the fact that I exist, because the fact that I exist is a necessary condition for the possibility of my thinking or doubting (*cogito ergo sum*).

Self-verifying propositions are not necessarily true in the sense that mathematical judgements are true. Logically, it is possible that Descartes does not doubt, does not think, and does not exist. One can conceive of circumstances in which Descartes does not doubt, think, or exist.

Yet Descartes' self-verifying propositions provide a sounder basis for knowledge than necessary *a priori* propositions of mathematics. They are at least *factual* propositions and therefore not analytic but synthetic; so that they do provide some information on the factual state of the world.

On the other hand this is not all that much of an advance. Self-verifying propositions are verified when they are doubted by the person whose doubt, thought, or existence is involved, and then only at the moment he attempts to doubt them. They are indubitable only in the first person present tense. Thus they, too, provide a much too narrow basis for all our knowledge. From self-verifying propositions in the first person present tense we can draw no indubitable conclusion that reaches beyond the first person present tense. Descartes' attempts to do so were not successful.

### 3. Direct experiences

Descartes himself found self-verifying propositions inadequate for his purpose. He felt the need for further indubitable truths. These he sought in the direct contents of introspection and sensory perception. Following Descartes example, I cannot doubt that I conceive of God as a perfect being; I know this directly through introspection. Nor can I doubt that I have some sensory impression (for instance the impression that there is a green dragon in my room). According to Descartes, errors arise only if I draw erroneous conclusions from these direct experiences: for example if I conclude from my *impression* of a green dragon that there is indeed a green dragon. I can doubt whether or not a green dragon does exist; I cannot doubt that I have a green dragonish impression. I can doubt whether or not what I remember has indeed occurred; I cannot doubt that I *remember* it. I cannot doubt that I have an *idea* (for instance an idea of God); all I can doubt is whether or not that of which I have an idea, does exist. According to Descartes no doubt is possible as regards the direct contents of our perception and our introspection.

According to empiricism (Hume) these direct contents of perception and introspection form an indubitable basis for all knowledge. A. J. Ayer[10] summed up this standpoint as follows:

> Suppose that I assert merely that I am seeing what now looks to me to be a bunch of grapes, without the implication that there is anything really there at all; so that my statement would remain true even if I were dreaming or suffering a complete hallucination. How in that case could I possibly be wrong? What other people may experience, or what I myself may experience at other times, does not affect the issue. My statement is concerned only with what appears to me at this moment, and to me alone: whether others have the same impression is irrelevant.

We could comment, first, that propositions about the contents of our sensory perception and introspection are not analytically true. I can deny without contradiction that I now have the impression of seeing a green dragon.

Secondly, such propositions are not self-verifying in the sense that Descartes' 'dubito', 'cogito', and 'sum' are. They are not verified when the person asserting them tries to doubt their truth.

Thirdly, propositions about the direct contents of my experience, unlike self-verifying and analytical propositions, are indubitable because I have the best of grounds for assuming that I have these direct experiences: the fact that I am having them! My having experiences are the best possible ground for my statement that I have them.

Fourthly, although I cannot now, while I am having the experience, doubt that I am having it, others may doubt it. They cannot examine my direct experiences and therefore cannot ascertain whether or not I am lying. Furthermore, I myself may at other times doubt the truth of statements about these experiences. It may occur to me to question whether I recall my experiences correctly.

Fifthly, this kind of certainty applies only to the direct experiences of the speaker and then only at the moment he has these experiences. Here, as with self-verifying propositions, we have a much too narrow basis for knowledge. From our direct experiences we can draw no necessary conclusion with regard to what lies beyond our direct experiences. From my having impressions I cannot necessarily conclude that realities exist outside my mind. Nor can I necessarily conclude from my experiences *now* that realities exist at other times than the immediate *now*.

Briefly: according to rationalism we have the right to be sure only with regard to propositions that are (1) indubitable or (2) can be necessarily deduced from indubitable propositions. The possibilities for indubitable propositions in this sense are: (1) *a priori* propositions, (2) self-verifying propositions and (3) propositions about the contents of our sensory experience and introspection. But these three form a much too narrow basis for knowledge. From them we cannot deduce with logical necessity everything that we wish to recognise as justified beliefs. On the basis of this strict rationalism no belief is justified if it transcends my immediate experiences at the moment I am having them. No beliefs about the past, about the reality of other minds or about a reality beyond my direct experience could be justified. As a consequence of Descartes' attempt to find an indubitable basis for all knowledge, virtually all knowledge becomes impossible! Rationalism leads to scepticism.

## 14.41 MODERATING RATIONALISM

If the rationalist is not to lapse into scepticism he will have to moderate his criteria for justified belief. These criteria could be made less stringent in two ways.

First, he could try to make his inference rules less stringent so that in terms of these weaker inference rules he could derive more from his indubitable premises. For instance, he could grant that I can infer the existence of a tree from my direct perception of a tree, the reality of the past from my clear recollection, or the existence of conscious persons like myself from my peception of other people.

Another possibility is that he could maintain the stringency of the deductive inference but make less stringent demands of his premises.

For instance, instead of starting with nothing but indubitable propositions he could start with propositions he does not consider to be open to reasonable doubt. After all, there are many propositions that we do not consider to be open to reasonable doubt, but in respect of which it is logically possible that we may be mistaken, for example: 'There is a tree outside my window', 'I went to bed early last night', 'My son wants a ball from Santa Claus', and so on.

It is possible to construe the views of R.M. Chisholm and Norman Malcolm, respectively, in such a way that they could serve as examples of these two ways of attempting to escape the rationalistic impasse.

(1) Chisholm[11] holds that all justified belief can be derived from direct evidence, that is from what appears to us directly or is directly evident to us as opposed to what we conclude from the directly evident. Since we cannot restrict *knowing* to that which is directly evident, we have to find means of including the *indirectly* evident, which is inferred in some way or other from the directly evident. Not everything that we accept as indirectly evident and therefore as justified belief can, however, be deductively inferred from the directly evident. If we are to avoid scepticism we must therefore seek some other means of deriving our justified beliefs from direct evidence. In order to achieve this Chisholm tries to follow and extend the sort of procedure proposed by Carneades of Cyrene (213–129 BC).

Carneades held that all belief must ultimately be founded on the direct content of our sensory perception. In order to be able to infer all beliefs that he considered justified and wished to admit as knowledge from such indubitable premises, Carneades laid down three rules of inference.

Carneades' first inference rule is formulated as follows by Chisholm: 'If a man has a perception of something having a certain property F, then, for him, the proposition that there *is* something having the property F is acceptable.' For instance, if he has a perception of something being a cat, the proposition that there really *is* a cat is acceptable for him. By introducing this inference rule, Carneades tried not to restrict knowing to our immediate experience and thus to create the possibility that we might infer the existence of further realities from our immediate experience.

It is always possible, of course, that our immediate perceptions may be illusory and that there may be no corresponding reality. Carneades, therefore, found it necessary to distinguish between perceptions from which we may infer a further reality and perceptions that are illusory and do not correspond with reality. With a view to this distinction Carneades laid down a second inference rule. Some of our perceptions, he told us, concur and reinforce each other, hanging together like links in a chain. Medical diagnosis provides an example of this kind of concurrence. Some doctors do not conclude that they have to deal with a genuine case of fever from one symptom only – such as a too rapid pulse rate or a very high temperature – but from a concurrence of symptoms, such as a high temperature accompanied by a rapid pulse rate, inflamed joints, feverishness, thirst, and other such symptoms.

Carneades' second inference rule is therefore as follows: 'Acceptable propositions that stand in this relation of concurrence are more reasonable than those that do not'. In other words, an acceptable proposition is reasonable if it is supported by other acceptable propositions; it is not reasonable if it is contradicted by other acceptable propositions.

From the class of uncontradicted and concurring perceptions, Carneades finally singles out a further sub-class, namely the perceptions that have the added merit of having been 'closely scrutinised and tested'. In testing a perception we carefully examine the circumstances in which such a perception occurred. We examine the conditions of observation, the intervening medium, our sensory organs, and our state of mind. Carneades' third rule, then, is as follows: 'Concurrent propositions that survive such a "close scrutiny and test" are more reasonable than those that do not'.

Carneades leaves open the possibility that propositions may be false even if they can be derived from our direct perceptions in accordance with his three inference rules. He therefore ends with a version of scepticism. Nevertheless, Chisholm believes that by following Carneades' general procedure, we have a way of showing how all our knowledge can be based upon what is directly evident, and thus indubitable. Do we in this way escape the rationalist impasse?

Rationalism takes *indubitability* as a *norm* for justified belief: we have the right to be sure of those propositions which can be deduced from indubitable premises. This norm is, however, so strict that most of what we consider justifiable belief cannot pass the test. If we argue like Carneades and Chisholm, however, we merely beg the question. We first decide which beliefs we wish to justify, and then adjust our inference rules in such a way that these beliefs can be derived from our indubitable premises. Whatever we want to be sure of, becomes the norm for deciding when we have the right to be sure!

(2) Norman Malcolm tries the second way out of the rationalist impasse. Malcolm's argument is founded on his distinction between the strong and the weak senses of the word 'knowing'. According to Malcolm:

> When I use 'know' in the weak sense I am prepared to let an investigation (demonstration, calculation) determine whether the something that I claim to know is true or false. When I use 'know' in the strong sense I am not prepared to look upon anything as an *investigation*; I do not concede that anything whatsoever, could prove me mistaken; I do not regard the matter as open to any *question*; I do not admit that my proposition could turn out to be false, that any future investigation *could* refute it or cast doubt on it.[12]

Malcolm's distinction is not identical with the distinction between analytical and synthetic propositions. According to Malcolm I know in the strong sense that 2 × 2 = 4 and also that there is an ink bottle in front of me on my desk. Malcolm maintains that one cannot conceive of any possible evidence that would disprove the truth of these two propositions. We know in the weak sense that 92 × 16 = 1472 and that the sun is about ninety million miles from the earth. Although we are sure that these two propositions are true, there are conceivable circumstances that would force us to concede that we are mistaken about them.

All knowing in the weak sense implies that there is also knowing in the strong sense. Knowing in the weak sense is knowing that is open to future falsification or verification. But proof for or against a specific proposition is adduced only in terms of propositions that need no proof and that we therefore 'know' in the strong sense.

> The concepts of proof, disproof, doubt, and conjecture *require* us to take this attitude [knowing in the strong sense]. In order for it to be possible that any statements about physical things should *turn out to be false* it is necessary that some statements about physical things *cannot* turn out to be false.[13]

We therefore see that, according to Malcolm, knowing in the strong sense is the basis of all knowledge. All other kinds of knowing are founded on strong knowing. We are justified to believe a proposition (and hence to call it knowledge in the weak sense) if we can derive it from a proposition or set of propositions which we hold to be indisputable (and hence knowledge in the strong sense).

This again is no satisfactory way out of the rationalist impasse. The problem of finding criteria in the light of which we can justify our beliefs, is just moved one step further back. We have the right to be sure about a proposition when we consider it beyond dispute. But when have we the right to consider it beyond dispute?

In brief: the rationalist approach makes epistemology into a *normative problem*: by what norm can we decide which propositions we ought to believe? The extreme rationalist holds that we ought to believe only what is logically impossible to doubt. This is obviously true, but so stringent that most of what we want to believe turns out to be unjustifiable. Attempts to moderate the rationalist criteria by adapting the rules of inference in order to allow more beliefs to be derived from indubitable premises, or by not requiring indubitable premises but premises which we consider beyond reasonable dispute, seem to beg the question. Hence these attempts at moderating rationalism do not help us out of the rationalist impasse.

## 14.42 WHAT MUST WE JUSTIFY?

There are obviously great difficulties in finding a satisfactory answer to the problem of epistemological justification as posed by the rationalist. Apart from the difficulties in finding an answer, there is something remarkable about the problem itself: When have we the *right* to be sure? When is our conviction *justified*? When *ought* we to believe? These questions require a norm or a criterion by which we can judge *actions* in order to decide whether or not we ought to perform them, whether or not we are justified in performing them, or whether or not we have the right to perform them. Questions of this kind can only be asked with regard to *acts* which, *per definition*, we can *decide* to perform or to refrain from performing, and not about that which happens to us or that we undergo. Let us examine this point more closely.

Supposing I were seized and abducted by a gang of thugs, it would make sense to ask: (1) Have they or have they not the *right* to abduct me? (2) *Ought* they or ought they not to abduct me? (3) Is their action in abducting me *justified* or not?

It would also make sense to ask: (1) Have I or have I not the *right* to offer resistance? (2) *Ought* I or ought I not to offer resistance? (3) Am I *justified* in offering resistance or not?

The following questions would also be meaningful: (1) Have I or have I not the *right* to go alone along dark alleys if this means taking the risk of being abducted? (2) *Ought* I or ought I not in this way to take the risk of being abducted? (3) Am I *justified* in taking this risk, or not?

It would, however, be meaningless to ask: (1) Have I or have I not the *right* to be abducted? (2) *Ought* I or ought I not to be abducted? (in contrast to: Ought they or ought they not to abduct me?) and (3) Am I or am I not *justified* in being abducted? 'Having the right to', 'ought to' and 'being justified' apply to *acts* that we can decide to perform or to refrain from performing. 'Abducting someone', 'offering resistance' and 'taking risks' are such acts. 'Being abducted', however, is not an act in this sense because it is done to us; we cannot decide to 'perform' it or to refrain from 'performing' it.

Thus, too, we cannot ask whether John has the right to fall in love with Mary, or ought to fall in love with Mary, or is justified in falling in love with Mary. Falling in love is not an *act* which John can decide to perform or to refrain from performing; it is simply something that happens or does not happen to him. John can, of course, decide whether or not to avoid a pretty girl like Mary, because of the obvious risk of falling in love with her! Then, too, having fallen in love, he can decide to hide this love in his innermost heart and not to reveal it to anybody. But if he does not avoid Mary and takes the risk of falling in love, falling in love is itself something that simply happens to him. It is not an act in the above-mentioned sense.

If the fundamental problem of epistemology is one of *justification*, the question arises: which *acts* are we required to justify in epistemology? From our discussion above it would seem that we have to justify the fact that we believe that $p$ or are sure or convinced that $p$, and thus to establish our right to believe that $p$ or to be sure or convinced that $p$. The trouble is, however, that believing that $p$ or being sure or convinced that $p$ are not *acts* which we could decide to perform or not to perform. They are states of mind which are caused in us by the evidence which we take into consideration. We are convinced by the evidence. We do not decide to be convinced. Of course this effect can be more or less strong. We are not always equally sure or convinced that $p$. Our belief that $p$ is not always equally strong. Even though the effect the evidence has on us can vary in this way, it remains an *effect* and not something we decide to do.

Although our beliefs are not acts they are closely connected with our acts. In section 12.33 we argued that we decide to act on the basis of our beliefs and our norms and ideals, that is, on the basis of our constative beliefs and our prescriptive beliefs. Constative speech acts are assurances about which possibilities for action are given us in the world. Constative beliefs are *expectations* that the possibilities assured in the constative will in fact be given to us. Thus when I believe that $p$ (or am sure or convinced that $p$) I expect that the possibilities for action assured in $p$ will indeed be given.

The possibilities which I expect are *given*. I do not decide what they are to be. I can of course decide which of the given possibilities I will realise – but not which possibilities are given. Because my possibilities are given, I also cannot *decide* which possibilities to expect. For this reason, again, believing that $p$, being sure or convinced that $p$ (or: expecting that the possibilities assured in $p$ will be given) are not acts which we can decide to perform or to refrain from performing. Therefore, too, it is meaningless to prescribe or prohibit them, to claim or deny the right to perform them, or to justify our performing of them. 'When do we have the right to be sure that $p$?', 'Ought we to be convinced that $p$?' and 'Are we justified in believing $p$?' are therefore very odd questions. They are prescriptive questions about things which cannot be prescribed since they are not acts.

Since believing is not an act, we could not meaningfully be asked to justify it. However, this does not imply that there is no problem of justification in epistemology. It only implies that this problem is not one of justifying our beliefs. There are, however, a number of important decisions which we have to take with respect to our beliefs and these could very meaningfully require justification.

In the first place, we will always have to decide which attitude we are to adopt towards our own beliefs. On the one hand we could adopt a rational attitude towards our own beliefs whereby we admit that our beliefs are always fallible and should therefore always be subjected to criticism. On the other hand, we could decide to claim infallibility for our beliefs and hence consider ourselves exempt from the moral and intellectual obligation to subject our beliefs to criticism. We could choose to be irrational obscurantists and immunise our beliefs from all criticism or counter-evidence whereby they might be falsified.

The fact that belief is not an act which can be prescribed, prohibited, allowed or justified, does therefore not imply an irrational attitude towards our beliefs. It only implies that the rationalist conception of rationality is incoherent. Being rational does not mean deciding to believe propositions only on sufficient (or irrefutable) evidence. There is no such decision possible. We are rational, however, when we adopt an open and critical attitude towards those beliefs which we have and which have been brought about in us by the evidence which we have considered.

The argument of W.K. Clifford[14] is instructive in this connection. On the one hand Clifford gives a classic statement of the rationalist ideal of rationality: 'It is wrong always, everywhere, and for anyone, to believe anything upon insufficient evidence.' His examples of such irrationalism are, however, not of people who believe things on insufficient evidence, but of people who refuse to submit themselves to arguments against their beliefs:

> If a man, holding a belief which he was taught in childhood or persuaded of afterwards, keeps down and pushes away any doubts which arise about it in his mind, purposely avoids the reading of books and the company of men that call in question or discuss it, and regards as impious those questions which cannot easily be asked without disturbing it – the life of that man is one long sin against mankind.

At this point a problem arises: If believing is not something we can decide to do, but the effect which evidence has on us, how can we criticise someone's belief? Is it not meaningless to criticise someone for something which is beyond his control? That depends on what we mean by *criticism*. If by criticism of someone's belief we mean an attempt to show that the proposition *p* which he believes is not the sort of proposition which he *ought* to believe since it does not fulfil some standard of adequate evidence, then criticism of someone's belief would indeed be impossible. We could, however, try to show that *p* is not the sort of proposition which he *can* believe, since it contradicts some of his other beliefs.

Believing a contradiction is not inappropriate (nor appropriate, for that matter!). It is logically impossible. In section 12.33 we argued that we determine our actions in accordance with our prescriptive beliefs (ideals and norms) and our constative beliefs (expectations). Entertaining prescriptive beliefs and constative beliefs therefore involves acting according to these beliefs. It is, however, logically impossible to act according to contradictory beliefs. This applies not only to our prescriptive beliefs, but also to our constative beliefs. Hence, believing that $p$ is true *and* that not-$p$ is true is impossible since we *cannot* act on the expectation that we will be able to do what we are assured in the proposition $p$ *and* in the proposition not-$p$.

In brief: it is possible to test our beliefs in order to determine whether they *can* be maintained. I *can* maintain my belief that $p$ as long as: (1) I do not have a stronger belief $q$, such that believing $p$ is inconsistent with believing $q$, and (2) I do not come across some further evidence which gives rise to my believing such a proposition $q$. Adopting a *rational* attitude towards my belief that $p$ would mean: (1) admitting the fallibility of my belief that $p$, and therefore the possibility that I may have or acquire a stronger belief $q$ which is incompatible with my believing $p$, and (2) a commitment to being on the look out for and not avoiding the possibility of acquiring such a belief $q$. Being rational about my own beliefs therefore means being open to the possibility of their falsification. This sort of rationality is not only possible, but is also an intellectual and a moral duty.

Are there limits to this sort of openness? I could show that my belief that $p$ can be maintained because it is consistent with my belief that $q$. But how do I know that I can maintain $q$? By showing that it is consistent with $r$? And what about $r$? Are we ever justified in putting an end to this regress, if all our beliefs are in principle fallible? I can show that my belief that $p$ can be maintained because I found no situations which provide evidence to the contrary. But have I been thorough enough in my search for counter-evidence? When have I been thorough enough to justify putting an end to the search? In science we can test our empirical hypotheses experimentally. But how do we know that we did not make a mistake in our experiment? We could of course repeat the experiment, but how often have we to repeat the experiment before we have the right to stop? In brief: because our beliefs are never infallible, we have an intellectual and moral duty to test them in order to find out whether they are consistent with each other and with the evidence which gives rise to further beliefs. But do we ever have the right to terminate the testing process, seeing that our tests are themselves never infallible? Do we ever have the right to 'close our case'?

If by 'closing our case' we imply that we have achieved infallible beliefs which therefore need not be tested any more, we never have the right to close our case. On the other hand, we sooner or later have to decide to *act* on our beliefs and in this sense to stop testing them. At some point I will have to stop testing the strength of the bridge and decide to walk over it – acting on the belief that it will hold me. There are, however, no *general* norms in the light of which we could decide when we have the right to 'close our case' in this latter sense. This is a pragmatic decision depending on the practical circumstances in which we find ourselves. Considerations which are relevant to this decision are, among others, the limits of our time, testing abilities and patience, the relative importance of the belief in question and of the consequences of acting upon it. If my life depends on the truth of some belief, I will make assurance doubly sure before acting upon it. If this is not the case I may be more easily satisfied.

Our beliefs can be divided into two classes: those which need testing and those which we have tested and consider certain enough in order that we may act upon them. For these latter beliefs we claim the status of *knowledge*, and use them as criteria to test the former. Since such knowledge claims are never infallible, they are not irreversible either. If fresh evidence should arise which throws doubt on what we claimed to know, we should be willing to re-open the case and reconsider our knowledge claim.

We test our beliefs by considering whether they are consistent with those beliefs for which we claim knowledge status. Thus I can maintain my belief that $p$ as long as it is consistent with what I (claim to) know. If my belief that $p$ can be inferred from what I know, then I claim knowledge status for it as well. If my belief that $p$ turns out to contradict what I know, then I must either reject my belief that $p$ or reconsider the knowledge status of those beliefs which contradict it. I can criticise somebody else's belief that $p$, by showing him that it is inconsistent with beliefs for which *he* claims knowledge status, or by giving him experiential evidence which could convince him of propositions which are inconsistent with $p$. I can prove $p$ to somebody else by showing him that $p$ is validly inferable from some propositions which he knows. (He must of course know these other propositions independently of $p$, otherwise our argument would be circular).

The concept of 'proof' is *person-relative*, in the sense that an argument can only be a proof *for some person* (or persons), depending upon whether its premises are taken from among the beliefs for which that person (or those persons) claim knowledge status. If someone does not believe the premises of an argument, then that argument can not be a proof for him.[15] The concept of 'evidence' is also person-relative. Evidence is always evidence for somebody in the sense that it gives rise to the belief of some person or persons. Evidence is not convincing in itself. It is always convincing for somebody or other. If it convinces nobody, it is not evidence. This applies to both experiential evidence, where somebody's experience gives rise to his belief and to argumentative evidence or proof, where somebody is convinced by an argument or a proof in the sense discussed above.

In brief: what must we *justify* in epistemology? Not the fact that we believe that $p$ or are sure or convinced that $p$. These are mental states caused in us by the evidence and not acts which we can decide to perform or to refrain from performing. We can, however, meaningfully be required to justify our attitude towards our beliefs and our decision to claim the status of knowledge for our beliefs.

# 15 Knowledge and Belief

## 15.43 JUSTIFIED TRUE BELIEF

IN this chapter we have to tie up some loose ends and draw some conclusions from chapters 12-14 with regard to the relation between knowledge and belief. As point of departure for our epistemological inquiry we took the traditional definition of knowledge as 'justified true belief'. It now appears, however, that there are some difficulties involved in this definition. First of all, we have seen that believing or being convinced is not something that we decide to do or not to do, and hence not an act which we could meaningfully be asked to justify.

Secondly, if truth is a defining characteristic of knowledge, we can never know whether we know something. What we think we know, can always turn out to be untrue, and therefore not knowledge at all. 'If knowledge is so defined that we are only knowing when ... that of which we are sure is in fact the case, then knowledge is elevated into something that we may have but can never know that we have.'[16]. The only exceptions are those propositions that the rationalists admit as knowledge, namely propositions that are indubitably true. But there are so few of these that we are not prepared to restrict our knowing to them. Because we often claim to know something and furthermore consider this claim *justified* even if it is possible that we may afterwards be shown to have been mistaken, (indubitable) truth cannot be a condition to our claims to know something.

Before considering these objections to our initial definition of knowledge we have to take note of the following distinctions:
(1) 'I know' and 'he knows';
(2) an *acceptable* and a *reasonable* claim to knowing;
(3) 'he knows' and 'he believes';
(4) 'I know' and 'I believe'.

*'I know' and 'he knows'*

'I know that *p*' and 'He knows that *p*' are not *reports* of my knowing and his knowing, respectively. The difference between these two speech acts is more complex.

The speech act 'I know that *p*' contains two elements: (1) an *expressive* element whereby the speaker expresses his belief that *p* is true and (2) a knowledge claim with respect to his belief that *p*, i.e. (a) a claim that he is sure enough of the truth of *p* to act upon it, because (b) his belief that *p* is consistent with the whole body of beliefs for which he makes knowledge claims – that is, with everything that he claims to know and on which he is prepared to act.

The speech act 'He knows that *p*' is not merely a *report* of his belief and his knowledge claim. If we only want to make such a report we would rather say 'he says that he knows', or 'he thinks that he knows' or 'he claims to know'. 'He knows that *p*' could rather be analysed as (1) a *report* of his belief and his knowledge claim and (2) an expression of *agreement* with this knowledge claim.

Briefly: 'I know that *p*' is an *expression* of my own belief that *p* is true and a knowledge claim with respect to this belief. 'He knows that *p*' is a *report* of his belief and his knowledge claim, as well as an expression of *agreement with* his knowledge claim.


*Acceptable and reasonable claims*

I base my knowledge claims with respect to my beliefs on their consistency with that body of beliefs for which I make knowledge claims. When I concur with someone else's knowledge claim my concurrence is similarly founded on *what I claim to know*. When I concur, on the grounds that the belief for which he makes a knowledge claim is consistent with my body of knowledge, I regard his knowledge claims as *acceptable*.

It is also possible, however, to consider someone's claim *reasonable but not acceptable*. In the thirteenth century most people believed that the earth was flat and would furthermore have claimed knowledge status for this belief. They would have said 'We know that the earth is flat'. Today we find their claim *unacceptable*, because this belief is not consistent with what we know today. Yet we regard their knowledge claim as *reasonable*, considering (1) the fact that they believed this and (2) considering what they knew then. In other words if we knew only what they knew then we would probably agree with their knowledge claim with respect to their belief that the earth is flat. As it is, however, we know more than they did and this convinces us of the contrary.

I therefore consider someone's knowledge claim with respect to his belief as *reasonable* if (1) I accept that he has this belief, and (2) if I would have agreed with his knowledge claim if I judge it on the basis of *his* body of beliefs.

From the foregoing example it is clear that we may consider someone's knowledge claim to be *reasonable though not acceptable*. It is also possible, however, to consider someone's knowledge claim *acceptable but not reasonable*. For instance, someone may claim knowledge status for his belief that the earth is round on the grounds that he has dreamt that in the middle ages people believed that the earth was round and because he is convinced that whatever people believed in the middle ages is true. We would consider his claim *acceptable*: on the strength of *our* body of knowledge we are, after all, also convinced that the earth is round, and we therefore agree with his claim that the truth of this belief is certain enough that we may act upon it. Yet we would not consider his knowledge claim to be reasonable since *his grounds* for making it are inadequate. Not only do we not share the body of beliefs on which he bases his claim, but we also find that the belief that the earth is round does not follow from them. Even if we had believed his grounds we would still find them inadequate as grounds for his knowledge claim.

## 'He knows' and 'he believes'

From the foregoing it is clear that 'He knows that *p*' and 'He believes that *p*' are not the same. '*He believes that p*' is a report of his belief; '*he thinks he knows that p*' is a report of his belief and his knowledge claim with respect to it; '*he knows that p*' is a report of his belief and his knowledge claim, as well as an expression of agreement with his knowledge claim.

Note that 'I knew' and 'I believed' differ in the same way as 'he knows' and 'he believes'. '*I believed*' is a report of my belief *in the past*; '*I knew*' is a report of my belief and of my knowledge claim *in the past* as well as an expression of my present agreement with this past claim of mine.

### '*I know*' and '*I believe*'

'I believe that *p*' is an expression of my belief that *p*. 'I know that *p*' is an expression of my belief that *p* and a knowledge claim with respect to this belief.

Bernard Williams makes an important point in this connection.[17] According to him the most elementary and straightforward way of expressing my belief that *p*, is the assertion that *p* and not the assertion 'I believe that *p*'. When I say 'I believe that *p*' I not only express my belief that *p*, but I do this in a qualified way: I express my belief and at the same time *withold* a knowledge claim with regard to it. Thus if I say 'I know that Jack lives in Australia' I make a knowledge claim with regard to my belief about the whereabouts of Jack. If I say 'I believe that Jack lives in Australia' I withhold this knowledge claim because I am not sure enough about the truth of my belief. If I say 'Jack lives in Australia' I express my belief without explicitly saying whether or not I am sure enough about the truth of this belief in order to claim knowledge status for it. Normally we only add such parenthetic comments to the speech acts expressing our beliefs, in those circumstances where the knowledge status of these beliefs is being questioned, or where we expect that it could be questioned.

We may now return to the objections, raised at the beginning of this chapter, to the definition of knowledge as 'justified true belief'.

(1) Is 'truth' a defining characteristic of knowledge, and does this make knowledge something that we may have but of which we can never know whether we do have it? This is a misleading question because it is founded on the assumption that knowledge is 'something' that we have or do not have. We shall get further if we start with the fact that 'I know' and 'he knows' are different speech acts. If I say 'I know that *p*', I claim to be sure enough about the truth of my belief to justify making a knowledge claim with respect to it. Hence making knowledge claims implies making truth claims. If I say 'He knows that *p*', I claim to be sure enough about the truth of *his* belief to justify my agreeing with his knowledge claim with respect to it. Hence agreeing with the knowledge claims of somebody else also implies making truth claims. But making truth claims with respect to our beliefs does not exclude the *possibility* that these truth claims may *later* prove to be invalid. Hence there is always an element of risk in making truth claims and hence also in making or agreeing with knowledge claims which involve making

truth claims. In fact our truth claims are not infallibility claims. All claims we make are in principle always fallible. Hence it would be unreasonable to allow our making such claims only when they are infallible!

In this regard we may distinguish between a 'strong' and a 'weak' knowledge claim (more or less parallel to Malcolm's distinction between the strong and the weak sense of 'knowing', as discussed in section 14.41), which in turn respectively imply strong and weak truth claims. We sometimes claim to know that *p* even if we can conceive of circumstances in which, if they were to occur, *p* would be proved false (weak claim). For example 'I know that Nelson's column stands in Trafalgar Square.' Sometimes we claim to know that *p*, when we cannot imagine any circumstances that would prove this assertion false (strong claim). For example, 'I know that I am now writing'. However, the fact that we cannot imagine falsifying circumstances does not exclude the possibility that they may exist!

Briefly: (1) For me to be able to claim: 'I know that *p*', *p* need not necessarily be true. Claims need not be infallible. (2) It is necessary, however, that we *claim* that *p* is true, since knowledge claims necessarily imply truth claims.

(2) Since 'believing' is not an act that can or cannot be 'justified' we cannot simply define 'knowing' as *'justified* true belief'. The qualification 'justified' is usually included in the traditional definition of 'knowing', since the definition of 'true belief' is considered inadequate. Such a definition would also apply to instances where someone makes a knowledge claim on inadequate grounds for a belief that happens to be true. For example, someone may be firmly convinced that the earth is round because he has dreamt that the people in the middle ages believed the earth to be round, and because he believes that the people of the middle ages were always right. Because one could hardly say that such a person *knows,* the definition of 'knowing' has to be extended to *'justified true belief'.*

As shown above, this example may be explained by means of our distinction between acceptable and reasonable knowledge claims. If someone says under such circumstances that he *knows* that the earth is round, he is expressing his belief and making a knowledge claim with respect to this belief. We find his claim *acceptable* because, on the basis of what we claim to know, we will also make a knowledge claim with respect to the belief that the earth is round. But his knowledge claim is *not reasonable* for us because his grounds for making it are not adequate.

Since we are not prepared to say that such a person *knows* that the earth is round, we say, 'He knows that *p*' only if (1) he believes that *p* and makes a knowledge claim with respect to this belief; (2) this knowledge claim is *acceptable* to us (on the grounds of our own body of knowledge) and (3) we find this claim *reasonable* (acceptable also on the basis of those beliefs which he has and which we would be prepared to grant the status of knowledge).

# 16 Religious Belief

## 16.44 THE RATIONALIST CHALLENGE

WHEN Job was plunged in deepest misery, deprived of everything and deserted by all, he turned to his friend Bildad in his grief. Despite his miserable circumstances, however, Job ended his lament with a spontaneous confession of faith, 'But I know that my Redeemer liveth' (Job 19:25). Popularised by the aria from Händel's *Messiah*, these words of Job have come to be among the best-known utterances in the Old Testament. And if we consider the profound misery of Job's situation at the time, we cannot but be impressed by the resilience of his faith and the strength of his hope.

When we moderns, however, consider Job's words critically apart from the circumstances in which they were spoken and from the moving context in which Händel placed them, we are not wholly satisfied. Job may claim to *know* that his Redeemer lives, but *how* does he know that? Has he adequate grounds for saying so? Job is, however, expressing a religious belief, and grounds are usually problematic with respect to religious beliefs. Immanuel Kant argued that 'believing' must be distinguished from 'knowing' because, although it is founded on adequate subjective grounds, the objective grounds for it are inadequate. Job's subjective religious experiences may be such that they convince him that his Redeemer lives, but he cannot prove this on grounds that would be objectively evident to everybody. May Job, under these circumstances, claim to *know* that his Redeemer lives? Should he not be more modest in the profession of his religious beliefs? Many would agree with Kant that Job is perhaps somewhat brash in claiming to *know* in this case. Maybe it would be more appropriate if Job had said that he *believed* his Redeemer lives, or that he firmly trusted or was firmly convinced that He lives.

But this does not dispose of all our problems. The feeling of uneasiness with Job's words remains, even if Job were merely to say that he believes or is firmly convinced that his Redeemer lives, because it could then still be asked whether belief on purely subjective grounds is justified. It is true that there are people who subjectively experience what, with absolute conviction, they call encounters or confrontations with God. That they have such experiences, however, does *not* provide adequate grounds for concluding that their beliefs are true. In fact, if we accepted subjective experiences as adequate grounds for belief in objective realities, there would be no limits to what people would be justified in believing. In fact all beliefs would then be equally justified – the Buddhist's in Nirvana, the Mohammedan's in Mohammed's Mi'rai, and the Mormon's in the golden tablets of Joseph Smith! All beliefs could be justified equally well through an appeal to the personal religious experiences of those holding them. If Job's belief is founded on no better, more objective grounds than the belief of the Buddhist or the Mormon, the question remains: why should we consider Job's belief justified, yet refuse to accept the beliefs of others?

We remain, then, with a feeling of uncertainty at Job's words. Has he adequate grounds to justify his belief, and *a fortiori* to justify his claim to know? That we often ask these questions and remain uneasy about the answers given to them reveals that we are unconsciously influenced by the authoritarian character of Western thought and especially of the rationalist tradition.

W. W. Bartley[18] points out that the authoritarian character of the western philosophical tradition is shown by the fact that the primary philosophical questions have always been: On what grounds do you believe that? On what grounds are you certain? How justified is your belief? How do you know that? and so on. All these questions demand authoritarian answers, that is a specification (and ultimately a defence) of the authority on which one believes something or claims to know something, whether it is the Bible or the prophet, tradition, religious experience, sensory perception, reason, or whatever else. In fact, the history of western thought is largely a history of attempts to defend the claims of these alternative authorities.

Rationalism is not a reaction to this authoritarian tradition, as is often supposed, but part of it. It is the view that only an appeal to an intersubjective authority is allowable. That is, we may believe only that which we can justify on grounds which are evident *to everybody*. Our ultimate epistemological authority, then, is either reason, or sensory perception. Belief is justified only if we can prove it by an appeal to observable data which are in principle equally accessible to everybody, or if we can demonstrate that it would be contradictory to deny our belief. Any appeal to an epistemological authority which is not evident to everybody in this sense, is rejected as irrational; therefore any appeal to the people, the state, the leader, the tradition, the prophet, the Bible, individual religious experience, etc., is inadmissable.

It is clear that this sort of rationalism must reject religious belief. The Christian faith, for instance, implies belief on the authority of the Bible or Christian tradition and is thus a belief on the grounds of an authority of which the reliability is not equally evident to everybody. For this reason it is rejected as irrational when judged by rationalist criteria for rationality.

This does not mean, however, that we may never believe anything on someone else's authority. We must, however, be able to prove the reliability of the authority on grounds that are evident to everybody. For example, if we accept certain doctrines on the authority of the Bible (or the church) we must, if we wish to be rational, be able to prove through an appeal to grounds evident to everybody that (1) these doctrines (of the church or the Bible) are from God and (2) this God exists and is reliable. Therefore, the argument concludes, reason (an appeal to grounds evident to everybody) remains the ultimate authority by which all other authorities must be justified.

The challenge of rationalism to religious belief may be summed up as follows: we may believe only that which can be proved on grounds evident to everybody. If we are to believe the doctrines of Christianity we either have to prove these doctrines on rational grounds (evident to everybody), or we must justify, on such grounds, the authority by which we believe. The rationalist conclusion is, therefore, that we cannot accept the doctrines of the Christian faith, since these demands cannot be met.

The most important attempts to answer this rationalist challenge have taken two forms. On the one hand the challenge was accepted and an attempt was made to prove the truth of Christian belief by appealing to grounds evident to everybody. Here one may refer in particular to attempts to construct some kind of *rationalist theology*. The alternative possibility is to draw a sharp distinction between 'knowing' and 'religious belief'. 'Knowing' is taken to mean assenting to true propositions. Here the rationalist criteria are applicable, so that one cannot claim to know something unless this claim can be defended on rational grounds. 'Relivious belief', however, is existential rather than intellectual. It is the manifestation of a certain way of life, not a matter of assenting to propositional truth. Consequently, the rationalist demand does not apply to religious belief. Here one could think of various attempts to construct an *existentialist theology*, and also the attempts of some of Wittgenstein's followers to interpret religious belief as a separate language game, quite different from assenting to propositional truths.[19]

Both of these attempts to meet the challenge of rationalism are founded on the assumption that the rationalist criteria for rationality are valid, so that no proposition may be accepted without rational grounds (evident to everybody alike). Rationalist theology endeavours to *defend* Christian belief in terms of these criteria, whereas existentialist theology attempts to *distinguish* Christian belief from the sort of beliefs which do require this kind of defence.

Let us first consider these two attempts to provide an answer to rationalism, and finally consider whether the rationalist challenge as such is valid.


## 16.45 RATIONALIST THEOLOGY


One example of attempts to make the Christian faith acceptable on the grounds of rationalist criteria for rationality is found in the view of belief that is held, according to some neo-thomist interpretations, by *St Thomas Aquinas*. (There are other possible interpretations of St Thomas but those do not concern us here. The views of St Thomas are to be found in the *Summa Theologica* II, 2, questions 1-7). According to this interpretation St Thomas holds that belief is assent to propositional truth. In the case of religious belief this means assent to the doctrines of the church. However, these doctrines are mainly mysteries, that is, propositions of which the truth is (at least in this life) not evident to everyone and which can therefore be accepted only *on authority*.

Here St Thomas draws a sharp distinction between 'knowing' (*scientia*), that is, regarding propositions as true on evidence that convinces everybody, and 'believing' (*fides*), that is, accepting, on authority, propositions that are not acceptable on evidence that convinces everybody. What I know or do not know (*scientia*) depends, therefore, on the amount of generally acceptable evidence at my disposal. What I believe or do not believe (*fides*) depends on the authority I accept. Thus belief depends ultimately on my *choice* of an authority: I choose my authority, and thus also what I will or will not believe. In the words of St Thomas, faith is 'an act of the intellect assenting to the truth at the command of the will'.

But my choice of an authority is not arbitrary; it is by no means a leap in the dark. According to St Thomas it is possible to demonstrate rationally (that is, on grounds evident to everybody) that the authority to which the Christian appeals, is reliable. Thus St Thomas accepts the rationalist demand that when we accept something on authority, we must justify our authority on grounds that are evident to everybody. Belief (as assent to the truth of propositions on authority) is therefore preceded by a justification of the authority to which that belief appeals (the so-called *praeambula fidei*). This *praeambula fidei* consists of two steps. First, St Thomas provides five proofs of the existence of God (the so-called *quinque viae*) in which he endeavours to deduce, from premises evident to everybody, that God exists and is perfectly reliable. He then attempts to prove, by appealing to miracles and signs, that the church has divine authority and that the doctrine of the church therefore derives from the infallible God whose existence was proved in the *quinque viae*.

The Thomistic answer to the rationalist challenge may be summed up as follows: belief does mean assent on authority, to propositions of which the truth (at least in this life) is not evident to everybody; it is nonetheless rational, because the authority on which it is founded can be justified on rational grounds (evident to everybody).

The validity of the Thomistic answer to the rationalist challenge depends on the validity of the *praeambula fidei*. And that is where the weak point lies, because the *quinque viae* are by no means logically compelling proofs. All of them beg the question: the conclusion that God exists follows from the premises only if the premises are interpreted in the light of belief in God's existence. Only if, for example, we see the world as God's creation, can we conclude from our experience of the world as a creation that God exists as its Creator. But this means that these premises are not evident *to everybody* in the required sense. They are evident only to those who believe already. Therefore the *quinque viae* cannot serve as rational evidence of God's existence.

Nor is an appeal to miracles as evidence of the divine authority of the church convincing to everybody: we may be able to show that the history of the church has recorded all kinds of extraordinary (even inexplicable) events, but that merely makes the church a remarkable, or exceptional institution, not an institution with divine authority. It is only *through the belief* that the extraordinary events in the history of the church are *miracles,* that the church itself can be seen as an institution with divine authority. In both steps, therefore, the *praeambula fidei* presupposes belief instead of *proving* it.

If one bears in mind that the Christian appeals to what he calls *revelation* to justify his belief, the failure of the *praeambula fidei* becomes understandable. The revelation of God is not something that we can see, nor is it something that can be logically deduced from what we can see. It is, rather, something that we can *discern* or *recognise* in what we can see. Thus the people of Israel saw some events in their history as extraordinary; they *discerned* something that they called the glory (*kabod*) and the holiness (*qadosh*) of Yahweh. Their faith was a response or reaction to this glory and holiness, which they discerned or repeatedly recognised in their own history as a people. Glory and holiness are not, however, *directly observable* characteristics (like red and heavy), nor *dispositional* characteristics (like fragile and intelligent) but rather *impressive* characteristics (like sublime and mysterious) (see section 9.24). Impressive characteristics are discerned only by those who are impressed. That the view from a mountain top is sublime, for example, can be noticed only by those upon whom this view makes an impression. That something is a revelation or a sign of God's glory and holiness can be discerned only by those in whom this revelation has inspired belief.

The first Christians were aware of this glory and holiness in Jesus. In Him they recognised the same glorious and holy God whose actions they saw in the history of Israel. They expressed this awareness by saying that Jesus was the Son of God. Their belief was evoked by the impressive glory and holiness that they recognised in Jesus. Here too, however, only those in whom belief had been inspired, noticed the glory and holiness of Jesus. This is why Jesus could speak both of those who had seen him, yet did not believe (John 6:36) and of 'everyone that *beholdeth the Son* and believeth in Him' (John 6:40).

Briefly: religious belief is not founded on empirically observable data. All those who believe (that is, are impressed) are aware of this impressiveness. The kind of evidence on which religious belief is founded is therefore not equally convincing to everybody. Consequently, religious belief must always fall short when measured by the rationalist criteria for rationality.

Attempts to meet the rationalist challenge with an appeal to rationalist criteria for rationality are therefore never satisfactory. If religious belief means assent to propositional truth on the ground of a (impressive) religious authority, it would appear that religious belief must be rejected if tested by the rationalist criteria for rationality. The question is, however, whether belief is in fact assent to propositional truth, as assumed in both the rationalist attack on it and attempts to defend it in the way described above. Let us take a look at attempts to meet the rationalist challenge by denying this very assumption on which it is based.

## 16.46 EXISTENTIALIST THEOLOGY

In the second kind of answer to the rationalist challenge it is conceded that belief, in the sense of assent to propositional truth, is rational only if it can be justified on grounds evident to everybody, so that the rationalist criteria for rationality do apply to our *constative beliefs*. What is denied, however, is that Christian belief is assent to propositional truth and therefore requires justification in terms of these criteria. Christian belief is existential belief, not intellectual belief. Existential belief is concerned with *prescriptive beliefs*, not with constative beliefs. Prescriptive beliefs are not justified by the rationalist criteria that apply to our constative beliefs, but in a totally different way.

In chapter 10 we argued that our prescriptive beliefs can be justified only in the light of prescriptive norms. Our norms are justified in the light of higher norms or ideals, and these in turn are justified in the light of a total view of life. Ultimately, a person's view of life is determined by his final norm, that is, by that which inspires him or appeals to him as more important or more determinant of meaning than anything and everything else. As we put it in section 10.28, any viable view of life must be able to refer to something or someone that has the power to inspire people. Christians, for example, are inspired by the person of Jesus, so that it becomes evident for them that a Christian way of life is the only appropriate one. In this way different views of life become evident to their followers because they can refer to someone or something that inspires them.

Briefly: the Christian faith is not concerned with constative beliefs that have to be justified by an appeal to evidence that everybody finds convincing. It involves, rather, the *prescriptive beliefs* of a view of life, and these can by their nature be justified only through an appeal to *impressive experiences* which lead to existential insight. They cannot be justified on the grounds of empirical observations that lead to intellectual cognition. The Christian belief is not a *belief that* certain propositions about God are true: it is *belief in* God, having faith in Him and living by this faith.

Defenders of an existentialist theology of this sort, sometimes appeal to the way the Bible speaks of belief in God. In the Bible, belief (*pistis*, *hè-èmin*) is not primarily an attitude to propositions about God, but an attitude (relationship) to God as person.[20]

In the Old Testament this attitude to God has two primary aspects. (1) firm *trust* in Yahweh and, with this, firm *hope* on Yahweh's promises; and (2) 'the fear of the Lord', which is manifested in *obedience* to His commandments and veneration and worship of His person.

In the New Testament *pistis* is the usual term for man's relationship to God. There are references to *belief in God's Word*, but in such cases belief is mainly a matter of obedience. Here, too, we therefore find the Old Testament emphasis on 'the fear of the Lord', with the obedience that forms part of it. The Old Testament emphasis on belief as trust in God and faith in His promises is found in the New Testament too. Here it is mainly a matter of faith in the promises made through Jesus.

When the Bible speaks of belief or unbelief it is therefore not a matter of regarding propositions about God as true or false. Thus, for example, the question whether or not the proposition 'God exists' is true, never occurs in the Bible. The Bible is concerned solely with the question whether or not someone stands in the proper relation to God. Even when the Bible speaks of knowledge (*da'at*) of God it does not refer to propositional knowledge but to a personal relationship which someone does or does not have with God. *Unbelief*, too, is not treated as an *error* (rejection of a true proposition) in the Bible, but as *guilt* (unwillingness to adopt the proper attitude towards God).

From this standpoint one could try to deal with the rationalist challenge as follows: (1) belief in the Biblical sense is a way of life (trust, obedience, etc.) to which one is led by impressive experiences; it is not assent to propositional truth on the strength of intersubjective evidence. Therefore belief is *fiducia* (a belief *in* God), not *fides* (belief *that* certain propositions about God are true). (2) It is therefore an *ethical* question (what way of life am I to adopt?) which must be justified with reference to a view of life; it is not an *epistemological* question (what propositions am I to regard as true?) that needs epistemological justification. (3) Therefore the rationalist demand for an epistemological justification, which appeals only to grounds that are evident to everybody, is not applicable to religious belief.

What are we to say to this answer? First, it is correct in asserting that religious belief is not a (neutral) acceptance of propositions but a personal attitude of trust and obedience (*fiducia*) towards God. It is wrong, however, to separate this personal attitude (*fiducia*) from assent to propositional truth (*fides*). This is absurd because *fiducia* presupposes *fides*. Trust in God and obedience to God presuppose, for instance, the belief that He, in whom we trust and whom we obey, does exist and has the characteristics that make it appropriate to trust Him and obey Him. If we do not accept as true the fact that God exists and that He is indeed what He is professed to be, then trust in Him and obedience to Him become absurd. It is true that the question whether or not the proposition 'God exists' is true is never raised in the Bible. But this is not because the existence of God is not relevant to the Biblical context; it is simply because it is taken for granted that He exists, so that the only question that arises is: what attitude are we to adopt towards God?

Faith in God's promises implies *believing that* something will happen in the future. Furthermore, according to the New Testament the resurrection of Christ is the foundation of our faith. There can be no hopeful faith in the future without the *belief that* Christ has risen (see 1. Cor. 15:12-19, and Rom. 10:9). 'Acknowledgement of Jesus as Lord is intrinsic to Christian faith along with acknowledgement of the miracle of His resurrection, e.c., acceptance of this miracle as true.'[21]

It is clear that *fides* and *fiducia* cannot be separated. Religious belief cannot be reduced to a way of life, in contrast to assent to propositional truth. Even if the Christian faith is concerned with prescribing a way of life, and thus contains prescriptive beliefs, these nonetheless *presuppose* constative beliefs. We cannot, therefore, evade the rationalist challenge by supposing that the Christian faith involves no constative beliefs. (In chapter 19 we shall elaborate on this question).

## 16.47 'I KNOW THAT MY REDEEMER LIVETH'

We have argued that neither of these attempts to meet the rationalist challenge is successful: neither the attempt to justify faith rationalistically, nor the attempt to make such justification superfluous by reducing belief to a way of life. Both attempts are, however, founded on the rationalist demand that a proposition be accepted as true only if its truth can be proved on grounds evident to everybody. It remains a question whether this demand is valid.

In section 14.42 we argued that belief (being convinced, being certain) was not an act one can decide to perform, but a case of being convinced by the available evidence. We cannot, therefore, ask how much evidence we need for a proposition before we *may decide* whether to believe it. We do not decide that the evidence is sufficient to convince us; we simply find that it is or is not sufficient to convince us. The evidence is sufficient when it is effective, that is, when it convinces us. Our belief (conviction, certainty) is brought about by the convincingness of the evidence. We do not decide whether or not to believe (become convinced, be certain) on the grounds of the evidence.

The question, 'On what grounds do you believe that?' is therefore only meaningful if it is interpreted as a request for a *testimony* (What evidence convinces you of that?') and not if it is interpreted as a demand for justification of the belief in question. In this sense the rationalist demand, that a proposition be believed only if its truth can be proved by intersubjectively convincing evidence, is meaningless.

Let us now take another look at Job's confession of faith. It is clear that if the impressive evidence at Job's disposal convinces him that his Redeemer lives, it would be absurd to ask whether Job was really justified in believing that. Job has every right to express his own belief by saying, 'I believe that my Redeemer liveth', or even, 'I am firmly convinced that my Redeemer liveth'.

The question is, however, whether Job would also be justified in saying, 'I *know* that my Redeemer liveth'. Is not knowing something quite different from being subjectively convinced? Should we not agree with Kant that in order to know we have to be able to appeal to intersubjectively convincing evidence? Have we not after all reached a point where we cannot escape the rationalist challenge?

In sections 14.42 and 15.43 we argued that in saying 'I know that $p$' I do not only express my (firm) belief that $p$, but also claim knowledge status for this belief. I am justified in making this claim if (1) my belief that $p$ is consistent with the whole body of beliefs for which I claim knowledge status, and (2) I am convinced strongly enough, by the evidence at my disposal, that $p$ is true, in order to stop testing it and to add it to my criteria for testing other beliefs. Whether or not my belief is strong enough depends on the nature and the context of this belief.

These are factors which could vary with different beliefs and with different believers. If, therefore, Job's belief that his Redeemer lives is consistent with his other knowledge claims, and if in the context of this belief, the evidence at his disposal convinces him strongly enough of its truth, then no rationalist can deny him the right to claim knowledge status for it.

That everyone has the right to claim knowledge status for firm beliefs which are consistent with the body of beliefs for which he claims knowledge status, does not, of course, imply that I am obliged to concur with every claim. If the evidence at my disposal does not make the beliefs of the Buddhist or the Mormon reasonable and acceptable for me, I shall not concur with their claims. I shall say that they believe, or that they claim to know, or that they think they know; but I shall not say that they know. I shall thus report their claims with respect to their beliefs, without denying them the right of making these claims, but also without concurring with these claims. If, however, Job's belief is reasonable and acceptable for me, nobody can deny me the right of concurring with it by saying, 'Job knows that his Redeemer lives'.

The nature of a belief and the context in which it arises are important factors in deciding whether to make or concur with knowledge claims with regard to it. What, then, is the nature of Job's belief that his Redeemer God exists and in what sort of context does this belief arise? More generally: in what sense of 'exist' do religious believers believe God to exist, and in what sort of context does this belief arise? We have now to turn to these questions.

# PART FOUR

# ONTOLOGICAL CONCEPTS

# 17 Introduction

## 17.48 ONTOLOGICAL QUESTIONS AND THE EXISTENCE OF GOD

AMONGST others, three important questions can be asked about any statement in the form 'x exists': What x is involved? What is said of x? and On what grounds is this said of x? These three questions may be called, respectively, the *referential* question, the *ontological* question and the *epistemological* question.

In section 3.8 we noted that in speech acts with a subject-predicate form, the subject term has a referential function. The speaker uses this term as it were to isolate a 'segment' from all things that could be talked about, and to indicate that this is what he is concerned with in his speech act. This reference fails if the hearer cannot understand precisely what 'segment' is meant. Such an unsuccessful reference may induce the hearer to ask the *referential question*: what are you talking about? What x is your speech act about? In reply to this referential question the speaker will have to explain the relation between that with which he is concerned and the things that are known *to his hearer*. The things known to someone form a *frame of reference* within which he has to 'place' that which is discussed. There is therefore no sense whatsoever in replying to the referential question by relating that of which I am speaking to things that are unknown to my hearer or which he does not believe to exist. Such things are not part of his frame of reference.

The *epistemological question* with regard to the statement 'x exists' is a request for the grounds on which the predicate 'exists' is ascribed to the subject x. This question could be a request for information on the grounds for the speaker's claim to know that x exists ('On what grounds do you claim that x exists?') and/or a request to the speaker to produce grounds that would convince the hearer of the existence of x ('On what grounds do you think I would claim that x exists?'). In the latter instance the question calls for *proof* that x exists (see our discussion on proof in section 14.42).

The *ontological question* is a question about the meaning of the predicate in the statement '*x* exists': what are we saying of something when we say that it exists? While the epistemological question is concerned with the *truth* of the statement '*x* exists' (on what grounds can we claim that the statement is true?), the ontological question (and the referential question) is concerned with the *meaning* of this statement. Logically the ontological question precedes the epistemological question: we can question the truth of a statement only if we already know what this statement means.

In this section we shall examine the ontological question more closely. But we must take care to distinguish clearly between the ontological question and the referential and epistemological questions, because confusion of these three questions makes it impossible to find a sound answer to the ontological question.

The distinction between ontological questions and epistemological questions with regard to the existence of something is of the utmost importance when the *existence of God* is at issue. The objections that are usually raised to belief in the existence of God are in the main either epistemological objections (for example that the grounds for the claim that God exists are insufficient), or *ontological objections* (for instance that the statement that 'God exists' is meaningless, nonsensical). Either the *truth* of the statement 'God exists' is questioned, or the *meaning* of this statement is questioned. The traditional 'arguments for the existence of God' were usually attempts to answer the epistemological objections and therefore attempts to prove the statement that God exists by an appeal to *intersubjectively* acceptable grounds.

In Part Three we examined epistemological questions and discussed the problems about the search for adequate grounds. We shall therefore leave aside the question whether or not we have adequate grounds for believing that God exists, and deal here with the ontological questions: what are we saying about something when we say that it exists? and: can we say that God exists, or is the statement 'God exists' meaningless?

The *ontological* objections to the statement 'God exists' arise mainly from two quarters: (1) in *theology* it is often held that God is such that we cannot say of Him that He exists, and (2) in *philosophy* it is often held that the concept of 'existing' is such that we cannot ascribe it to God.

## 1. Ontological objections in theology

In chapter 10 we pointed out that from the Christian viewpoint God is the primary determinant of meaning. This implies that God is a *unique* being, differing from His creatures in all *factual* respects. God is *the Wholly Other*. But our descriptive terms derive their meaning from their use in talking about the created things that we know from our ordinary human experience in this world. None of them are, therefore, applicable to God, who is totally different. Consequently, we can say of God that He is quite different from the world of our experience and that our descriptive words are inapplicable to Him because He transcends their field of application (our world of experience). Therefore: God is non-temporal, non-spatial, infinite, and so on. By this means one is brought to a so-called *negative theology*, which was characteristic for neo-platonism and had great influence in the middle ages.

In his *Summa contra Gentiles* St Thomas Aquinas, for instance, follows his discussion of the proofs of God's existence with an examination of the characteristics of this God, whose existence he considers proven.

> We have shown that there exists a first being, whom we call God. We must, accordingly, now investigate the properties of this being. Now, in considering the divine substance, we should especially make use of the method of remotion. For, by its immensity, the divine substance surpasses every form that our intellect reaches. Thus we are unable to apprehend it by knowing *what it is*. Yet we are able to have some knowledge of it by knowing *what it is not*. (*Summa Contra Gentiles* I, 14,1 – 2).

Maimonides (a twelfth century Jewish philosopher) went even further than St Thomas and held that no descriptive term was applicable to God, not even the term 'exists'. God is so totally different from all existing things that we cannot even say of Him that He exists!

Such considerations were not confined to the middles ages. According to Paul Tillich[1]:

> The question of the existence of God can be neither asked nor answered. If asked, it is a question about that which by its very nature is above existence, and therefore the answer – whether negative or affirmative – implicitly denies the nature of God. It is as atheistic to affirm the existence of God as it is to deny it. God is being-itself, not *a* being.

These examples will suffice to show how in theology, it is often held that God's transcendence implies that the term 'exist' is not applicable to Him. In this sense the statement 'God exists' is therefore meaningless!

## 2. Ontological objections in philosophy

A speech act in the form '*x* exists' is one in which one tries to state a *fact*: it is a factual statement. But when is a statement factual? According to logical positivists such as A. J. Ayer a statement can *by definition* be factual only if it is in principle possible to determine by empirical observation whether it is true or false. God, however, is a being that absolutely transcends the world of our empirical observations; He is therefore *in principle* not empirically observable. This implies that all assertions about God are in principle neither empirically verifiable nor empirically falsifiable. But this means that they cannot be statements of fact. It follows that 'God exists' cannot be a statement of fact, even though it purports to be just that. Therefore 'God exists' is meaningless!

Ayer realises that this conclusion agrees with what is often said in theology too.

> An interesting feature of this conclusion is that it accords with what many theists are accustomed to say themselves. For we are often told that the nature of God is a mystery which transcends the human understanding. But to say that something transcends the human understanding is to say that it is unintelligible. And what is unintelligible cannot significantly be described. ... If one allows that it is impossible to define God in intelligible terms, then one is allowing that it is impossible for a sentence both to be significant and to be about God. If a mystic admits that the object of his vision is something which cannot be described, then he must also admit that he is bound to talk nonsense when he describes it.[2]

Any attempt to describe a transcendent God as 'existing' is therefore meaningless.

Once again: we are here concerned with a denial of belief in the existence of God on *ontological* and not on epistemological grounds. Ayer explicitly distinguishes himself from the *atheist* (according to whom the statement 'God exists' is meaningful but false) and from the *agnostic* (according to whom the statement 'God exists' is meaningful, although it is not certain whether it is true or false). According to Ayer the statement 'God exists' is meaningless; so that the epistemological question concerning its truth cannot even be asked!

What are we to say of these arguments? *Negative theology* is founded on a very special view about the *transcendence* of God. The question is whether this view is correct. *Logical positivism* is founded on a very special view about the nature of *factual statements* (and thus also of a statement that something exists). It is also debatable whether this view is correct.

To get clear about these matters, we have to answer the following questions:

(1) The general *ontological* questions about the meaning of the concepts 'exist', 'fact', and 'reality' (sections 18.49 – 18.53);

(2) The question whether and in what sense we can apply *these* concepts – 'exist', 'fact', and 'reality' – to God (sections 19.54 – 19.56);

(3) The question as to the implications of all this for the *transcendence* of God (section 19.57).

# 18 Existence, Fact, Reality

## 18.49 IS 'EXISTENCE' A PREDICATE?

IN his *Meditations* (chapter V), Descartes puts forward his 'ontological' argument for the existence of God. His argument is founded on the correspondence which according to him exists between the following three propositions: (1) 'A triangle has three angles that total 180 degrees', (2) 'A mountain is adjoined by a valley', and (3) 'God (as a perfect being) exists'. Descartes maintains that these three propositions are similar in the following respects:

(1) It belongs *by definition* to the idea of a triangle that its angles total 180 degrees; it belongs *by definition* to the idea of a mountain that it is adjoined by a valley; *likewise*, it belongs *by definition* to the idea of God (as a perfect being) that He possesses all perfect properties (including the property of 'existence').

(2) Therefore it cannot be said without contradiction that the three angles of a triangle do not total 180 degrees; nor can it be said without contradiction that a mountain is not adjoined by a valley; likewise, it cannot be said without contradiction that God does not exist.

(3) It follows that these three propositions about triangles, mountains and God are all *necessarily true*: to the *subjects* of these propositions (triangles, mountains and God) the *predicates* ('having angles that total 180 degrees', 'being adjoined by a valley', and 'existence', respectively) necessarily belong, because these predicates form part of the *definitions* of the respective subjects.

This argument may be criticised in different ways, but we shall confine ourselves to one particular counter-argument, which has been put forward often since Kant: according to Kant, Descartes erred in assuming that 'existence' is a predicate (like 'being adjoined by a valley') that might or might not be ascribed to a subject (in this case God). It is not a predicate, but rather the condition something has to fulfil if we are to ascribe a predicate to it. In other words, something can be a subject of predication only if it exists.

In an illuminating essay[3] W.P. Alston explains the view that 'existence' cannot be a predicate as follows:

Before we can attach any predicate to anything ('round', 'heavy', 'in my pocket', 'belongs to Jones', 'difficult to understand'), we must presuppose that it exists. If we were not making that assumption we could not even raise the question whether a given predicate attaches to it. To predicate sweetness of the pie in the oven without presupposing that there is a pie in the oven would be as self-defeating as asking you to take the pie out of the oven, or asking you whether the pie in the oven is done, without that supposition . . . I can *deceitfully* say that the pie in the oven is sweet, knowing all along that there is no pie in the oven . . . [But] one (logically) could not openly admit that *a* does not exist (or doubt, wonder, or express ignorance about whether *a* exists) and still predicate *P* of *a*. . . . 'There is no pie in the oven, and the pie in the oven is sweet' cannot be used to make a predication, though it might be used to propound a riddle, be ironical, or test one's voice.

If 'existence' is not a predicate it cannot form part of a definition. The *predicate* of a proposition in the form *S* is *P* indicates a *characteristic* ascribed to the subject. But unlike 'green', 'large', and 'being adjoined by a valley', 'existence' is not a characteristic that can be ascribed to something. Nor, therefore, can existence be a defining characteristic. It is rather the condition for having characteristics: unless something exists it can have no characteristics. Since 'existence' is neither a characteristic nor a defining characteristic of something, Descartes cannot maintain that 'existence' is a defining characteristic of God. Furthermore, since 'existence' is not a characteristic, it cannot be a predicate in a proposition of the form *S* is *P*.

This view, that 'existence' is not a characteristic and therefore not a predicate either, has the following remarkable consequences.

(1) If 'existence' is a condition something has to fulfil before it can be the subject of predication, it follows that only *existing* things can be the subject of predication. We can then speak of something only if it exists, since it would be logically impossible to speak of something if it did not exist. Thus it would be impossible to say that unicorns (which do not exist) have only one horn, or that Cinderella has two wicked sisters, or that Zeus is Hera's husband. In fact, we would then be unable to say anything whatsoever about Zeus, Cinderella, Little Red Riding Hood, and unicorns, since none of these exist and therefore none of these can be the subject of predication! This consequence of the view that 'existence' is not a predicate is absurd.

(2) If, in spite of these considerations, we still want to speak of Zeus, Cinderella, Little Red Riding Hood and unicorns whilst maintaining, on the other hand, that 'existence' is a necessary condition for being the subject of predication, we are compelled to admit that it is a tautology to say that '*x* exists'. The fact that *x* (no matter what *x*) is the subject of predication in this assertion, presupposes that it exists. In saying that *x* exists we are adding nothing to what is implied by the mere fact that we are talking about it. Consequently the proposition '*x* exists' is always true, regardless of what *x* is. In this sense the proposition 'God exists' is tautological, like any other proposition of the form '*x* exists'. It follows that the ontological argument is valid but at the same time meaningless. But surely the proposition 'God exists' is not meaningless in this sense? The entire discussion on whether or not God exists cannot be a dispute about nothing?

(3) If '*x* exists' is a tautology, '*x* does not exist' is a contradiction, and that means that it is impossible to deny the existence of anything whatsoever! In other words, if something has to exist for us to be able to say something about it, it has to exist before we can say that it does not exist, which in turn implies that we cannot deny the existence of something without contradicting ourselves!

We are faced with a dilemma: either 'existence' is not a predicate, in which case we cannot speak of non-existent things, or it is a predicate, in which case we should be able to ascribe characteristics to non-existent things. Both of these possibilities seem absurd.

We might try to avoid this dilemma by means of Bertrand Russell's distinction[4] between 'being' and 'existence'. According to Russell, 'being' applies to any entity *about which* we can speak or of which we can think ('every possible object of thought'). Thus we cannot say that something has no 'being', because in doing so we are *saying* something about it, which implies that 'being' does apply to it. ('To mention something is to show that it is.') 'Existence', however, cannot be ascribed to everything we can speak of. We can, therefore, say that something (of which we can speak and which therefore has 'being') does not exist.

Let us first of all take a closer look at the concept 'being'. In the next section we shall deal with the concept 'existence'. As regards the concept 'being', which is so *general* that it applies to *everything about which we can speak*, we have to consider the following points:

(*a*)The view that 'existence' is not a predicate has absurd consequences. It is, however, quite in order to say of the concept 'being', which Russell distinguishes from 'existence', that it is not a predicate. In the proposition 'The cat is black', the cat is the *subject* to which a predicate is ascribed, and 'black' is this *predicate*. Of 'the cat' (subject) it is said that it is 'black' (predicate). But the fact that 'the cat' (in the proposition 'The cat is black') is the *subject* of predication, is *not an additional predicate* ascribable (like 'being black') to the subject 'the cat'. Thus: the subjecthood of the subject in a proposition is not an additional predicate ascribable to that subject, but rather the condition for ascribing predicates to the subject. Since a predicate is by definition that which is ascribed to the subject of predication, it is logically impossible to ascribe a predicate to something unless that thing is the subject of predication. Therefore the subjecthood of the subject in a proposition is a condition for the possibility of ascribing predicates to it. It is only because 'the cat' is something of which I can speak (subject of predication) that I can say that it is 'black' (predicate). Therefore Russell's concept 'being', which is so general that it applies to everything we can speak of, is nothing but the subjecthood of the subject of predication. '*A* is (has being)' is equivalent to: '*A* is the subject of predication'. By its nature this concept '*being*' is not a predicate but the general condition for the possibility of predication. '*Existence*', however, is not a condition for predication (after all, I can say something about things that do not exist) and therefore it is not implied in the subject-function of the subject of a proposition that this subject must *exist*. Therefore 'existence' (as opposed to 'being') can be a predicate ascribed to a subject of predication (for instance in the statement 'Black cats exist').

(*b*) If '*A* is (has being)' is equivalent to '*A* is the subject of predication', it follows that we can only speak about things that *are*. We can only speak about things about which we can speak (= things that are the subject of predication)! We can, however, speak about things that do not *exist*, for example about unicorns (saying that they have one horn), about Cinderella (saying that she has wicked sisters), and about Zeus (saying that he is Hera's husband).

(*c*) To deny that something *is* (has being) is contradictory. In doing so, we would be saying that the subject of predication is not a subject of predication. But to deny that something *exists* is not contradictory. Therefore it is not absurd to say of the subject of predication that it does not exist.

(*d*) It is a tautology to say that something *is* ('has being'). All this would say is: 'The subject of predication is a subject of predication'. In saying this, however, we are saying nothing (= are ascribing no predicates to the subject). But it is not a tautology to say that something *exists*; '*x* exists' is not tautological, and therefore 'God exists' (as opposed to 'God is the subject of predication') is not a tautology either.

It seems, then, that we can avoid the absurd consequences of the view that 'existence' is not a predicate by accepting Russell's distinction between 'being' as a condition for predication and 'existence' as a predicate. It is not clear, however, whether this resolves all our difficulties. Is 'existence' in fact a predicate on a par with other predicates, and therefore not a necessary condition that something has to fulfil if we are to ascribe predicates to it? Is not the *existence* of something presupposed by the predicates that we ascribe to it? What are we to say of Alston's example, cited above? Is Alston correct in maintaining that we would contradict ourselves if we said that the pie in the oven was sweet without presupposing that there existed a pie in the oven? To gain further light on this problem we shall have to pay closer attention to the concept of 'existence', as opposed to 'being'.

## 18.50 THE SYSTEMATIC AMBIGUITY OF THE CONCEPT OF EXISTENCE

There are two possible answers to the question: 'Do fictitious persons exist?' On the one hand we could say: 'Yes, fictitious persons do exist. Cinderella is one.' On the other hand we might say: 'No, fictitious persons do not exist. After all, fictitious persons are *fictitious* and therefore non-existent.' Both answers are correct, of course, but they use the word 'exist' in different senses. In the first answer 'exist' is used in the sense in which (1) Cinderella's *stepmother* does exist, but (2) Cinderella's *stepfather* does not exist (she does not have one). In the second answer 'exist' is used in the sense in which (1) *the Prince of Wales* does exist but (2) Cinderella's *Prince Charming* does not exist.

It is clear that the word 'exist' is not always used in the same sense. It is used in different senses in each of the following examples:

'People with long hair do *exist*, but hippopotami with long hair do not.'

'A prime number does *exist* between 11 and 15, but not between 7 and 11.'

'Electrons do *exist*, but phlogiston does not.'

'An Egyptian sun-god does *exist*, but not an Israelite sun-god.'

Briefly: the meaning of the concept 'exist' is ambiguous: its meaning varies according to the language game within which it is used. Whether or not we can say that something exists depends on the language game within which we are asking the question about its existence.

In this regard it is illuminating to consider the views of Rudolf Carnap[5] on questions about the existence of entities. Carnap maintains that if we wish to speak of a new kind of entity (for instance numbers or fictitious persons), we have to construct a *language game* (Carnap calls it a 'linguistic framework') in terms of which to speak of that kind of entity. Such a language game sets the rules according to which we can speak of these entities as well as the procedures to be followed in order to ascertain whether or not an entity of that kind exists. Carnap distinguishes between two kinds of questions that may be asked about the existence of entities. First, there is the question whether or not a certain entity or certain entities of the kind in question exists/exist. This kind of question is asked and answered according to the rules and procedure of the relevant language game. Carnap calls such questions *internal questions*, because they are asked and answered within the relevant language game. Secondly, there is the question of the existence or the reality of the entire system of entities that can be spoken of in terms of the relevant language game. In this regard Carnap speaks of *external questions*, because these questions apply to the language game as such, and cannot be answered within this language game. Let us adopt Carnap's distinction. In section 18.51 we shall discuss the external questions, but before we do so we shall first have to consider the nature of internal questions.

Every entity we can talk about is part of some or other system of similar entities. Nothing exists in isolation. A fictitious person, for example, can exist only in a story (or myth, or fairy tale, etc.), and therefore as one of the entities talked about in that story. Nobody can be a fictitious person outside a story. Numbers can exist only as part of a numerical system. No numbers can exist outside a numerical system. A concrete, observable thing exists only within the spatio-temporal system of observable things among which we live. Briefly: when we say that something exists, we are stating its existence as a member of some system of similar entities.

Our speaking about some system of entities always occurs within the specific language game in which we speak of that system. That language game is constituted by rules that determine what can or cannot be said meaningfully about the entities that belong in the relevant system.

Thus, for example, we speak of the numerical system within the language game of arithmetic. This language game is constituted by arithmetical rules which determine what can or cannot be said meaningfully about the numbers that belong in the numeral system. Thus it can be said meaningfully of a certain number that it is even (or uneven), that it is (or is not) a prime number, that it is larger (or smaller) than 100, etc. But it cannot be said meaningfully of a number that it is red or blue, fast or slow, intelligent or stupid. Such terms have no function within the language game of arithmetic.

The constitutive rules of a language game also provide the criteria by which we can ascertain whether or not a certain entity exists (that is, is a member of the system of entities spoken about in that language game). If the question of existence is asked within the language game of story-telling, questions such as 'Has Cinderella a stepmother?' (yes) 'Has Cinderella a stepfather?' (no) can be answered by consulting the relevant text, in this case, the fairy tale. If a question is asked within the language game of arithmetic, questions such as 'Is there a prime number between 7 and 11?' (no) and 'Is there a prime number between 11 and 15?' (yes) can be answered according to the formal procedures of arithmetic. If we are dealing with theoretical entities within the language game of physics or biology, questions such as 'Do electrons and genes exist?' (yes) and 'Do phlogiston and aether exist?' (no) can be answered in terms of the acceptability of the biological or physical theories within which the existence of these entities is presupposed. If the question is asked in what we will call the *real-world language* (Carnap's 'thing-language') in which we speak about the real world, that is, the world of things and events among which we live and act, questions such as 'Do long-haired people exist?' (yes), 'Do long-haired hippopotami exist?' (no), 'Does the Prince of Wales exist?' (yes), and 'Does Prince Charming exist?' (no) can be answered by empirical inquiry. (Of course these examples are not meant to be a complete inventory of possible language games; it would be impossible in practice to give one. They do, however, provide an illustration of the way such language games may be distinguished from each other.)

In the light of this analysis, which shows that the question about the existence of something is an *internal* question, within some or other language game, the argument in the previous section, on whether or not 'existence' is a predicate, must be augmented with two propositions:

(1) 'existence' is indeed a predicate;
(2) 'existence' is also a condition for predication.

## 1. 'Existence' is indeed a predicate

As a predicate, however, it is *systematically ambiguous*: its *meaning* varies systematically according to the language game within which it is used. Abstracted from all language games, the concept 'existence' has no meaning. A general concept of existence, which would apply *unambiguously* to everything we speak of, irrespective of the language game in which we are participating, cannot be a predicate because it would say nothing. We would then have reduced it to the concept of *being* discussed in section 18.49.

W.P. Alston explains this point as follows:

> There is one and only one mode of existence, which things can be said to have in various places – Australia, Tahiti, or the Milky Way. But once we stretch the notion of place to include fiction, mythology, imagination, and the real world, it becomes very unclear what could be meant by the existence which could indifferently be exercised in these locales. We can understand one sort of existence being possessed either in Australia or Greenland, but that is because we are holding it constant to, say, real as opposed to fictional existence. Vary that, too, and with what are we left? I can say 'There (really) is a key to this box' without saying where the key is, and I have told you something, though perhaps you would like to have fuller information. But if I say 'Sea serpents exist', and leave it open whether I mean in mythology, in literature, in reality, or in my imagination, what have I told you? Have I excluded anything? Can I conceive of anything which would not exist in at least one of these 'places'? It seems that I must, implicitly or explicitly, add one of these qualifiacations in order to get any assertion at all.[6]

Briefly: any entity that can be spoken of can be spoken of only *within* some language game. Therefore, if I say (in language game *x*) that something *exists*, I am saying of it that we can speak of it within language game *x* (for example, in our discourse about the real world or in mathematics or in story-telling). If I do not make it clear what language game I have in mind when I say that something exists, I say nothing about it. Instead of saying 'This thing can be spoken of within language game *x*', I am merely saying 'This thing can be spoken of', that is, this thing is the subject of predication, or this thing has 'being'. With that I would be saying nothing, because, as argued above 'being' is not a predicate.

## 2. 'Existence' is a condition for predication

Since we can speak of something (ascribe predicates to something) only *within* some language game, it is a *condition* for predication that the subject of predication must be a member of the system of entities which can be spoken of in the relevant language game. For this reason we can agree with Alston's view as quoted in section 18.49: unless it is assumed that there is a pie in the oven it would be as absurd to say that the pie is sweet as to ask someone to take the pie out of the oven. To say that a pie is *sweet* and is *in the oven* is to ascribe predicates to it within the real-world language. This presupposes, however, that the pie exists in the real world about which we speak in the real-world language, otherwise no predicates can be ascribed to it within this language game. It is of course possible to say within the language game of telling fairy tales that the pie is sweet and yet to deny that it really exists; for example, the witch in the tale about Hansel and Gretel baked sweet pies, but those pies (like the witch) did not exist in the real world. They existed only in the fairy tale. But such a statement involves different language games. The predication occurs within the language game of telling the fairy tale in which the pies do indeed exist.

From this example it is clear that we can deny the existence of an entity without contradiction, and that we can affirm the existence of an entity without tautology, even though 'existence' is a condition for predication. Speaking within one language game, I can deny without contradiction and affirm without tautology that the subject of predication (which I assume to exist within the system of entities talked about in that language game) exists also within the system of entities talked about in some *other* language game. We can say without contradiction or tautology that Cinderella (who exists in the fairy tale) does not exist in reality; that Cinderella's stepfather (who exists in my imagination) does not exist in the fairy tale; that King Arthur (who exists in the legend) existed in reality (or did he?); that the city of London (which exists in reality) exists in stories about Sherlock Holmes, etc. In this way we can avoid the problems we encountered in section 18.49 with regard to the view that existence is a condition for predication.

Briefly: the *existence* of the subject of predication within the system of entities spoken of in a language game, is a condition for the possibility of ascribing predicates to that subject *within that language game*, and even for the possibility of denying or affirming the existence of that subject within the system of entities dealt with in some *other* language game.

## 18.51 THE STATUS OF THE REAL-WORLD LANGUAGE

In section 18.50 we examined the nature of questions such as: Does a prime number exist between 7 and 11? Has Cinderella a stepfather? Are there hippopotami with long hair? We arrived at the conclusion that all of these were *internal* questions, asked and answered within some language game. We would have to answer these internal questions affirmatively if – according to the rules of the language game within which we are asking the question – we can incorporate the entity in question in the system of entities that can be spoken of in that language game. In this sense all three questions mentioned above would have to be answered negatively if we asked them within the language game of arithmetic, the language game of the fairy tale, and the real-world language respectively. In the system of numbers dealt with in the language game of arithmetic, there is no prime number between 7 and 11; among the dramatis personae featuring in the fairy tale there is no stepfather of Cinderella; in the spatio-temporal system of entities spoken of in the real-world language there are no long-haired hippopotami.

All these questions are *specific*. More problematic, however, are the following quite *general* questions: Do numbers exist? Do fictitious persons exist? Do spatio-temporal things exist? If these general questions are interpreted as *internal* questions, they are quite readily answered. Their answers are then determined by the language game within which they are asked and depend upon whether the relevant language game admits of such entities. Therefore: yes, numbers do exist (within the numerical system) – 2 is an example; yes, fictitious persons do exist (in the fairy tale) – Cinderella is an example; yes, things do exist (within the spatio-temporal system of things) – this pen is an exam ple. But if these questions are all asked within the real-world language, only real things can be said to exist, and no fictitious persons or numbers.

From these examples it is clear that such internal questions can be asked only of the elements in a system of entities and not of the system as such. After all, the system as a whole is not an element within itself! The conflict between realists (who maintain that a world of spatio-temporal things exists outside our minds) and subjective idealists (who deny the existence of such a world) is therefore founded on a mistaken formulation of the problem. Since 'really existing' means 'being an element in a system', it is clear that the concept 'really existing' cannot be applied to the system as a whole.

According to Carnap, it may be possible that those who ask this nonsensical question about the world of real things, are actually confusing it with a different question, namely an *external* question about the real-world language. External questions are questions *about* some or other language game, and as such they cannot be answered in the light of the criteria that apply *within* that language game. They are questions about the acceptability or unacceptability of the language game as such, not about the existence of something within the system of entities spoken of within the language game. In asking the (in itself nonsensical) question 'Does there exist a system of spatio-temporal things?', one would actually have in mind an external question about the real-world language: shall we speak about things existing in the real world and use the criteria of the real-world language to ascertain what things do or do not exist in this world?

According to Carnap these external questions are not theoretical ones but questions of *practice*; they are not questions that can be answered within the relevant language game, but questions about the usefulness or necessity of participating in that language game in the course of practical life. This external question about the real-world language is in fact superfluous: practical life simply demands that we ask ourselves what things and situations occur in the real world. The external questions about most other language games are not superfluous; arithmetic is very useful, but not absolutely essential. Story-telling is also useful, but even less essential than arithmetic!

Arising from this analysis, two questions have to be considered more closely:

(1) What is the nature of the real-world language?
(2) How is the real-world language related to other language games?

## 1. The real-world language

In section 9.24 we argued that as human beings our possibilities for action are always determined by the situation within which we act. We are always free in our choice between various possibilities for action: we can choose which of the given possibilities we shall or shall not realise.

But the possibilities between which we can choose, are given; we do not choose them. In this regard Heidegger speaks of the *facticity* of human existence: our possibilities for action are *given* by the factual situation into which we are '*thrown*'. The real world, that is, the world in which we live, consists of the *total* acting-situation in which we find ourselves, the complete set of determinations of our possibilities for action. *By definition* we cannot act or exist outside of the real world. The *real-world language* is the language game within which we can say that something exists as an element in the real world. If I say in the real-world language that something exists, I am giving my hearer the assurance that there is one (or more) situation(s) within the real world in which that 'something' makes a difference to what we can or cannot do.

In this way we might say that long-haired people exist (we might meet them in the real world, where they make a difference to our possibilities for action). Long-haired hippopotami do not exist (we cannot encounter long-haired hippopotami, although we may imagine them existing and imagining is a human activity that we perform in the real world). Cinderella does not exist (we cannot come across her in the real world, although we can read about her in a real book of fairy tales). The number 7 does not exist (we do not meet any numbers in the real world, although we do encounter arithmetic as a human activity).

The answer to the external question, 'Why do we use the real-world language as a language game in which to ask whether or not something exists?' is, therefore: 'Because life within the real world in which we find ourselves makes it necessary to know, to ask and to say what things and situations determine our possibilities for action in this world'. Because we have to act, we need to know what our possibilities for action are. This question is (as Carnap points out) a question of *practice* to be answered in terms of the practical demands of our lives on earth. Our 'choice' for the real-world language is necessitated by the practical needs of human life on earth. Because our practical needs make this language game indispensable, it is misleading to speak of a *choice* in this context. Since we do not 'choose' to live but simply do so, we also do not 'choose' to employ the real-world language; we simply do so. There is usually no deliberate choice because we all have accepted the real-world language early in our lives as a matter of course.

## 2. *The primacy of the real-world language*

Like the external question about the real-world language, external questions about all other language games are of a *practical* nature:

whether or not we can accept the existence of a prime number between 7 and 11 is an *internal* question, settled within the language game of arithmetic within which we speak of numbers. Whether or not we are to participate in the language game of arithmetic itself, is an *external* question and as such a question of *practice*: does our concrete situation in the real world demand that we do arithmetic? Have we, in our situation as human beings in the world, practical needs that make the language game of arithmetic necessary or desirable? Whether or not we accept the existence of a stepfather of Cinderella is an *internal* question, to be settled within the language game of the fairy tale. Whether or not it is necessary or desirable to tell or to read tales is an *external* question (external to the fairy tale), and as such a question of *practice*: does our human situation in the real world pose practical demands that make it necessary or desirable to tell or to read fairy tales? Whether we shall pursue physics on the assumption that non-observable entities such as electrons (yes) and phlogiston (no) exist, depends upon their usefulness as explanatory hypotheses. Whether or not they are useful in this respect is an *internal* question within the language game of physics. Whether or not we seek physical explanation and thus take part in the language game of physics is an *external* question (external to physics) and thus also a question of *practice*.

Briefly: whether we accept the existence of an entity can be decided only *within* some or other language game. But whether we take part in a language game is a question *external* to the language game, and therefore a question that cannot be settled *within* that language game. All these external questions are question of practice, to be settled in the light of the demands made by our human situation in the real world.

In this sense the real-world language enjoys primacy over all other language games. It is within this language game that we speak of the real world in which we live and act and within which we perform the speech acts constituted by all the various language games (including the real-world language itself). Of each language game we might ask: what concrete practical needs make it necessary to take part in this language game within the real world? It follows then, that any discussion of the existence or non-existence of something occurs either directly or indirectly within the real-world language. *Directly*: when we ask whether or not something exists as determinant of our possibilities for action in the real world; London, the Kremlin, this pencil and elephants do exist, while fairyland, Prince Charming, Hercules, centaurs and the number 7 do not exist. *Indirectly*: when we ask within some language game other than the real-world language, whether or not something exists; the Kremlin does not exist in fairyland, while Hercules and centaurs do exist in Greek mythology. But we must in such cases be able to fit our participation in the relevant language game into the real world and thus be able to speak of it within the real-world language. *Indirectly* our speech acts about the number 7 are therefore speech acts about arithmetic, and speech acts about Cinderella are speech acts about a fairy tale, and speech acts about Hercules are speech acts about Greek mythology.

Therefore, if we say (in the real-world language) that something exists, we must be able to specify in what (kind of) concrete situation it would determine our possibilities for action. If, in some other language game, we say that something exists, we must be able (1) to show that it exists in the light of the criteria of that language game, and (2) to show how the use of that language game fits into our concrete human situation in the real world. We shall return to this distinction in the next chapter. In brief: since external questions about the various language games in which we participate are all questions of *practice*, asked and answered in the light of the practical demands made by our human situation in the real world, the real-world language enjoys *primacy* over other language games: our participation in all language games takes place in our concrete human situation in the real world and it must therefore be possible to speak in the real-world language about our participation in all language games.

Our use of the term 'primacy' must not be misunderstood. It is a systematically ambiguous term in the sense that something can enjoy primacy only in some or other *respect*. In chapter 10, for example, we suggested that for Christians God is the *primary determinant of meaning*. It does not follow that God enjoys primacy also as an explanatory principle in physics or as an axiom in mathematics. The real world in which we live has no primacy as determinant of meaning (unless we were to adopt some form of 'materialism' or 'secularism'). Nonetheless, it remains the world in which we as questioners find ourselves. *We* do not 'exist' in a fairy tale or in a mathematical system! It must therefore be possible directly or indirectly to locate within the real world everything about which we, as inhabitants of this world, can speak. This locating is performed in the real-world language within which we ask and answer questions about what exists in the real world, that is, about the entities, events, situations etc., which determine our possibilities for action in the real world.

## 18.52 FACTS

Is it a *fact* that God exists? Or is the concept 'fact' not at all applicable to God's existence, because God transcends the world of facts? Before we can answer these questions we must first clarify what we mean by 'facts'. Here the following questions are relevant: (1) How are facts related to knowledge? (2) How do facts differ from fictions? (3) What is the relation between facts and states of affairs? (4) What are questions of fact?

### 1. Facts and knowledge

It is under exactly the same circumstances and on the same grounds that we say 'I know that *p*' and 'It is a fact that *p*'. Hence, too, we cannot assert one of these and deny the other without contradiction. Nevertheless, 'I know that *p*' is not synonymous with '*p* is a fact'.

In section 14.42 we argued that in saying 'I know that *p*' I claim a certain *status* for my *belief* that *p*; that is, I claim (*a*) that this belief is beyond doubt and therefore not in need of further testing and (*b*) that it can now be used as criterion to test the truth of other beliefs. The truth of other beliefs can be proved by showing that they are consistent with those beliefs for which we claim the status of knowledge.

In saying 'It is a fact that *p*' I claim a similar *status* for the *state of affairs* asserted in *p*. In saying that a state of affairs is a fact, I claim (a) that its existence is beyond doubt and therefore not in need of proof, and (b) that it can serve as basis for proving the existence of other (possible) states of affairs. In this sense facts can be distinguished from theories or hypotheses. These can be proved by showing that they follow from or are founded on the facts.

### 2. Facts and fiction

Whether or not we are to accord a state of affairs the status of fact, is an issue to be resolved in the real-world language. In this sense facts are opposed to *fictions*. A history book gives us *facts* about historical persons; a story does not report facts about the characters in that story. The brothers Grimm do not report the facts about Snow White. Thus it is not a *fact* that Snow White stayed with the seven dwarfs. We can, however, state facts *about the story* which is told by the brothers Grimm. For example, it is a fact that the brothers Grimm portray Snow

White as living with seven dwarfs. In this case, however, we are stating facts in the real-world language and not in the story, because, as we argued in section 18.51, every story is given as such within the real world as something that we can read, hear, tell, etc. and therefore as something about which we can talk in the real-world language.

### 3. Facts and states of affairs

The following things could be said about states of affairs. (*a*) Within every *state of affairs* we can distinguish *things* and *relations* between things. In this sense, things (and relations) are elements of states of affairs. (*b*) *States of affairs* (like the things and relations occurring within them) can arise (be brought about), change (be changed), and end (be terminated). *Events* are changes in states of affairs and thus in the things and relations within the states of affairs. (*c*) *States of affairs* are, one might say, the 'furniture' of the real world, setting the limits of our acting-situation and determining our possibilities for action. Events are changes in the real world and thus changes in our possibilities for action. (*d*) It follows that we can *in principle* always observe, experience, encounter, etc. states of affairs, events and things. In other words: we are in principle able to experience that our possibilities for action are determined by the relevant state of affairs, things or event. (*e*) States of affairs, things and events are always *describable*. With regard to the way they determine our possibilities for action we can always ask and answer the questions: How? Where? and When? Such descriptions (as answers to the questions: How? Where? and When?) may be accurate or inaccurate, correct or incorrect, vague or precise. We can therefore always ask whether a state of affairs, thing or event is (was) indeed as stated in a description.

In contrast to states of affairs, *facts* cannot be *described*; they can only be *stated*. (*a*) We can *state* facts: a fact is a state of affairs which is, first, described in a statement, and secondly, declared to be beyond doubt as described in the statement. Therefore, to describe a state of affairs and to declare it beyond doubt to be as described, is to *state* it as a fact. For example, I may *state* (as a fact) that Nelson's column is in Trafalgar Square, that is, describe the state of affairs (Nelson's column being in Trafalgar Square) in the statement 'Nelson's column is in Trafalgar Square' and declare this state of affairs, which has *thus been described*, to be beyond a doubt. (*b*) *We cannot describe* facts, since *facts* (states of affairs which have been described and declared to be beyond doubt) are by definition already described and therefore cannot be described again. *States of affairs* can be described *anew* if we question a description that has already been given of them. *Facts* cannot be described *anew* because facts are by definition states of affairs of which the description is considered to be beyond doubt. For example, we may question whether *Ajax* won the race, but not whether the *winner* won the race. Likewise, we may question whether a state of affairs has been described correctly, but not whether a correctly-described-state-of-affairs (fact) has been described correctly. By definition, therefore, *facts* are beyond doubt, although we may doubt whether we are justified to consider a (described) state of affairs as a fact. Similarly, I may doubt whether my belief is true, but not whether what I *know* (i.e. my belief which I claim to be true beyond doubt) is true. I could of course doubt whether I have correctly claimed the status of knowledge for my belief.

### 4. Questions of fact

Such questions are the sort of questions which are decided in the real-world language. They could be formulated as follows: 'Is *S* (a state of affairs described in a proposition) a fact?' 'It is a fact, (that is, a state of affairs established beyond doubt in the real-world language) that the Eiffel Tower is in Paris, an d hence a *question of fact* (that is, a question to be decided in the real-world language) whether or not the Eiffel Tower is in Paris. I would, however, not call it a *fact* that the Eiffel Tower contains 3,602,341 bolts (I do not know how many bolts it contains and therefore cannot confirm this hypothesis as beyond any doubt), but it is a *question of fact* whether the Eiffel Tower contains so many bolts (that is, a question to be settled in the real-world language).

Hypotheses, opinions, suppositions, etc., do not state *facts*: they are not established beyond a doubt. All of them do, however, pose *questions of fact*, because it must be settled in the real-world language whether the states of affairs which are stated in the hypotheses, opinions, suppositions, etc., are to be accorded the status of *facts*.

An extremely important condition that a question has to meet if it is to be a *question of fact* is that it must be possible to conceive of circumstances in which it would make a difference to our possibilities for action whether or not the state of affairs in question is a fact. This point may be explained as follows: states of affairs determine our possibilities for action, therefore propositions in which states of affairs are stated as facts are assurances regarding our possibilities for action.

Whether or not a state of affairs is a fact (and hence whether or not the proposition in which that state of affairs is stated is true) therefore has a bearing on our possibilities for action. Whether or not it is true that Nelson's column is in Trafalgar Square makes a difference to what I could or could not observe or do if I went to Trafalgar Square. It is therefore always meaningful to ask in respect of a *question of fact* how and under what circumstances it would make a difference to our possibilities for action whether or not the proposition in which the relevant state of affairs is stated as a fact, is true. If there is *no* conceivable situation in the real world in which it would make a difference to our possibilities for action, whether or not the proposition in question is true, such a 'proposition' would be giving us no assurance regarding our possibilities for action and would thus be raising no question of *fact*.

The by now standard example used to illustrate this point, is the following parable:

> Once upon a time two explorers came upon a clearing in the jungle. In the clearing were growing many flowers and many weeds. One explorer says, 'Some gardener must tend this plot.' The other disagrees, 'There is no gardener.' So they pitch their tents and set a watch. No gardener is ever seen. 'But perhaps he is an invisible gardener'. So they set up a barbed-wire fence. They electrify it. They patrol with bloodhounds. (For they remember how H.G. Wells's *The Invisible Man* could be both smelt and touched though he could not be seen.) But no shrieks ever suggest that some intruder has received a shock. No movements of the wire ever betray an invisible climber. The bloodhounds never give cry. Yet still the Believer is not convinced. 'But there is a gardener, invisible, intangible, insensible to electric shocks, a gardener who has no scent and makes no sound, a gardener who comes secretly to look after the garden which he loves.' At last the Sceptic despairs, 'But what remains of your original assertion? Just how does what you call an invisible, intangible, eternally elusive gardener differ from an imaginary gardener or even from no gardener at all?'[7]

Let us consider what this story is all about.

(1) The 'believing' explorer maintains that the clearing in the jungle is tended by a gardener. He is therefore stating that they can consider their possibilities for action to be determined by the existence of a

gardener. The sceptic denies that their possibilities for action are determined by the existence of a gardener. He maintains that there is no gardener.

(2) To find out who is right, they check their possibilities for action to see whether these are in fact determined by the existence of a gardener.

(3) When it becomes apparent that they never *see* a gardener (that is, that what they can or cannot see is not determined by the existence of a gardener), the believer amends his factual claim: their possibilities for action are determined by the existence of an *invisible* gardener, one who naturally has no effect on what they can or cannot *see*.

(4) Every time it becomes apparent that in some further respect, too, the existence of the gardener makes no difference to their possibilities for action, the believer adjusts his original claim. According to him there is a gardener, but one who does *not* determine their possibilities for action in these ways: one who is 'invisible, intangible, insensible to electric shocks, one whom the dogs cannot smell and who makes no sounds, a gardener who comes secretly . . . etc.'.

(5) The consequence of this line of argument is that the believer is ultimately saying: 'Our possibilities for action are determined by a gardener who is of such a kind that he does not determine our possibilities for action, in any way whatsoever!' It is clear that the believer no longer succeeds in asserting any factual proposition. The sceptic is justified in finally asking: 'What remains of your original assertion? How does what you call an invisible, intangible, eternally elusive gardener differ from an imaginary gardener or even from no gardener at all?'

Briefly: a factual proposition raises a *question of fact*, which has to be settled in the real-world language. But a 'proposition' raises no question of fact if it makes no difference to our possibilities for action whether or not the state of affairs in question is as stated. Thus, for example, it makes no difference to our possibilities for action whether the 'proposition' relates to 'an invisible, intangible, eternally elusive gardener' or 'an imaginary gardener, or no gardener at all'. Therefore, if we wish to raise a question of fact, we must be able to say under what circumstances in the real world the stated fact would make a difference to our possibilities for action. If we cannot say that we fail to raise a question of fact.

It may be asked whether this condition for raising a question of fact is not too stringent. Whether or not there are living creatures on the Andromeda nebula is a question of fact, even if their existence makes no difference to our possibilities for action because we shall never be able to reach the Andromeda nebula in order to encounter such beings and see how they determine what we can or cannot do. But even if it is *technically* impossible for us to reach the Andromeda nebula, it is *logically* possible to do so. For raising a question of *fact* it is merely necessary to say that if we find ourselves in the (logically possible) situation *S*, our possibilities for action will be determined in this or that way by the stated fact. We are therefore indeed concerned with a question of fact (a question about the determination of our possibilities for action in a *logically possible situation*), even if it is not technically possible to arrive at this situation.

Whether or not an event occured in the past is indeed a question of fact, but then about a state of affairs *in the past*. *Logically*, however, it is impossible to 'return to' the past. I can return to a *place* where I have been before, but not to a *moment* in the past. It is in fact contradictory to speak of 'returning in time', since by definition time is irreversible. It follows that it is logically impossible to arrive at a situation where our possibilities for action are determined by a state of affairs in the past. Although it is a matter of fact that Napoleon lost the battle of Waterloo, it is (logically) impossible to visit the scene of the battle in 1815 and to witness his defeat. Have we not in this case come up against a question of fact that makes no difference to our possibilities for action under any (logically) possible circumstances?

To this question one could reply that all past evens have *consequences in the present,* and that these consequences do make a difference to our possibilities for action. *We* cannot witness Napoleon's defeat, but we can indeed witness its consequences. Such consequences make a difference to what we can or cannot do or observe in our *present* world. This answer is borne out by the methods of historical research: whether or not something has taken place in the past is determined not by witnessing the event in question (which would be logically impossible), but by examining its (often documentary) consequences in the present.

There are two main objections to this answer. (1) It leads to the conclusion that propositions about the past are *reduced* to propositions about the present. Propositions state that something makes a difference to our possibilities for action. In terms of the answer given above, propositions about the past provide no indication of how events in the *past* make a difference to our possibilities for action, but only of how the effects that such past events have in the *present* make a difference to our possibilities for action. Thus propositions about Napoleon are reduced to propositions about documents etc. about Napoleon. (2) According to this view, we cannot speak of questions of fact in cases of past events that have *no* consequences in the present. The classic example of this is the question Carl Hempel[8] asks – whether the largest dinosaur whose skeleton may be seen in the New York Natural History Museum had a blue tongue when it was alive. On the one hand it is logically impossible to 'return in time' to observe that possibly blue tongue. On the other hand it is impossible to say what consequences this long-decayed tongue, observed by no man, could have for the present. Yet it remains a fact that it was blue (or that it was not blue). Therefore Hempel's question is a *question of fact*.

To meet this kind of objection we have to formulate the condition for raising questions of fact as follows: we can speak of a question of fact only in cases where it is logically possible that *someone* (no matter who) has been/is/will be in a position where the state of affairs in question would make a difference to his possibilities for action. It is not necessary that that person must be one of us; it is not a question of *our* possibilities for action, nor, *a fortiori*, of *everybody's* possibilities for action; it is a question of the possibilities for action of a *favourably situated person* (which implies that it must be logically possible for a real person to have been/be favourably situated). Nor is it necessary that someone must in fact ever have been/be in the circumstances in question; but *logically* it must be *possible* that such a person really existed/exists/will exist. For example, it is a question of fact whether or not Peter has a headache, because his possible headache forms part of what *he* may possibly come to experience. Peter is, however, the only person favourably situated to experience his headache. Others can only observe the (external) symptoms of his headache. Whether or not there are people on the Andromeda nebula is also a question of fact, because a person's possibilities for action would be determined by the presence of such people if he reached the Andromeda nebula. In the (logically possible, but technically impossible) event of someone arriving at the Andromeda nebula, he might be able to encounter such people, observe them, speak to them, etc. Whether or not tyrannosaurs lived in the year 3,689,235 BC is a question of fact, because the possibilities for action of anyone living then would have been determined by the existence of tyrannosaurs. In the (logically possible, but empirically unlikely) event of someone having lived in the year 3,689,235 BC he would have been able to encounter tyrannosaurs, be eaten by them, etc. Whether or not there is a gardener who is *in principle* imperceptible is not a question of fact, because it is logically impossible for such a gardener to affect the possibilities for action or observation of anyone whatsoever. We cannot conceive of any situation in which the existence of such a gardener would make a difference to what someone can or cannot do or observe. Or can we?

Briefly: a question of fact arises only if it is logically possible that there could be (or could have been) a situation in the real world in which the state of affairs in question would make (or would have made) a difference to the possibilities for action of a favourably situated person.

## 18.53 REALITY

Does God *really* exist? What does it mean if we say that He *really* exists? What is *reality*, after all? After our analysis of the concepts 'existence' and 'fact' we can be brief about the concept 'reality' because it is related to these two concepts.

In section 18.51 we argued that the *real world* (or *reality*) could be defined as the total acting-situation in which we find ourselves, the complete set of determinations of our possibilities for action. To say of something that it is *real* is therefore to say that it is an entity in the real world, and hence that its existence makes a difference to our possibilities for action.

Usually the predicate 'real' is employed in direct relation to its opposite, 'unreal', just as the predicate 'true' is used in relation to 'untrue'. We say that Nelson's column is in Trafalgar Square to give our hearer some information. But we say that it is true that Nelson's column is in Trafalgar Square, only if our information is queried or if it is suggested that it is *untrue*. 'True' is used to deny 'untrue'; 'untrue' is used to deny 'true'. Similarly, we say that something is *real*, really exists, or really occurred, only if there is doubt about the reality of that thing or event, and we call something unreal if there is doubt about whether it can justly be considered real.

There are two senses in which we could claim that something is not an element in the real world and hence call its reality into question: when it is claimed to be an *illusion* and when it is claimed to be *fictitious*.

In the first case the question is whether an observed state of affairs is *illusory* or real. For example, if we put a stick into a tub of water it *appears* to be crooked but in reality remains straight. The oasis seen on a desert horizon is a *mirage*, not a reality. The pink elephants one might see at a carnival are *hallucinations* (resulting from inebriation) and not real. The utopian situation you are talking about does not really exist; you have probably *imagined* it.

In all these examples our concrete possibilities for action are not determined in the way our observation of the situation has led us to believe. For example, I may *see* an oasis on the desert horizon and conclude that I will find something to drink there, but if I go there, I shall find nothing. This discrepancy between our observation of a situation and our actual possibilities for action in that situation may be explained in terms of the *perceptual circumstances* within the situation.

An observed state of affairs is *illusory* if it does not make a difference to our possibilities for action in the way our observation would lead us to believe. For example, I may be *seeing* an oasis on the horizon, but this has no effect on my chances of obtaining water. An observed state of affairs is real if it does make a difference to our possibilities for action in the way our observation leads us to believe. For example, I see a fountain at the bottom of the garden, and this does affect my possibilities for obtaining water.

We also speak of real as opposed to *fictitious*. For example, there is not *really* any such person as Cinderella. She is a character from a fairy tale. It is not certain that King Arthur *really* did exist; many people think that he is merely a legendary figure. It is merely a rumour that the British Government intends abolishing the monarchy; they will not *really* do so. Centaurs and unicorns do not *really* exist; they are mythological animals.

A thing, person, event, situation, etc., is therefore *fictitious* if it belongs to a system of entities talked about in some language game other than the real-world language. It is then not an element in the real world but an element in a story, rumour, myth, etc.

We conclude that there is a close relation between the three concepts dealt with in this chapter, viz. 'existence', 'fact', and 'reality'. A *fact* is a state of affairs the *reality* of which is considered to be beyond doubt. A state of affairs is *real* if it *exists* within the *real world*. The real world is the world in which we live and act and which determines what possibilities for action we have.

In denying the reality of something we either hold it to be an *illusion* and hence only seemingly an element in the real world; or, we hold it to be a *fiction* and hence an element in the system of entities talked about in some language game other than the real-world language.

Can we say that God *really exists*? Is the existence of God a *fact*?

# 19 God's Existence

## 19.54 INTRODUCTION

IN chapter 17 we pointed out the importance of the distinction between the *ontological* and the *epistemological* questions with regard to God's existence. Since these two questions are often confused, we need to make the distinction between them quite clear before we can discuss the ontological question about God's existence. In the light of our analysis of the concepts 'existence', 'fact' and 'reality' in chapter 18 we are now able to distinguish more clearly between the ontological and epistemological questions than we could do in chapter 17.

The statement '*x* exists (in reality)' is a statement of fact in which a certain state of affairs (the existence of *x*) is stated as a fact. By making this statement the speaker gives his hearer the assurance that there is a situation in the real world in which our possibilities for action are determined by the state of affairs that has been stated as fact. With regard to this statement we may ask questions about the *content* of the assurance that has been given (ontological question) and about the *grounds* for the assurance (epistemological question). Briefly: how are our possibilities for action determined by the existence of *x*? (ontological question) and on what grounds do you claim to know that our possibilities for action are determined by the existence of *x*? (epistemological question). Both questions are concerned with one or more situations in the real world. In reply to the *ontological* question we have to refer to the situation(s) in which the existence of *x* would make a difference to the possibilities for action of a favourably situated person. In reply to the *epistemological* question we have to refer to the situation(s) in which we could find the evidence on the basis of which we would claim to know that *x* exists in reality.

An example will serve to illustrate this distinction. If we state that the Dalai Lama exists, we are making a statement of fact in which we give our hearers the assurance that there is a situation in the real world in which the existence of the Dalai Lama would make a difference to what a favourably situated person could do. In reply to the *ontological* question with regard to this assertion we have to refer to a situation (at this moment probably in India) in which the Dalai Lama's being there would make a difference to someone's possibilities for action: someone might encounter the Dalai Lama in that situation, converse with him, touch him, etc. In reply to the *epistemological* question about this statement we could say that we base our knowledge claim on the fact that we (being in the presence of the Dalai Lama) now see him standing in front of us, that we can converse with him, touch him, etc. In other words, in the situation in which we now find ourselves we experience that his being there makes a difference to our possibilities for action.

In this case we reply to the *epistemological* question by referring to *the same* situation as that to which we refer in reply to the *ontological* question, that is, the situation in which we meet the Dalai Lama in person and perceive that our possibilities for action are determined by the fact that he exists. Usually, however, we refer to *different* situations in reply to epistemological and ontological questions respectively. We could, for instance, reply to the epistemological question with regard to the Dalai Lama's existence by referring to the situation in which we have seen him on television, or have read a report about him in the newspaper, or have heard him over the radio.

Briefly: in order to answer the *ontological* question with regard to a statement of fact we have to refer to the situation(s) in which the state of affairs stated as a fact makes a difference to our possibilities for action. To answer the *epistemological* question with regard to a statement of fact we have to refer to the situations in which we might find the *evidence* on the basis of which we would claim to know that the relevant state of affairs exists in reality. These two situations need not be identical: I may claim to know that something exists (= that it determines our possibilities for action) because I encounter it in my experiential world as such. I may also claim to know that something exists because I have indirect grounds for my claim that it exists. There may conceivably be instances where these two situations *cannot* be the same because the state of affairs stated as a fact is not (no longer) accessible to us and we can claim to know it exists or existed only on the basis of indirect evidence. Let us examine a number of examples of statements of fact in which there is a difference between the situations in terms of which the ontological and the epistemological questions, respectively, can be answered.

*'There are living beings on the Andromeda nebula'*

(a) Here I am giving an assurance regarding a state of affairs that would determine our possibilities for action if we were on the Andromeda nebula. To answer the *ontological* questions one would therefore have to refer to a situation on the Andromeda nebula.

(b) To answer the *epistemological* question ('what evidence would provide grounds for claiming to know that there is life on the Andromeda nebula?') we *cannot* refer to the situation on the Andromeda nebula because it is *technically* impossible for us to get there. Unless tremendous technical advances enable us to reach the Andromeda nebula, we shall in practice have to appeal to a *different* situation if we want to find evidence in support of this knowledge claim (for example, the situation in which we might collect evidence by radio telescope from the Andromeda nebula).

### 'President Kennedy was assassinated in Dallas'

(a) To answer the *ontological* question in this regard we have to refer to a situation in Dallas (Texas) on the morning of 22 November 1963.

(b) To answer the *epistemological* question we *cannot* refer to this situation, because it is not only technically but also *logically* impossible to 'return' to 1963. We shall have to do this by referring to the situation in which we could find as evidence the documentary and other consequences of Kennedy's assassination. In this case we could also appeal to the *memories* which people (possibly we ourselves) have of the situation in 1963. This is, however, a reference to the memories that we have *now*, not a 'return' to the situation *at that time*.

### 'Nelson died in the battle of Trafalgar'

(a) As in the previous example, we have to answer the *ontological* question by referring to a situation in the past (a situation on HMS Victory off Cape Trafalgar on the afternoon of 21 October 1805).

(b) As in the previous example, we have to answer the *epistemological* question by referring to the situation in the *present* where we might encounter evidence, not to the situation in 1805. Here we cannot, however, (as in the previous example) appeal to the memories of eye-witnesses, because they no longer exist.

### 'The moon was once part of the earth'

(a) Here, too, the *ontological* question relates to a situation in the past and therefore a situation to which it is logically impossible for us to return ourselves. This example differs from the previous one, however, in that there was (probably) no-one who experienced it (man did not yet exist). The statement therefore gives an assurance about a situation that would have determined someone's possibilities for action *if* there had been someone (even though in fact there were no people). *Ontologically* this is, therefore, still a *question of fact*.

(b) In reply to the *epistemological* question we also have to refer to the situation in which we might now find evidence to suggest that the moon was once part of the earth. Geological and astronomical evidence can be found which make this probable.

*'The largest dinosaur, of which the skeleton is to be seen in the Museum of Natural History in New York, had a blue tongue when it was alive'*

(a) As in the previous example, the *ontological* question here relates to a situation in the past that was (probably) not experienced by man because man did not yet exist at the time when this dinosaur roamed the earth. Here, too, it remains a *question of fact* whether or not this situation existed, because we are able to refer to a situation in which the state of affairs in question would have made a difference to what someone might have experienced *if* he had been in that situation.

(b) As regards the *epistemological* question, this example differs from the previous one in that no consequences are to be found at present of the colour of the dinosaur's tongue. It is therefore difficult to conceive of a situation in which we might now find relevant evidence for or against this statement. Even though it is difficult (if not impossible) to answer the *epistemological* question, this does not affect the *ontological* question because the situation (during the life of the dinosaur) with which the ontological question is concerned, can be specified.

*'Jesus rose from the tomb'*

(a) Here the *ontological* question relates to a situation in a garden near Jerusalem early on the morning of the first Easter day. In this statement we are given the assurance that if someone had been in this situation it would have been possible for him to see Jesus appear from His tomb, to speak to Him, etc. In this instance there is no problem about the kind of *existence* at issue; the question is about the *factual* existence of the state of affairs in question.

(b) To answer the *epistemological* question we have to refer to Biblical testimony, even though not everybody will accept this as adequate grounds for a knowledge claim with respect to the resurrection of Jesus.

*'It is going to rain tomorrow'*

(*a*) Here the *ontological* question is concerned with a situation in the future, not one in the past, as in the previous example. We are given the assurance that our possibilities for action will be determined by the rain tomorrow.

(*b*) We cannot relive events of the past. We can, however, experience states of affairs or events in the present of which the relevant event in the past was the cause or to which it gave rise in some way or other. Such states of affairs in the present could serve as evidence on the basis of which we might claim to know that the relevant event did occur in the past. To answer the *epistemological* question with regard to such events in the past we have to refer to evidence of this kind. Similarly, we cannot (now) experience events of the future. But to answer the epistemological question with regard to such future events we cannot appeal to their consequences either, since these also lie in the future. Here we have to refer to the present *antecedents* of the future event in question. Thus meteorologists base their statements about tomorrow's weather on the occurrence of high-pressure zones, cold fronts, oceanic depressions, etc., which they can observe in the present.

*'The next king of France will be a German'*

(*a*) Here, again, the *ontological* question relates to a situation in the future. It is not stated, however, when the German will accede to the French throne. It may be next month, or it may be in 200 years' time! Even if we are not told *when* this event will occur, we are told *that* it will occur and we can form some conception of the effect this event would have on our possibilities for action.

(*b*) Here, too, we have to answer the *epistemological* question by referring to possible *antecedents* in the present, such as sociological or political data about France and Germany. Even though we may not be able to find adequate grounds for a knowledge claim with respect to this statement, or even for a claim that this statement is probable, this does not imply that the ontological question cannot be answered: we understand quite well what assurance we have been given regarding the future, even though we have no way of knowing whether this assurance will prove to be true.

*'Jesus Christ will return to judge the living and the dead'*

(*a*) Here the *ontological* question relates to a situation at an unspecified moment in the future. Although not all particulars of this situation have (as yet) been made known to us, and although we have no indication as to when this situation will arise, the context in which we are told of this future situation does not leave us completely in the dark as to what we could or could not do or experience if and when it does occur.

(*b*) In answer to the *epistemological* question one would once again have to refer to Biblical evidence. Even though not everybody will accept this evidence as adequate grounds for a knowledge claim, this has no implications for the *content* of the assurance given here about what one could or could not do or experience at the unspecified moment in the future to which the statement refers.

In summary we may say the following.

(1) Two questions may be asked in respect of any statement that a state of affairs exists/existed/will exist or arises/arose/will arise:

(*a*) the *epistemological question*: what grounds do we have for the truth or falsehood of this statement?

(*b*) the *ontological question*: what is the content of the assurance regarding the possibilities for human action (and experience) given to us in this statement?

(2) To answer either of these two questions one has to refer to a concrete situation in the real world.

(*a*) To answer the *epistemological* question one has to refer to the situation in which one might find grounds for the truth or falsehood of the statement in question.

(*b*) To answer the *ontological* question one has to refer to the situation in which the relevant state of affairs itself would make a difference to the possibilities for action of a favourably situated person.

(3) The situation demanded by *epistemology* (that is, that in which one might find the relevant grounds) must in principle be accessible to *us*. If *we* are to make knowledge claims, *we* must have access to the grounds on which to base these claims. If such grounds could be found only in situations which are inaccessible to us, as in the case of the question whether the dinosaur had a blue tongue, we can never be in a position to know whether the statement in question is true or false. If only some people have access to the relevant evidence (or consider the evidence adequate for a knowledge claim, as in the case of statements about the

resurrection or second coming of Christ), only some people will be able or willing to make a knowledge claim with respect to the statement in question.

(4) The situation required by the *ontological* question (that is, that in which the relevant state of affairs itself would make a difference to the possibilities for human action), need not in principle be accessible *to us*. It is not a matter of *our* possibilities for action, but of those of some or other favourably situated person (cf. all statements about situations in the past). There need not even *actually* have been anyone in the situation in question (compare the statement 'the moon was once part of the earth'). All that is required here is that it should be possible to refer to a situation in which it is *logically* possible for *someone* to be, so that his possibilities for action would be determined by the state of affairs in question *if* he were in that situation. If it is impossible to refer to such a situation we have stripped the 'statement' in question of all factual content. We are then left with a 'statement' such as that of the believer in the story told by Flew (compare section 18.52 above), that a gardener 'exists' whose 'existence' is such that it makes no difference whatsoever to the possibilities for action of anyone at all. In such a 'statement' we have stated nothing.

(5) If we are unable to give an answer to the ontological question with regard to a 'statement' we have not succeeded in making a statement at all. An assurance with no specifiable content is not an assurance. If we make no statement, there is nothing that could be true or false. It is therefore not possible to ask the epistemological question if we are not able to answer the ontological question. But the reverse does not apply. If we can give no (satisfactory) answer to the epistemological question this does not imply that the ontological question cannot be asked and answered. A statement may have factual content, even if we are unable to determine whether or not the statement is true. Logical positivism errs in this respect by attempting to make the factual content of a statement dependent upon its verifiability or falsifiability.

In the light of these conclusions we are now able to clearly formulate and distinguish the ontological question with regard to God's existence from the epistemological question.

*Epistemological question*: In what situation could we find adequate grounds for a knowledge claim with respect to God's existence? *Answer*: Those who claim to know that God exists, usually base this claim on Biblical testimony. In section 19.56 we shall return to the question whether these grounds are adequate.

*Ontological question*: What assurance regarding the possibilities for human action is given to us in the statement that God exists? In other words: in respect of what (logically possible) situation within the real world are we given the assurance that God's existence would make a difference to the possibility for human action?

The question arises here whether we are not making a mistaken assumption, namely that God is an entity among the entities whose existence determines what we can or cannot do in the universe. Is not God the transcendent Origin or Ground of the universe as a whole and thus, by definition, not a part *within* this whole? Does this question not imply a denial of the transcendence of God? If by 'existence' we mean 'being an element in the real world in which man lives and by which his possibilities for action are determined', should we not agree with Paul Tillich that both the affirmation and the denial of God's existence imply a denial of His transcendent being, since by virtue of His nature He transcends all that exists (compare section 17.48)?

In the light of our analysis of the concept 'existence' in chapter 18 we are now able to say more about this problem. In section 18.50 we suggested (1) that we always speak of something *within* some *language game*, and (2) that a condition for being able to speak of something is that we must be able to say that it exists in terms of the criteria of the relevant language game. In other words we cannot speak of something while denying its existence in terms of the criteria of the language game within which we are speaking. We cannot (in the real-world language) say that a pie is sweet while denying that it exists as a pie within the real world. We cannot (within the language game of the fairy tale) say that Cinderella has a stepmother and yet say, *within the same language game*, that Cinderella does not exist. If we wish to speak of something we must, therefore, be able to say within what language game we are speaking of it. By doing so, we indicate at the same time in what sense we must be able to say that it exists. It is clear that we are able to speak of God and that we in fact do so. Therefore the question is: *within what language game do we speak of God?*

(1) If we speak of God within *the real-world language*, we must be able to say in the real-world language that God exists. God's existence is then a *factual existence*, since in the statement 'God exists' we wish (as in any statement in the real-world language) to state a *fact within* the real world. The implication of this is that God is taken to be 'a being beside others and as such a part of the whole of reality. He certainly is

considered its most important part, but as a part and therefore subjected to the structure of the whole.'[9]

The question is whether we are not denying God's *transcendence* when we try to speak of Him in the real-world language. If we wish to maintain that we can speak of God in the real-world language, we must be able to (*a*) specify the sort of situation in the real world in which God's existence is claimed to make a difference to the possibilities for human action, and (*b*) give an answer to the objection that in doing so we are denying God's transcendence.

(2) If we agree with Paul Tillich that this objection is valid, and we nevertheless wish to speak of God, we must be able to (*a*) specify within what other language game we can speak of God; (*b*) show how God's existence is presupposed (or stated) within that language game; (*c*) show in what sort of concrete situations within the real world, we take part in the language game (compare section 18.51 above).

Let us begin by examining this second possibility. The question is therefore within what language game other than the real-world language do we speak of God?

## 19.55 GOD'S EXISTENCE AND THE MEANING OF LIFE

If we cannot speak of God in the real-world language, within what language game can we then speak of Him? What springs to mind is the language game of a *view of life*. Thus, for example, we speak of the God of the Bible within the language game of a Christian view of life, which derives its norms from the Bible. In chapter 10 we urged that within the Christian view of life the God of the Bible is the *primary determinant of meaning*. Speaking of this God therefore has a central place within this language game.

Speaking of God as the primary determinant of meaning raises a special problem. In section 10.27 we argued that something can be a primary determinant of meaning only if it is also descriptively unique. In some way or other it must be completely different from everything else. The most consistent way to maintain God's unique character, would be to say that He had *no descriptive characteristics* in common with His creatures (including man). We would then avoid all *anthropomorphism* when we speak of Him and ascribe no human (or creaturely) characteristic to Him.

St Thomas Aquinas has pointed out, however (*Summa Theologiae* 1, 13,3), that all our descriptive words derive their meaning from our talk about creatures. If, therefore, we can ascribe no creaturely characteristics to God, none of our descriptive words are applicable to Him. Does this imply that we can actually say nothing about God?

The main problem that confronts us when we wish to speak of God as the primary determinant of meaning is, therefore, how can we do justice to His unique character and yet be able to speak about Him?

One possible solution to this problem is that of negative theology: we cannot say what characteristics God does have but we can say what characteristics He does *not* have. He is infinite, non-temporal, incorporeal, etc. By doing this consistently, however, we would simply be saying that none of our descriptive words apply to God. We would ultimately be saying nothing about God; we would merely decline to say anything.

Another possible solution is to argue that the descriptive words that we use in speaking of God are not used literally but *analogically*. The descriptive words apply to God in a way that is not identical but *analogous* to the way they are used of creatures. The characteristics that we ascribe to God with these words are analogous but not identical to the characteristics that we ascribe to creatures in using such words. This solution is an attempt to have it both ways. An analogy is a *partial similarity*. Such an analogous use of descriptive words would therefore imply that God's characteristics are *partly* the same as those of His creatures. In respect of this part, therefore, God would be identical to His creatures and not the Wholly Other that He would apparently have to be if He is to be regarded as the primary determinant of meaning.

At first sight, the following seems to provide a more satisfactory solution to the problem: we do speak of God, but we cannot *describe* Him (that is, ascribe descriptive *characteristics* to Him). As soon as we try to describe Him we fail because we are then ascribing creaturely characteristics to Him. The words that we apply to Him are therefore to be construed as *prescriptive* rather than *descriptive* words: they do not say what characteristics God has but what attitude we as human beings ought to have towards Him. Thus we may say of God that He is worthy of praise, of veneration, that He is holy, etc., or that we ought to obey Him, love Him, trust in Him, honour Him, etc. We also speak of God in parables (parabolic onlooks). Thus we may say that we ought to look on God as a wise Father, as a just Ruler, as a mighty Defender, etc. In these parables God is *not* given the descriptive characteristics of (earthly) fathers, rulers, defenders, etc., but a similarity in *prescriptive properties* is asserted: God is worthy of being treated like a wise father (whom we ought to obey, love, etc.), a just ruler (whom we ought to honour, acknowledge, etc.), a mighty defender (whom we ought to trust, on whom we rely, etc.) Briefly: there is no analogy between God's factual characteristics and those of His creatures. There is, however, an analogy between the attitudes that we ought to have towards God and those appropriate towards His creatures. On the one hand we ought to obey God as we do a father and trust in Him as in a mighty defender. On the other hand there are also differences. The obedience we owe an earthly father is conditional; there are, conceivably, circumstances under which we might have to disobey our earthly father. God, however, is worthy of unconditional obedience. There are no conceivable circumstances under which we would not have to obey Him. Similarly He is also, by contrast with earthly defenders, worthy of unconditional trust. There are no conceivable circumstances under which we would not be able to trust in Him. Briefly: if we speak of God in prescriptive terms within the language game of a view of life, His unique character as the Wholly Other is not questioned because we do not ascribe to Him any of His creatures' characteristics. We do not say what descriptive characteristics God has, but what *attitudes* are proper towards Him.

The following problem arises: how can we adopt attitudes towards a God whom we cannot directly encounter in the world of human experience? In other words: what sense does it have to say that a certain attitude (for example, love or obedience) is appropriate towards God if in the world of our experience we can never meet God to show Him this love or obedience? In reply to this we could say that someone's attitude to something is expressed not only in his acts, conduct, feeling, etc., in respect of the thing concerned, but also in his acts, conduct, feeling, etc., in respect of all other things related to that thing. For instance, someone's sense of responsibility towards his family implies that he is industrious in his daily work (which he sees as a source of his family's livelihood); someone's loyalty to a leader implies that he opposes everybody whom he regards as his leader's rival; someone's love for his children implies that he will fend off anything that he considers dangerous to his children. In the same way our attitude to God finds expression in our attitudes to everything that we relate to God: my love for God is expressed in my love for my neighbour, whom I see as created in God's image; my trust in God finds expression in my faith in the future, which I believe to be in God's hands; my obedience to God finds expression in my obedience to the commandment of love, which I consider to be the will of God. Because the Biblical God is the *primary determinant of meaning* in the Christian's view of life, the meaning of *everything* or every situation in our world is ultimately determined for the Christian by the way this thing or situation is related to God. In this sense the Christian's entire way of life expresses his attitude to the God whom he regards as the primary determinant of meaning.

If our attitude to the God whom we cannot encounter finds expression only in our attitude to the things that we do encounter and can relate to God, the question arises: in what sense is my attitude to God *more* than the sum of my attitudes to all such entities within my world of experience? If my love for God finds expression only in my love for my neighbour, in what sense is love of God *more* than love for my neighbour? If my trust in God finds expression only in my faith in the future, in what sense is trust in God *more* than faith in the future? If my obedience to God finds expression only in my obedience to the commandment of love, in what sense is obedience to God *more* than obedience to the commandment of love? If it is true that the attitude a Christian shows towards God is not different from or more than his total attitude in life in respect of all situations and things that he encounters in his daily experience, the question arises whether this concept of God is not superfluous in a Christian's view of life. Is it not possible to express the Christian view of life, *with no difference in content*, without employing the idea of a transcendent God?

Briefly: in terms of this argument, God functions merely as an idea that enables us to express in words the meaning things have in the world of our experience. We assert the meaning of things in onlooks which relate such things to God. But is it not also possible to ascribe the *same meaning* to something in a direct way, without relating it to a transcendent God? Instead of saying 'I regard the future as being in God's hands', can we not simply say 'I consider it appropriate to have faith in the future'? Instead of saying 'I regard the commandment of love as an expression of God's will for me', can we not simply say 'I regard the commandment of love as authoritative'? In this way we might steer clear of all transcendent metaphysics in the Christian faith without losing anything of the essential content of this faith. The Christian view of life would thus become more *understandable*, because it would express exactly *the same* attitude to life without introducing transcendent metaphysical entities that modern man finds incomprehensible.

If we accept this conclusion we adopt a viewpoint more or less like that defended by Paul Van Buren in his book *The Secular Meaning of the Gospel*. According to Van Buren, religion (including the Christian religion) is primarily a view of the world, of ourselves and of other people from which life as a whole derives meaning and by which our way of life is determined: 'Statements of faith are to be interpreted ... as statements which express, describe or commend a particular way of seeing the world, other men, and oneself, and the way of life appropriate to such a perspective.'[10]

This perspective or view of ourselves and our world is not arbitrarily chosen. The Christian comes to see the world in this way because he has been inspired by the *historical* person of Jesus and through this inspiration strives to model his own way of life on that of Jesus. Jesus is therefore the *norm* from which Christians derive their way of life and in terms of which they evaluate their actions and attitudes. 'The norm of the Christian perspective is the series of events to which the New Testament documents testify, centering in the life, death, and resurrection of Jesus of Nazareth.'[11] This way of life, which we adopt when we are inspired by the person of Jesus, may be described in *secular* terms, that is, in terms derived from *this* world in which we live. We can formulate such a way of life *without* speaking of transcendent metaphysical entities. We should in fact rather not speak of a transcendent God at all, since to modern man the word 'God' is dead.

Van Buren admits that by this reasoning he reduces the Christian faith to its *ethical* dimension (in reply to the question: which way of life is the proper one?) and its *historical* dimension (the historical Jesus, whom we know through the Gospels, as origin of and norm for this new way of life). He denies, however, that this reasoning affects the *content* of the Christian faith. 'Although we have admitted that our interpretation represents a reduction of Christian faith to its historical and ethical dimensions, we would also claim that we have left nothing essential behind.'[12]

One could raise various objections to this view. Let us concede that Van Buren is correct in seeing the Christian faith primarily as a total *attitude to life* or way of life ('a particular way of seeing the world, other men, and oneself, and the way of life appropriate to such a perspective'). The question is, however, whether it is possible (as Van Buren thinks) to formulate this way of life in words *without* using metaphysical terms. Can the meaning that we ascribe to things by relating them to God be formulated *equally well* if we do not speak of God? Can the 'metaphysical' onlooks (by which we indicate the meaning of things by relating them to a metaphysical God) be adequately 'translated' into non-metaphysical onlooks? Or does such a 'translation' alter the concrete *meaning* ascribed to something in such an onlook? Such 'translations' are inadequate in two respects.

(1) Onlooks are always *interrelated* within the context of a particular view of life. The meaning ascribed to something in an onlook is always dependent on its relation to other onlooks since onlooks always qualify each other. The meaning ascribed in every onlook can, therefore, only be grasped in terms of this relation with other onlooks.

Hence, if an onlook is isolated from others (or worse: if we take it out of its context), its concrete sense does not remain unchanged. Consequently no 'translation' can succeed if it ignores this coherence between onlooks.

In chapter 10 we argued that the inner coherence of a view of life is ultimately determined by the *basic conviction* underlying it. The relation between the various onlooks within the Christian view of life is thus ultimately dependent on their relation to the basic conviction, that the God and Father of Jesus Christ is the primary determinant of meaning. It is clear that this basic conviction of the Christian faith cannot be eliminated without affecting the content of the faith in all its aspects.

If, for example, we 'translate' the words 'I look on the future as in God's hands', as 'I consider it appropriate to have faith in the future', we have *severed* this onlook from the context that determines and colours its concrete content, and then the *concrete nature* of this *faith* has been affected. Thus *faith in the future* is given a different content and has quite different implications for my further attitudes when I say 'I have faith in the future because I think that life is more bearable when people are optimistic than when they are pessimistic', or 'I have faith in the future because it is controlled by a despotic God, who could not do without mankind and will therefore see to it that we are not destroyed', or 'I have faith in the future because it is controlled by the almighty Father of Jesus Christ, who has shown us in Christ that He loves His children'.

The following provides a further example. What attitude is appropriate toward our *enemies*? We could *love* them 'that ye may be the children of your Father which is in Heaven: for he maketh his sun to rise on the evil and on the good, and sendeth rain on the just and on the unjust' (Matthew 5:45). The nature of this attitude of *love* toward the enemy is determined by the context: it is coupled with gratitude towards God (who makes His sun rise on sinners like us) and humility (following the example God sets us). We may also treat our enemies with love because we regard this as the will of a vengeful God who demands it from us despotically. This places our love for our enemies in a very different context, thus changing its nature: here it is coupled with fear of the consequences if we hated our enemies and thus brought the anger of a vengeful God upon ourselves. We may also love our enemies because we regard the command to love one's enemies as a pragmatic rule, or a worthwhile ideal. This context again changes the nature of the love said to be appropriate toward one's enemies: here it becomes an ideal, the achievement of which could lead to pride or self-satisfaction.

Briefly: (a) In the Christian way of life the meaning of everything is ultimately determined by the way in which it is related to a transcendent God. (b) Onlooks in which meaning is ascribed to things by relating them to God, cannot be replaced by onlooks that assert the meaning of things directly without relating them to God, for by doing so one would abstract such onlooks from the context that determines their concrete content. (c) We cannot eliminate the 'metaphysical form' without affecting the content. (d) Van Buren's attempt at a *'secular' translation* of the Gospel cannot, therefore, succeed.

(2) There are, furthermore, some attitudes which are appropriate toward God and which cannot be *fully* reduced to attitudes to things which we encounter in the world. These are attitudes that a Christian would have to show in this world but which can be expressed in words only in terms of a relation to God. If, therefore, we try to translate away the word 'God', we can no longer account for these attitudes in our view of life.

For example: 'I am *thankful* to God for my Christian perspective on life, which is a gift from Him'. This 'thanksgiving' is so essentially relational that it cannot be expressed in words if the word 'God' is eliminated. Van Buren does, however, try to translate into secular terms our thanksgiving to God for our freedom as Christians. He writes that that

Thanksgiving may be understood as the expression of the joy of a man who has found a measure of freedom and who sees signs of this freedom in the world about him. Thanksgiving and adoration express his joy and wonder before the fact that the world is and that he is, and that his historical perspective gives him a way of understanding both himself and the world'[13].

What Van Buren has given us here can hardly be called a *translation*. Van Buren simply replaces 'thanksgiving' with 'joy' because thanksgiving cannot be expressed in words without reference to the God to whom such thanksgiving is due. Thanksgiving for my being a Christian is possible only if I regard my being a Christian as a *gift* from God. If, however, I eliminate God the Giver, I can no longer speak of *gifts*, nor of *thanksgiving*. *Joy* is then still possible, but this is no longer the attitude of *thanksgiving*, which is properly derived from the 'historical perspective' found in Christ. *Joy* over my Christian perspective may well be combined with self-satisfaction (or even pride) because I have achieved this perspective on life. Thanksgiving for God's gift, however, implies humility and is therefore at variance with any self-satisfaction or pride.

Briefly: Van Buren's attempt to eliminate all references to a transcendent God from the Christian faith cannot succeed. The content of such a view of life cannot be expressed in words without the metaphysical form. We cannot eliminate God from our talk within the language game of the Christian view of life because He is necessarily presupposed as the centre that determines the meaning of everything. Many relational attitudes of the Christian are necessarily related to this centre and cannot be expressed in words without it. Furthermore this centre determines the unity and coherence of all onlooks for the Christian, and thus determines and colours their concrete *content*.

At the end of section 17.48 we were faced with the question: can we speak of God in the real-world language, in which case we would have to interpret His existence as a *factual existence*? Or can we speak of God only within some language game other than the real-world language? In what sense would we then be able to say that He exists? In this section we have pointed out that within the language game of the Christian view of life we do not merely speak of God, but that we also *have to* speak of Him. We cannot eliminate the word 'God' from our talk within this language game without far-reaching consequences for the *content* of the Christian view of life expressed in this language game.

In what sense, then, is the *existence* of God presupposed in the language game of the Christian view of life? In what sense must we be able to say that God *exists* if He is to provide this view of life with a *centre of meaning* without which we cannot express in words the meaning that things have for the Christian? We are again faced with the choice set out in section 17.48: Does the Christian view of life, in expressing the meaning of our life and of the world in which we live, presuppose a God who exists *factually* as centre of meaning? Is it not possible to ascribe precisely the *same meaning* of things by relating them to an *ideal of God*, without presupposing that this God exists *in fact*?

Let us examine this view more closely. Compare the following speech acts: (1) 'I look on the future as something that can be faced with confidence.' (2) 'I look on the future as being in God's hands.' (3) 'I look on the future *as if* there is a God in whose hands it is.' From our discussion of Van Buren's view it is clear that (1) does not ascribe the same meaning to the future as (2). In this sense we cannot eliminate references to God. In (2) and (3), however, precisely *the same* meaning is ascribed to the future. There is no difference between the attitude said to be appropriate to the future in onlooks (2) and (3). The only difference is that in (3) the future is related to a God of whom it is stated by implication that He does *not* exist in fact but merely as an idea. At the beginning of this section we suggested that we speak of God in onlooks or parables. For example the parable of the Prodigal Son deals with God and compares Him with the father of the prodigal son. The view we are now examining takes a step further by suggesting that God Himself is merely a character in a parable. Not only is God's relation to us like the relation of the father to his prodigal son, so that the attitude we ought to show towards God is like that of the (returning) son to his loving father, but God is seen as existing in the same way as the father in the parable, namely as a character in a *story* and not in reality. The Christian view of life (as, in fact, most views of life) is concerned with a *way of life* which is expressed in these parables; and God is the central figure in these parables. But all these parables are *stories* (or myths, etc.) and not descriptions of states of affairs in the real world. Such stories (myths) are essential for formulating the Christian way of life in words. They cannot, therefore, be eliminated in an attempt to *demythologise* them, as Van Buren has tried to do. But this does not detract from the fact that they are *stories*, and not descriptions of real states of affairs.

This view is defended by someone to whom Van Buren himself refers approvingly, namely *R. B. Braithwaite* in his essay 'An Empiricist's View of the Nature of Religious Belief'.[14] According to Braithwaite, a religious statement is 'the assertion of an intention to carry out a certain behaviour policy, subsumable under a sufficiently general principle to be a moral one, together with the implicit or explicit statement, but not the assertion, of certain stories'. Braithwaite concedes that some of the 'stories' in which a Christian expresses his way of life are also historical, for instance those dealing with the life and death of Jesus of Nazareth. Since it is not plausible to assumt that these reports are mere myths, a Christian will believe that what is said in these reports has really happened. But *to the verbal expression* of the Christian way of life it is not relevant whether or not these stories are true in fact. They are merely the essential *form* in which the Christian expresses his way of life. According to Braithwaite, stories about the origins of the world and about the last judgement as well as those about Jesus' resurrection and ascension are effective means for expressing the Christian way of life and thus also of the meaning of our existence, even though they are merely stories and not reports of real events. In fact, Jesus would have served equally well as an example for our way of life if He had been merely a mythological and not an historical person.

Briefly: Braithwaite agrees with Van Buren that the Christian faith is not concerned with factual statements about reality, but with the *verbal expression of a certain way of life*. But unlike Van Buren, Braithwaite realises that we cannot express this way of life in words without using stories or parables. We cannot eliminate these stories (even though they refer to metaphysical entities and unhistorical events). Some of the stories may be historically true, but this is not relevant to their use in expressing a way of life.

The phrase 'verbal expression of a way of life' is ambiguous. It is only because of this ambiguity that we can succeed in camouflaging the weakness of Braithwaite's argument. This argument is valid only if by 'expressing in words' we mean 'describing'. As soon as we give a wider meaning to it, Braithwaite's position becomes untenable. Let us explain this in more detail.

In section 10.26 we argued that someone's *way of life* is verbally expressed in his *view of life*, that is, 'the total complex of norms, ideals and eschatological expectations in terms of which someone directs and assesses his way of life'. If, therefore, we wish to *describe* someone's way of life we shall have to do so in terms of his norms, ideals and eschatological expectations. Often these norms, ideals and eschatological expectations can only be *described* by means of stories or parables, regardless of whether these stories are believed to be *true*. Thus we are able to describe the norms, ideals and eschatological expectations of the Hindu, for example, only in terms of stories about the various Hindu gods. My description could be quite accurate even though I did not believe these stories to be true. Similarly, the Christian norms, ideals and eschatological expectations could be *described* by means of the various 'stories' told in the Bible, and such a *description* might be quite accurate even if these stories were not regarded as true.

But difficulties arise when I come to formulate my *own* way of life in a view of life. It is then no longer merely a matter of *description*, but also of *subscription*. Braithwaite in fact concedes this by saying that the typical function of all Christian professions of faith is to proclaim the Christian's 'intentions to follow an agapeistic way of life'. But *subscribing* to a way of life is possible only, if we believe that the *factual* presuppositions of this way of life are true. In section 16.46 we pointed out that religious belief cannot be reduced to commitment to a way of life, in contrast to the acceptance of certain factual statements as true. Even if the Christian faith were a matter of prescribing and subscribing to a way of life, and thus of accepting certain prescriptive beliefs, these would always *presuppose* a number of constative beliefs.

This is most clearly seen in the case of eschatological expectations. It is impossible to live in accordance with certain eschatological expectations if one does not believe that these expectations will in fact be realised. It would be absurd to live in accordance with the expectation of a resurrection and a last judgement if one assumed that the resurrection and last judgement were merely stories for which no factual claims were made.

The same difficulty arises with regard to the norms and ideals by which a Christian directs his way of life. We may confine ourselves to two examples. Two characteristic elements of the way of life that a Christian tries to follow are *thanksgiving* and *trust*. Both are attitudes with a *dual directedness*. I am always thankful (1) to someone (2) for something that I regard as a gift from him. My trust is always trust (1) in someone (2) for something that I expect of him. This dual directedness is also found in the thanksgiving and trust that characterise the Christian way of life. Here it is, after all, a matter of thanksgiving to God for all that I consider His benevolent gifts, and trust in God for all that I expect of Him. But fundamental to an expression of thanksgiving and of trust is the factual presupposition that the objects of this dual directedness really exist. Therefore I can be thankful to God for His benevolence only if I believe that God exists in fact and that certain things that exist in fact are the gifts of His benevolence. I can put my trust in God for the things that I expect from Him only if I believe that God exists in fact and that what I expect of Him will in fact be realised by Him.

Briefly: I can *describe someone else's* thanksgiving to and trust in God by using the word 'God', without myself believing that such a God exists in fact. But I cannot *express my own* trust in God and *my own* thanksgiving to God without presupposing that this God exists in fact and not merely as a character in a parable by means of which I formulate my way of life in words. Therefore Braithwaite's attempt to demonstrate that in the framework of the Christian faith it is sufficient to suppose that God exists merely as a character in a story, can hardly succeed.


## 19.56 THE FACTUAL NATURE OF GOD'S EXISTENCE


In section 19.55 we argued that we speak of the Biblical God within the language game of the Christian view of life. Within this language game God is the primary determinant of meaning. The meaning of all things is determined by their relation to God. The concept of God is *necessary* within this language game. We cannot, as Paul Van Buren suggests, do without the word 'God', since we would thereby be eliminating the basic conviction underlying this view of life. This cannot be done without affecting the entire view of life as such.

Since God is the primary determinant of meaning in the Christian view of life, the existence or non-existence of God makes a fundamental difference to the *meaning* that the world in which we live has for the Christian, and thus also a difference to the way of life that we *ought* to pursue in this world. Braithwaite is correct in maintaining that talk of God is necessary to the Christian view of life. He errs, however, in suggesting that for the Christian, God exists as a character in a story, a *symbol* of meaning used in expressing the Christian way of life. On the contrary, God's *factual existence* is a constitutive presupposition of our talk within the language game of the Christian view of life. Within this language game it is claimed not merely that God's existence affects the *meaning* of our world, but also that it makes a *factual* difference to it. God's existence determines not only what we *ought* to do and pursue in the world but also what we *can* do and pursue in it.

If we thus assert the *factual* nature of God's existence, we have to answer two questions that were posed at the end of section 19.54: (1) in what situations and in what way would it make a difference to man's possibilities for action (and not only to the meaning of the world) whether or not God exists factually? (2) Does the view that God exists factually imply a denial of His transcendence as the Wholly Other? In this section we shall try to find an answer to the first question, and in section 19.57 we shall deal with the second.

In what situations and in what way does the Christian claim God's existence to make a difference to our possibilities for action? The main difficulty about answering this question is that we cannot conceive of any situation in the universe where we could *perceive* God or *meet* God. Nelson's column determines our possibilities for action because we can see or bump into it, etc., in Trafalgar Square in London. The Dalai Lama determines our possibilities for action because we could (probably at this moment) meet him in India, shake hands with him, etc. But one cannot conceive of any situation in the universe in which God's existence would make a difference to our possibilities for action in these ways. Therefore the question is whether, and if so how, the existence of a God whom we cannot perceive or encounter can make a difference to our possibilities for action. Is it not, in fact, contradictory to deny on the one hand that we can encounter or perceive God anywhere in the universe, and yet to insist, on the other hand, that He exists factually and therefore determines our possibilities for action?

One possible approach to this problem is the following. It is true that God is not a directly observable entity whom we can encounter somewhere in the universe. We can, however, observe and encounter God's *works* in the universe. Through His works (*per suos effectus*) God's existence does, therefore, affect our possibilities for action. If there were no God, His works would not have been there to determine our possibilities for action.

We could distinguish four aspects of these 'works of God': (1) God is the Creator of all that exists. He is therefore the cause of there being anything (apart from Himself) instead of nothing. If there were no God as a Creator, the entire created universe would not be there to determine our possibilities for action. (2) God is the origin of the order and regularity that we find in nature. If there were no God, there would be no order and regularity in nature to determine the possibilities for human action. (3) In the course of history God has revealed Himself in numerous miracles and signs (for example the exodus and the resurrection of Christ). If there were no God, these miracles and signs would not have been there to determine the possibilities for human action. (4) As Christians we experience the power of God's regenerating grace, by which He changes our lives and makes 'new beings' of us. If there were no God we could not experience His regenerating power in our lives, nor could we observe its effect on the lives of others.

Briefly: even though we cannot observe God directly, His existence does *through His works* make a demonstrable difference to our possibilities for action in this world. Thus the Christian's claim that God exists in fact is not without content.

We have pointed out repeatedly that the ontological and epistemological questions regarding God's existence must be carefully distinguished. The greatest confusions in our dealing with these problems often arise from the fact that these two questions are not clearly distinguished. For the sake of clarity it may therefore be useful first to consider whether an appeal to God's works provides a satisfactory answer to the epistemological question, and then to see whether it is satisfactory to answer the ontological question with such an appeal.

### God's works and the epistemological question

Because we cannot observe God directly, we have to appeal to His works in order to answer the epistemological question regarding His existence ('On what grounds do you claim to know that God exists?'). We *known* God only *per suos effectus*. The various traditional arguments for the existence of God (with the exception of the ontological argument) may therefore be seen as attempts to answer the *epistemological* question by appealing to one of the above-mentioned aspects of God's works. According to the *cosmological argument* we know that God (the Creator) exists because apart from Him there is something (a creation) instead of nothing. According to the *teleological argument* we know that God exists because there is order and regularity in nature instead of chaos. According to the *argument from miracles* we know that God exists because we see his miraculous signs in history. According to the *argument from religious experience* we know that God exists because we experience His regenerating power in our lives.

Appealing to God's works as ground for religious knowledge claims is problematic, however, because our experience of God's works is ambiguous. This ambiguity is very well illustrated by the following examples.[15] Perhaps the greatest event in the history of the people of Israel was the crossing of the Red Sea, for this was, so to speak, the birth of the nation which trekked towards freedom and thus found itself. Previously there was little to tell about this nation because they were still strangers to themselves, living as slaves of the Egyptians. The sudden exodus, the pursuit by the renowned Egyptian chariots – at the time a new form of warfare and as fearsome as the advent of heavy tanks in recent times – and then finally the miraculous and strange crossing of an arm of the sea, during which the swift Egyptian columns were destroyed; all this caused a considerable stir in the world of the time, as we gather from the Biblical reports. The Israelites stood facing the water and were in danger of being hemmed in. But an east wind drove the water back, and in addition a mass of cloud – Jozua later spoke of a bank of mist that formed – lay between the Egyptians and the Israelites. The Israelites trekked through the drained arm of the sea, followed by the Egyptians, whose heavy chariots were soon bogged down in the sand. Both parties noticed the wind and saw the passage before them. But whereas the Egyptians saw only the east wind, it instantly became clear to the Israelites that something more was happening: their miraculous salvation by the strange Power of whom Moses had spoken and who was different from the gods of the Egyptians. Moses had addressed them in the name of the strange divine Power and, standing by the sea, had pointed his rod over the sea as a sign of the decisive events that they were soon to experience. Thus the Egyptians and the Israelites saw virtually the same things, the sea and the wind and the mist, but only the Israelites recognised a liberating Power in these events and moved on, whereas the Egyptians were vanquished. One event followed another, and the Israelites gradually came to know their God, whose significance for them became clear in the history they shared. Something similar occurs in the stories of the New Testament. Here it was the followers of Jesus who did not quite know who their Master was. They and their contemporaries saw the same events, but through quite different eyes. There are reports from which it appears that the opponents of Jesus saw Him performing various miraculous signs, including healings, but they explained this by saying that He had studied under Egyptian magicians who had occult powers. His followers, however, saw something quite different: an astonishingly rich haul of fish, the healing of the sick and many other events which convinced them that He was the one in whom the wildest expectations of Israel's entire history were being fulfilled.

The people of Israel recognised God's work in their crossing of the Red Sea. Similarly, the followers of Jesus recognised God's work in their Master's action. The Egyptians and the opponents of Jesus, however, did not perceive the work of God in these events. There are two main reasons for this ambiguity in man's experience of God's works.

First, the examples show that there is a great difference between the situation in which we see something as the work of God and the situation in which we see that a painting is a work by Picasso or that a building is the work of Plaster, Strutt & Co. We can see Plaster and Strutt's artisans working on the house and from the distinctive style and unmistakable signature one can clearly conclude that a painting was done by Picasso. But one cannot perceive in this way that a certain directly observable phenomenon or event is the work of God, nor can one deduce this from what is directly observable. It is an *impressive* experience when we see something as the work of God. In this regard the Bible speaks of Jahweh's glory (*kabod*) and holiness (*qadosj*), which are recognised in His works. As we pointed out in section 9.25, glory and holiness are impressive characteristics.

D.D. Evans points out[16] that three aspects are involved when the Bible speaks of the glory (*kabod*) of a human being. (1) Sometimes someone's 'glory' refers to his inner nature or character, his inner dignity, majesty, moral strength, etc. (2) More often, however, someone's glory relates to the externally observable characteristics that distinguish him and make him impressive: his wealth, his clothing, his bearing, his shining face and eyes, or his achievements and personal influence, his weight in the community. (3) Sometimes a person's glory relates to the acknowledgement and response of others, the honour or respect they show him. These three aspects apply to both the glory (*kabod*) and the holiness (*qadosj*) of Jahweh. His glory and His holiness relate to His inner nature, to the observable, impressive events and phenomena that are perceived to be expressions of His inner nature, and to the recognition of His glory and holiness by men and by personified nature.

Briefly: God's works are expressions of His glory and holiness. When we perceive something to be the work of God it implies that we recognise God's glory and holiness in that thing. Since this is an impressive experience it does not occur to everyone in equal measure. The Israelites saw their miraculous crossing of the Red Sea as an expression of Jahweh's glory and holiness; the Egyptians saw only the east wind, the sea and the mist. The followers of Jesus recognised God's glory and holiness in the person and acts of their Master, whereas his opponents saw only Egyptian witchcraft. In this sense experiencing God's works is ambiguous.

A second reason for this ambiguity is that in a certain sense the experience of God's works *presupposes* belief in God. The Israelites saw their miraculous crossing of the sea as an act of God – but only in the light of their belief in the strange Power of whom Moses had spoken and who differed from the gods of the Egyptians. The disciples saw in Jesus the one in whom the wildest expectations of Israel's entire history were being fulfilled. But they could see Jesus as such only in the light of these expectations, which they shared. Experiencing God's works induces people to say 'It is Him again!' But they can say so only because it is not the first time they have experienced His impressive works.

Any attempt to *prove* God's existence by appealing to His works is therefore always circular: an attempt to prove God's existence by appealing to an experience which we have only in the light of a belief in God's existence. We claim to know that God (the Creator) exists because we experience His creation. But we experience the universe as creation only in the light of our belief in the Creator. We claim to know that God (the Designer) exists, because we perceive order and regularity in creation. But our conception of order and regularity is determined by the kind of Designer in whose existence we believe. We claim to know that God exists because we see His miracles in history. But events in history can only be *signs* of God in the light of our belief in God's existence. We claim to know that God exists because we experience His regenerating power in our lives and see its effect on the lives of other believers. But this regenerating power is experienced only by those who believe, and it is only in the light of their belief that they see regeneration in the lives of other Christians as the work of God.

Briefly: experiencing God's works is not only an impressive experience, but in addition an experience in the light of faith. In this connection Paul Tillich speaks of the 'theological circle'. A Christian theologian speaks within a circle: he speaks about faith in the light of faith. The question is whether this is not a vicious circle since the Christian bases his claim that God exists on his experience of God's works, though he can experience something as God's work only in the light of his belief that God exists. If, in this sense one can find faith only by the light of faith, it is in principle impossible for anyone to enter this circle from outside!

The impression that this is a vicious circle arises from a confusion between (1) the impressive experience by which someone is convinced, and (2) the impressive tradition in the light of which he interprets this experience. The impressive experiences by which people come to believe may differ widely. In principle it is different for every believer. Someone may come to believe because he is inspired by the glory and holiness of Jesus of Nazareth. It may also be that he recognises this glory and holiness in some event or situation or person that he encounters in his own life. Thus someone might find the impressive experience of God's glory and holiness in the way some Christians live. We have seen that God's glory and holiness are also revealed in their acknowledgement by people. In the Christian tradition the saints are people in whose lives God's holiness (and glory) is manifested. In Matthew 5 we read that Jesus commands believers to live in such a fashion that others might recognise God's glory and holiness in their lives. 'Let your light so shine before men, that they may see your good works, and glorify your Father which is in heaven' (Matthew 5 : 16).

In the epistemological sense, the achievement of faith is more than experiencing the impressive character of some situation or event, or of the lives of the saints, or of the Christian community, or of the person of Jesus of Nazareth. One has to see these impressive events as part of an impressive tradition, so that one may say of that which inspires one personally: It is He once again – as it was He who has repeatedly revealed Himself in Israel's exodus, in Jesus, in the Church through the ages, and in the lives of all the saints.

The question 'How do you know that the rhinoceros exists?' could be a request for a demonstration or proof on grounds that are acceptable to the questioner. One could answer this question by taking the questioner to the zoo. The question 'How do you know that God exists?' cannot be answered by demonstration or proof but only by the believer testifying to his own impressive experiences on which he bases his claim that God exists, and to the impressive tradition within which he interprets his experiences. The believer might, for instance, answer this question by saying 'I know that God exists because I recognise His glory and holiness in Jesus as well as in the lives of His followers, for whom He is the primary determinant of meaning.' Although arguments for the existence of God *per suos effectus* are, therefore, ineffectual as *proof*, they could still be interpreted as a testimony in which the believer provides an answer to the epistemological question: on what grounds do *you* claim to know that God exists?

### God's works and the ontological question

Although we cannot see or encounter God in our world in the way we can see and encounter Nelson's column in Trafalgar Square, we may observe and encounter the things and events that are held to be God's works. We have suggested that a reference to these works of God, despite their ambiguity, is in one sense an adequate answer to the epistemological question about God's existence. But such a reference is not an adequate answer to the ontological question about God's existence. This becomes clearer if we compare the following assertions:

1. 'God exists'.
2. 'The universe exists, there is order and regularity in nature, there have been extraordinary events in history, and some Christians live impressive lives as a result of a regenerating power that they experience in their lives.'

In each of these statements we give our hearers an assurance regarding the way in which our possibilities for action are determined. But since the two statements do not contain the same assurance, they state different facts. In other words, the fact that God exists determines our possibilities for action in a different way from the facts stated in the second assertion. If that were not so, the statement that 'God exists' would say no more and nothing else than the other statement. The second statement does state as fact the *consequences* of God's acts and thus of God's existence, but the fact that God exists cannot be *reduced* to the facts that are recognised as consequences of His existence. If God's existence is something different from the existence of the facts that we recognise as consequences of His existence, then we must be able to state the difference between the way in which we claim that God's existence determines our possibilities for action and the way in which we claim that they are determined by the consequences of His existence.

Briefly: even if God's works can convince us of His existence, His existence must be distinguished from the existence of His works. The way in which His existence determines our possibilities for action must therefore also be distinguishable from the way in which they are determined by the existence of His works. An appeal to Gods works is therefore inadequate as answer to the ontological question regarding God's existence.

*God's existence and eschatology*

In what way does God's existence determine our possibilities for action, if we cannot conceive of any situation in our human life-world in which we might see or encounter Him? John Hick tries to answer this question with an appeal to eschatology in his essay, 'Theology and Verification'.[17] Hick explains his answer with the following story:

> Two men are travelling together along a road. One of them believes that it leads to a Celestial City, the other that it leads nowhere; but since this is the only road there is, both must travel it. Neither has been this way before, and therefore neither is able to say what they will find around each next corner. During their journey they meet both with moments of refreshment and delight, and with moments of hardship and danger. All the time one of them thinks of his journey as a pilgrimage to the Celestial City and interprets the pleasant parts as encouragements and the obstacles as trials of his purpose and lessons in endurance, prepared by the king of that city and designed to make of him a worthy citizen of the place when at last he arrives there. The other, however, believes none of this and sees their journey as an unavoidable and aimless ramble. Since he has no choice in the matter, he enjoys the good and endures the bad. But for him there is no Celestial City to be reached, no all-encompassing purpose ordaining their journey; only the road itself and the luck of the road in good weather and in bad. During the course of the journey the issue between them is not an experimental one. They do not entertain different expectations about the coming details of the road, but only about its ultimate destination. And yet when they do turn the last corner it will be apparent that one of them has been right all the time and the other wrong. Thus although the issue between them has not been experimental, it has nevertheless from the start been a real issue. They have not merely felt differently about the road; for one was feeling appropriately and the other inappropriately in relation to the actual state of affairs. Their opposed interpretations of the road constituted genuinely rival assertions, though assertions whose assertion-status has the peculiar characteristic of being guaranteed retrospectively by a future crux.

Hick uses this story as a *parable* to explain the Christian eschatology and the way in which this relates to our lives in the present. The parable deals with the distinction between an existence *in via*, that is, in our life-world as we experience it now, and an existence *in patria*, that is, in the fulfilment of God's kingdom in which, in terms of the Christian faith, we shall share at the resurrection.

In principle there is no difference of opinion between the beliver and the non-believer about the factual situations that they encounter or observe *in via*. The two travellers do not entertain different expectations regarding the details of the journey around the next corner. The believer, and the non-believer do, however, differ in their eschatological expectations. The believer believes in the resurrection and in the fulfilment of God's kingdom. The non-believer expects something quite different or nothing at all. Their claims therefore differ with regard to the facts of a possible life *in patria*. In chapter 10 we suggested that a person's eschatological expectations help to determine the meaning that life has for him. The difference in their eschatological expectations therefore also implies that the believer and the non-believer will disagree on the meaning of life *in via*. In Hick's parable one traveller sees the journey as a pilgrimage to a Celestial City, the other sees it as an unavoidable and aimless ramble.

The believer claims to know about the future kingdom and of the existence of the King of that kingdom because of certain events and phenomena *in via*, which he sees as impressive signs (revelations) of the King and His kingdom. We have seen, however, that these signs are ambiguous. It will always be possible to fail to see such events and phenomena as signs and thus to remain unconvinced of the coming kingdom and of the existence of a King of this kingdom. An appeal to such signs is, therefore, inadequate as an unambiguous verification of faith. It can serve only as testimony to that on which the beliver himself bases his knowledge claim. The believer, however, assumes that there will be a situation *in patria* in which his faith (founded on ambiguous signs) will be verified unambiguously. In this sense an appeal to eschatology is relevant to the epistemological question.

Is an appeal to eschatology relevant to the ontological question too? In respect of the Christian's eschatological expectations it clearly is, because such eschatological expectations are factual expectations. How the Christian lives in the present depends in part on his expectation that at the end of the journey a factual situation will arise in which his possibilities for action will be determined by the resurrection and by the fulfilment of God's kingdom. In specifying the factual content of these eschatological expectations the Christian will have to refer to the situation that, in his view, will arise *in patria*. The question, however, is whether he can also refer to this eschatological situation when specifying the factual content of his claim that God exists. The Christian view of life does not claim that God can be met or observed *in via*. God's existence is not said to make a difference to our possibilities for action *in via* in this sense. But it is part of the Christian claim that man will see God in some way or other *in patria*. Do we have here a situation in which God's existence would make a difference to our possibilities for action, and thus an answer to our ontological question?

The problem with this answer is that it reduces God's existence to an eschatological event. God *will* exist in the eschatological future. His existence will make a difference to our possibilities for action *in patria*. This is not an adequate representation of the Christian's claim regarding God's existence. In the Christian view of life it is not merely maintained that God will exist (and that we shall meet Him *in patria*) or that He existed in the past (and may have been met by Moses on Mount Sinai); it is also claimed that God exists *now*. We are therefore left to face the question of the content of *this* claim. In what way does God's existence make a difference to our possibilities for action *in the present*, even though we cannot observe or meet Him in the present?

### God's existence and living in the sight of the Lord

We cannot meet or observe God *in via*. In terms of the Christian faith we do, however, encounter God's works, the consequences of His actions, *in via*. The believer is always in some way or other personally involved in what he sees as God's work. For this reason we can never say in a disinterested way that something is the work of God, as we could say in a disinterested way that a house was built by Plaster, Strutt & Co., or that a shower of rain is the result of a cold front. It would be absurd for a believer to say: 'I know that is the work of God, but it does not concern me.' God's works always concern us because His acts are always directed at us in some way or other.

God's acts are directed at us in various respects. (1) As suggested above, they are impressive manifestations of His glory and holiness. In His acts God reveals His glory and holiness *to us*. (2) God's acts are saving acts. Whatever He does is done for the good of mankind. Thus the believing traveller in Hick's parable saw the prosperity he enjoyed along the way as encouragement and his adversities as trials of his purpose and lessons in endurance. Both prosperity and adversity were *gifts* prepared for him by the King with the object of making him a more worthy citizen of the Celestial City when he arrives there. In this sense God's works are gifts of grace and His acts are acts of salvation, directed at those for the good of whom they are performed. (3) The believer interprets God's acts of salvation in the context of the *covenant*. This means, on the one hand, that God's gifts are seen by the believer as signs of God's faithfulness to His promises. Thus regularity in nature, for example, is frequently interpreted in the Bible as an expression of God's faithfulness to His covenant. 'For ever, O Lord, thy word is settled in heaven. The faithfulness is unto all generations: thou hast established the earth, and it abideth. They continue this day according to thine ordinances: for all are thy servants' (Psalm 119 : 89-91). Through His acts God reaffirms His promises. On the other hand God's covenant gifts are always seen by the believer as bound up with His commandments. The believer regards his own life not only as a gift but also as a *commission* to obey, to serve and to love God.

It is clear that God's acts cannot be seen as mere exercises of causal power. Through His acts God also reveals His glory and holiness, manifests His love and faithfulness and calls upon the believer to serve and obey. Within the framework of the Christian faith the acknowledgement that something is the work of God or an act of God is, therefore, not an existentially neutral statement that God has brought about a causal effect. Such acknowledgement of God's acts is, furthermore, an acknowledgement of God's glory and holiness by honouring and worshipping His person, a profession of thanksgiving for His gifts and of trust in His promises, and a commitment to obedience and service in response to the injunctions of His covenant. The Christian community expresses this acknowledgement of God's acts in liturgy. In response to the proclamation of God's works the believer worships God's person, professes his gratitude for God's gifts, expresses his trust in God's promises and commits himself to the service of God. But for the Christian these actions are not confined to the liturgy. We could also say that the Christian's entire way of life should be characterised by the elements of honouring God, trusting in God, thanksgiving to God and obedient service to God. In the Heidelberg Catechism this entire way of life is in fact defined as a life of thanksgiving. All that the Christian does should be most profoundly an expression of thanksgiving to God.

In this regard, however, we should avoid a possible misconception. I can express my gratitude for all that I have received from my late parents. I cannot now, however, give them thanks, because they are no longer alive. The Heidelberg Catechism calls the Christian's life a life of thanksgiving in this latter sense. All that the Christian does should be a form of thanksgiving 'in the sight of the Lord'.

In section 19.55 we discussed R.B. Braithwaite's view that the Christian way of life is quite possible without a belief in God's factual existence; that we need God only as a symbol to express this way of life in words. This is, however, untenable if we are concerned with a life of thanksgiving 'in the sight of the Lord'. One of the constitutive conditions for the possibility of thanksgiving is that the one to whom one gives thanks must exist. It is logically equally impossible to thank someone who does not exist, as it is to open a door that does not exist, or to bump into a non-existent column in Trafalgar Square. In this sense the existence of God is a constitutive condition for the entire Christian way of life, as a life of thanksgiving 'in the sight of the Lord'. If God did not exist it would be logically impossible to thank Him or to pledge Him obedience, or to praise or worship Him, or to show our love for Him. It is not so much a matter of the Christian way of life being *appropriate* because God exists; it is, rather, (logically) *possible* only if God exists.

We may ask ourselves whether we have not now found a satisfactory answer to the ontological question with regard to God's existence. Within the Christian view of life it is held that God exists in fact, and therefore that His existence makes a difference to our possibilities of action. It now appears that the entire Christian way of life as a life of thanksgiving 'in the sight of the Lord' is (logically) possible only if God exists. Have we not found here a way in which God's existence makes a difference to our possibilities for action at every moment in the most comprehensive sense?

It might be objected that the *belief* that God exists, and not the *existence* of God, is a constitutive condition for the possibility of thanking God, etc. It would be contradictory to say: 'I thank God, even though I do not believe that He exists', or: 'John thanks God, even though he does not believe that God exists'. It is not contradictory, however, to say that someone else is thanking a God that according to him does exist but that you do not believe to exist. Thus a phenomenologist of religion who is not a Hindu and therefore does not believe in the existence of Shiva might well state without any contradiction that the Hindu devote themselves to serving Shiva, or that they give thanks to the (non-existent) Shiva in their prayers.

Briefly: it is not contradictory for someone to give thanks to a non-existent God, as long as he believes that this God does exist. It follows that God's existence does not determine our possibilities for action in this sense and that this answer to the ontological question on God's existence is unsatisfactory.

But this objection is based on a misconception of what the phenomenologist of religion does when describing a Hindu's worshipping. If a Hindu believer said 'O Shiva, I thank thee', he would be doing what he *claims* to be a successful expression of thanksgiving because its constitutive factual presuppositions (including the assumption that Shiva exists) were true. If the equally believing son of this Hindu said, 'My father gives thanks to Shiva', he would not only be *reporting* his father's speech act; he would also be expressing *agreement* with his father's claim that such an expression of thanksgiving was successful because its constitutive factual presuppositions were true. The phenomenologist of religion, however, is performing a purely descriptive activity. He is merely *reporting* what the Hindu purports to be doing and what presuppositions are involved in the Hindu's activity. As a phenomenologist he expresses no opinion on the truth of these presuppositions, n or on the validity of the Hindu's claim. The phenomenologist would merely be trying to say the following. 'In his utterance the Hindu does something that he claims to be a successful expression of thanks and in which he presupposes, *inter alia*, that Shiva exists. As a phenomenologist I am merely reporting this claim and this presupposition. As a *non-Hindu*, however, I do not accept the validity of this factual presupposition and I therefore deny the validity of his claim. He *thinks* that he is successfully giving thanks, but he is mistaken.'

Briefly: it is possible to thank God only if He exists. It is, therefore, absurd to claim that one is giving thanks to God unless one believes in the truth of the assumption that God exists. It is equally absurd to *concur* with someone's claim that he is thanking God unless one accepts the truth of the assumption that God exists. The Christian *can* do all that he claims to be doing 'in the sight of the Lord' only if God exists in fact. If God did not exist the Christian would be under the *illusion* of doing these things; in fact he would not be doing them.

In this section we have tried to draw a clear distinction between the epistemological and the ontological questions with regard to God's existence and to suggest ways in which these two questions might be answered with regard to the Christian faith. These answers may be summed up in three points.

(1) The Christian claims that God exists in fact and that this determines our possibilities for action in such a way that we can act 'in the sight of the Lord' in the present. If God did not exist in fact this would be impossible. This answers the ontological question.

(2) The Christian bases this claim on the impressive revelation of God in His works. But since this revelation is ambiguous, not everybody would consider it an adequate ground for a knowledge claim. Hence not everybody will agree with the Christian's claim that he is successfully acting 'in the sight of the Lord'.

(3) On the grounds of the same impressive revelation the Christian also claims that *in patria* there will be a situation in which it will be unambiguously clear to everyone that God has always existed, so that the Christian has not lived under an illusion *in via* but did indeed succeed in acting 'in the sight of the Lord'. These last two points answer the epistemological question.

## 19.57 THE WHOLLY OTHER

Within the context of the Christian faith it is therefore assumed that God is not merely a character in a story told by prophets, but that He exists *in fact* and therefore forms part of the total life-world by which man's possibilities for action are determined. In section 19.56 we tried to show that this is no empty assumption. It does have a content which can be defined in terms of human possibilities for action. We are now left with the question whether this assumption does not contradict the doctrine of God's transcendence. Is Paul Tillich not perhaps correct in arguing that in terms of this assumption God is seen as 'a being beside others and as such a part of the whole of reality. He certainly is considered its most important part, but as a part and therefore subjected to the structure of the whole'?[18] Does this not deny God's character as the Wholly Other?

In section 10.27 we suggested that something can be the primary determinant of meaning only if it is also factually unique. For this reason the Christian claim that the God of the Bible is the primary determinant of meaning, implies the further claim that this God is also unique in all factual respects. But if God's being different were made absolute, it would imply that God is so different from all reality that He can no longer be real. A God who stands outside all reality would be unique, but would be so unreal that He could not effectively determine meaning for men. The question is, therefore: how can we conceive of God's being different without denying His reality? With regard to God's existence, this question may be formulated as follows: how can we hold without contradiction that God exists *uniquely,* without denying that He exists *in fact?*

To answer this question, theology has traditionally held that God's (factual) existence differs from that of all other factually existing entities in the following ways: God's existence is (1) necessary and not contingent, (2) eternal and not temporal, (3) omnipresent, and (4) independent from everything else. These aspects have consequences for (5) the nature of belief in and doubt about God's existence. Let us examine these five points more closely.

## Necessity (necessitas)

In his third proof of God's existence (*Summa Theologiae,* I, 2, 3) Thomas Aquinas distinguishes between entities that exist contingently and those that exist necessarily. All about us we see things coming into existence and dying away. According to St Thomas such things can exist, but at a given moment it is also possible for them not to exist. Both existence and non-existence are among their possibilities. In this sense their existence is *contingent.* God's existence, however, is different because for God it is impossible not to exist. His existence is *necessary.* But it is not clear what St Thomas means by saying that it is impossible for God not to exist. In what sense is this impossible?

In the third chapter of his *Proslogion* St Anselm draws a similar distinction. The non-existence of things around us is conceivable. God's existence, however, is different because His non-existence is inconceivable. God's non-existence is, therefore, impossible in the sense that it is *inconceivable.* But in what sense is it inconceivable? Are our powers of imagination inadequate here, so that it is not possible for us to imagine God's non-existence? Or is God's non-existence inconceivable because the statement 'God does not exist' is a contradiction? Is God's existence necessary because the statement 'God exists' is necessarily true? In what sense would this statement be necessarily true?

How we answer this last question depends on how we use the word 'God'. The word is ambiguous in an important sense. It is sometimes used like a proper name and sometimes like a descriptive predicate.

By a 'proper name' we mean the kind of names J. S. Mill analyses in the first chapter of his *A System of Logic,* that is, purely referential symbols with no descriptive content. According to Mill such names have no connotation, but rather a denotation with only one member. Such names may be used to *refer* to the person concerned ('This is Peter's book', 'Peter accompanied me yesterday') or to *address* him ('Peter, are you coming along?'). But since they have no descriptive content they give us no information about the person concerned (except that he can be referred to or addressed with this name). In the Bible the word 'God' is often used as an alternative name for Him who is also called Jahweh. Thus Jahweh is referred to with the word 'God' ('In the beginning God created the heaven and the earth') or addressed with it ('God, have mercy upon us'). On the other hand the word 'God' is also used as a descriptive predicate. In the statement 'Jahweh is God' the word 'God' is used to give information about Jahweh and not to refer to or address Jahweh. What, then, is the logical status of the word 'God'? Is it a proper name or a descriptive term?

Nelson Pike[19] argues convincingly that we are here faced with a pseudo-dilemma. According to Pike the word 'God' serves as a certain kind of descriptive term, namely a *title* term, designating the function of somebody having this title. The term 'mayor', for example, is such a title term, which serves as a form of address and as a referential symbol, but may also be used descriptively to say what function somebody fulfils. I may for instance *describe* Charlie Chainbearer as 'the Mayor' and also *address* him as 'Mr Mayor' or *refer* to him as 'the Mayor'. Let us follow Pike and interpret the word 'God' not as a proper name but as a *title term,* that is, as designating the function of the one who is the primary determinant of meaning. With St Anselm we may then define the word 'God' as 'that than which nothing greater is conceivable'. When we say that someone is God we are saying that He is that than which nothing greater is conceivable. The word 'Jahweh' is distinct from the word 'God' because it is not a title term but the *name* that we use to refer to or address the One who is, in terms of Biblical faith, the primary determinant of meaning. In the light of this distinction we can ask two questions with regard to God's 'necessary existence'. (1) In what sense is the statement 'God exists' necessarily true? (2) In what sense is the statement 'Jahweh exists' necessarily true?

Certain things are true of a functionary by virtue of his fulfilling his function. If they were not true he could not be said to be fulfilling this function. If someone is the King of England he is (by virtue of his office) the head of state. If such a person were not the head of state he could not be the King either. He might be a former king or a pretender to the throne, but not the King. 'Being head of state' forms part of the meaning of 'being King'. It would therefore be contradictory to say that someone is the King but not the head of state. The statement 'The King of England is the head of state' is necessarily true, because it could not be denied without contradiction. To be the Mayor of Oxford, someone has to fulfil certain conditions; if he does not fulfil them, he cannot be the Mayor. One of the conditions is that he must exist in reality, that is, that he is not a fictitious person. It would therefore be contradictory to say that someone is the Mayor of Oxford but that he does not really exist. The statement 'If someone is the Mayor of Oxford he exists in reality' is necessarily true, because it cannot be denied without contradiction.

In section 19.55 we tried to show that it is by definition impossible for a person who does not really exist to be the primary determinant of meaning in the sense in which the Christian believes that Jahweh is the primary determinant of meaning. Therefore we cannot say without contradiction that someone is God and yet deny that He exists in fact. St Anselm's ontological argument is plausible for this reason. In his *Proslogion* St Anselm examines the logical implications of saying that Jahweh is God ('*aliquid quo majus nihil cogitari potest*'). The first implication he notes is that one cannot deny without contradiction that Jahweh exists, because by definition someone can be '*aliquid quo majus nihil cogitari potest*' only if this someone exists in reality and not merely as a fiction of the human mind. 'Existing in reality' is one of the conditions for fulfilling the function of '*aliquid quo majus nihil cogitari potest*'. In this sense the statement 'God exists' is necessarily true and cannot be denied without contradiction.

The statements 'The King of England is the head of state', 'The Mayor of Oxford exists in fact' and 'God exists in fact' are all three *necessarily* true only when we construe them as statements about a *function* and not about a person. The terms 'the King', 'the Mayor' and 'God' in these examples all refer to functions and not to possible functionaries. That these statements are true in respect of the functions does not imply that there really exist functionaries who fulfil these functions. From the fact that only a really existing person can be '*aliquid quo majus nihil cogitari potest*' it does not follow that someone also really exists to fulfil this function.

Briefly: if the statement 'God exists' is construed as a statement about a function, it is necessarily true in the sense that it cannot be denied without contradiction, but this has no implications for the question of whether there is someone fulfilling this function.

The statement 'Jahweh exists' is not a statement about a function but one about Him of Whom the Christian says that He fulfils the function of being the primary determinant of meaning. This statement is not necessarily true in the way in which 'God exists' is necessarily true. Many people deny that Jahweh does in fact exist. According to them Jahweh exists only as an idea in the minds of believers or as a character in stories told by prophets. Such a denial of Jahweh's factual existence may be erroneous, but is it not contradictory. Therefore Jahweh's existence is not logically necessary. There is, however, another sense in which Jahweh's existence is necessary. J.J.C. Smart explains this by way of an example from physics.[20]

According to Smart it is not *logically* necessary that light should have a constant velocity in a vacuum. We may deny without contradiction that this is the case. Yet this proposition is so fundamental to all current physical theory that we cannot deny it without rejecting or at least radically revising all current physical theory. *Within current physical theory* this proposition cannot be denied without contradiction. In this sense the proposition that light has a constant velocity in a vacuum is not logically necessary but *physically* necessary.

The factual existence if Jahweh is not *logically* necessary either. But the statement that Jahweh exists in fact is so fundamental to the Christian view of life that we cannot deny it without rejecting or very radically revising this entire view of life. *Within the framework of the Christian view of life* this statement cannot be denied without contradiction. In this sense the statement that Jahweh exists in fact is not logically necessary but *theologically* necessary.

Perhaps St Anselm has succeeded in demonstrating in his *Proslogion* only that Jahweh exists necessarily in *this* sense. His entire argument is founded upon a belief in Jahweh as '*aliquid quo majus nihil cogitari potest*'. At the beginning of chapter II he professes: 'We believe that Thou art something than which nothing greater can be conceived'. St Anselm draws the conclusion that *within the framework of this confession of faith* the factual existence of Jahweh cannot be denied. In this sense Jahweh's non-existence is inconceivable within the framework of the Christian faith.

Briefly: the existence of Jahweh differs from the existence of the things around us firstly in being necessary within the context of our faith. Within this framework the things around us are contingent. It would not be in conflict with our faith to say that they do happen to exist but that we can also imagine the world without them. Within the framework of our faith their non-existence is conceivable whereas the non-existence of Jahweh is not.

### Eternity (aeternitas)

According to the Christian tradition the second difference between Jahweh's existence and that of all else is that Jahweh exists eternally and not temporally. Like His factual existence, Jahweh's eternity is also a *necessary* (or essential) characteristic in the sense defined above. If Jahweh were not eternal He would not be God. Within the framework of the belief that Jahweh is God one cannot deny, without contradiction, that He is eternal.

In what sense does the Christian faith maintain that Jahweh exists *eternally*? In chapter XIX of his *Proslogion* St Anselm writes as follows about Jahweh's eternity: 'Therefore didst Thou not exist yesterday, nor wilt Thou exist tomorrow, but Thou *art* yesterday, today, and tomorrow. Indeed Thou dost not exist yesterday, today or tomorrow, but Thou art absolutely beyond all time. For yesterday, today and tomorrow are entirely within time, but Thou art not within time'. According to this conception Jahweh exists timelessly, or 'absolutely beyond all time', in the sense that no temporal terms (yesterday, today, tomorrow) apply to Him. According to Schleiermacher,[21] Jahweh's timelessness implies that His existence can neither be localised temporally, nor does it have temporal duration. Dating predicates (yesterday', 'pre-Reformation', 'in the next decade', etc.) and predicates of duration ('from now until next year', 'for the past 500 years', etc.) do not apply to Jahweh.

The nature of this timelessness is perhaps best illustrated with reference to the existence of a number in a numeral system. There is a prime number (11) between 9 and 13. The existence of this prime number is timeless in the sense that it is absurd to ascribe temporal predicates to it. It would be absurd to say, for instance, that this prime number between 9 and 13 was also there yesterday at midday, or that it has been there for the past 500 years, or that it will still be there by the end of this century. Numbers are simply not the sort of entities to which such temporal predicates can be applied.

If we say that Jahweh is a timeless being, we maintain unambiguously that He is different. Timeless beings exist in a completely different sense from temporal entities. But it is questionable whether we are in this way doing justice to the Christian belief regarding Jahweh's existence. For example, a timeless being cannot act, because action can always be localised temporally, whereas Jahweh called Abraham from Ur before He led Israel out of Egypt, and He made Israel wander about the desert for forty years before He allowed them to enter the promised land. A timeless being cannot respond to human actions, because such responses always occur temporally after the actions. Jahweh, however, punished Israel for their sins and hears the prayers of His children. A timeless being can make no promises, because promises are always made before they are fulfilled. Jahweh, however, is a God of the covenant who always remains faithful to the promises He once made under the covenant. It is clear that we can hardly call a timeless being a person, since he can neither act nor respond to the actions of people. To the Biblical faith, however, it is essential that God should be personal. Furthermore, we cannot say that a timeless being exists in fact. A being that exists in fact is by definition a being that determines our possibilities for action, and these are all possibilities for action in time. Briefly: according to the Christian faith Jahweh exists eternally, but this eternity cannot adequately be construed as timelessness.

Jahweh's eternity has more to do with the fact that there are no temporal limits to His existence. According to the Christian faith Jahweh exists in fact as a determinant of the possibilities for human action. According to this faith there has never been a moment, nor could there ever be one, when His existence did not determine the possibilities for man's actions. If there had been people fifty million years ago they would have been able to live in the sight of the Lord. In this sense Jahweh's existence is eternal and therefore different from the existence of everything else.

## Omnipresence (omnipraesentia)

According to the Christian faith Jahweh's existence is not only temporally but also spatially infinite. In section 19.56 we pointed out that Jahweh does not exist as an entity that we can observe or encounter. Such entities determine our possibilities for action in places where we can observe or encounter them. In this sense their existence is spatially limited. According to the Christian faith Jahweh determines our possibilities for action in the sense that we can live in His sight. There is no possible place, however, where one would not be in the sight of Jahweh.

> Whither shall I go from thy spirit? Or whither shall I flee from thy presence? If I ascend up into heaven, thou art there: if I make my bed in hell, behold, thou art there. If I take the wing of the morning, and dwell in the uttermost parts of the sea; even there shall thy hand lead me, and thy right hand shall hold me. If I say, Surely the darkness shall cover me; and the night shall be light about me. Even the darkness hideth not from thee, but the night shineth as the day: the darkness and the light are both alike to thee. (Psalm 139 : 7-12)

Like His eternity, Jahweh's omnipresence is an essential characteristic of Him. If He were not omnipresent He could not be God in the way the Christian believes Him to be God. Within the framework of the Christian faith Jahweh's omnipresence cannot be denied without contradiction.

### Independence (aseitas)

We often ask for an explanation of the existence of something. 'How did *x* come to exist?' and 'What is the cause of *x*'s existence?' are demands for such an explanation. These demands for an explanation are meaningful only if they meet two conditions. First, we can meaningfully ask for an explanation of the existence of things only if we believe that they do in fact exist. It is absurd to ask for an explanation of the existence of non-existent things. For this reason an unbeliever can never ask for an explanation of Jahweh's existence. 'How did Jahweh come to exist?' and 'What is the cause of Jahweh's existence?' are absurd questions for those who do not believe that He exists.

Second, we ask for an explanation of the existence of something only if we consider it *possible* that it might not exist. 'How does it come about that there is a path through the forest?' is a meaningful question only if we consider it possible that there might not have been such a path. The Christian, too, cannot ask for an explanation for Jahweh's existence, since he believes that Jahweh exists eternally and has therefore neither come into being at some moment, nor will His existence come to an end. It would be absurd to ask for the cause of something's origin if it never came into being, or about the cause of the possible destruction of something that will in fact never come to an end. For the believer God's existence has no cause. In fact, as the Creator of heaven and earth He is the ultimate cause of the existence of everything else.

Briefly: Jahweh's eternity implies His *aseitas* or independence. Neither for His existence nor for His survival is He dependent upon some or other cause. Like His eternity, His independence is not logically necessary, but it is theologically so. Within the framework of the Christian faith the independence of Jahweh's existence cannot be denied without contradiction.

## Doubt and despair

It is theologically necessary that Jahweh should exist factually, eternally, omnipresently and independently. This means that one could deny that Jahweh exists in this manner only if one rejected the basic conviction underlying the Christian faith, namely the conviction that Jahweh is God. Doubt about Jahweh's existence is therefore essentially different from doubt about the existence of anything else. I shall not lie awake at night because I doubt the existence of living beings on other planets. This kind of doubt does not affect my existence. But doubting the existence of Jahweh implies despairing of the basic conviction by which the Christian directs, evaluates and gives meaning to his entire life.

We therefore come to the conclusion that a belief in Jahweh's factual existence is not in conflict with the conviction that He is the Wholly Other, the primary determinant of meaning. On the contrary this basic conviction necessarily presupposes that Jahweh exists in fact as the One whom we can thank for His acts of salvation, can trust, obey, love − briefly: in whose sight we can live.

# Notes and References

PART ONE: CONCEPTUAL INQUIRY

1.  J.L. Austin, *How to do Things with Words* (Oxford, 1962).
2.  Gilbert Ryle, *The Concept of Mind* (London, 1949) p. 102.
3.  Ibid., p. 183.
4.  Austin, *How to do Things with Words*, p. 151.
5.  R.M. Hare, *Freedom and Reason* (Oxford, 1963) pp. 59 ff.
6.  John Locke, *An Essay Concerning Human Understanding*, book 3, ch. 2.
7.  Gilbert Ryle, *Collected Papers*, vol. II (London, 1971) p. 407.
8.  Ludwig Wittgenstein, *Philosophical Investigations* (Oxford, 1953) I, 11.
9.  Peter Geach, *Mental Acts* (London, 1957) p. 12.
10. *Ibid.*, p. 14.
11. Wittgenstein, *Philosophical Investigations*, I. 19.
12. Quoted by Paul Henle in *Language, Thought and Culture* (Ann Arbor, 1958) p. 6.
13. John Hospers, *An Introduction to Philosophical Analysis* (London, 1967²) p. 44.
14. Henle, *Language, Thought and Culture*, pp. 5 f.
15. Quoted in Anthony Flew, *An Introduction to Western Philosophy* (London, 1971) p. 450.
16. P.F. Strawson, 'Different Conceptions of Analytical Philosophy', in *Tijdschrift voor Filosofie* (vol. 35, 1973) p. 824.
17. A.J. Ayer, *Philosophy of Language* (Oxford, 1960) p. 33.
18. Richard Robinson, *Plato's Earlier Dialectic* (Oxford, 1953) p. 59, see also Richard Robinson, *Definition* (Oxford, 1954) ch. 6.
19. Cf. Strawson, 'Different Conceptions of Analytical Philosophy', pp. 799ff.
20. Gilbert Ryle, *Dilemmas* (Cambridge, 1956) pp. 31–2.
21. Wittgenstein, *Philosophical Investigations*, I, 309.
22. Ibid., I. 255.
23. Ibid., I. 109.
24. Strawson, 'Different Conceptions of Analytical Philosophy', p. 803.
25. Karl Barth, *Church Dogmatics*, I, 1 (Edinburgh, 1975) p. 3.

PART TWO: AXIOLOGICAL CONCEPTS

1.  R.M. Hare, *The Language of Morals* (Oxford, 1952) p. 80f.
2.  B. Mayo, *Ethics and the Moral Life* (London, 1958) p. 71.
3.  A.J. Ayer, *Language, Truth and Logic* (London, 1936) p. 107f.
4.  Hare, *The Language of Morals*, p. 10.
5.  C.L. Stevenson, *Ethics and Language* (New Haven, 1944) ch. 1.
6.  Ayer, *Language, Truth and Logic*, p. 110.

7.    S.E. Toulmin, *The Place of Reason in Ethics* (Cambridge, 1950) p. 32f.
8.    Ayer, *Language, Truth and Logic*, p. 108.
9.    C.L. Stevenson, *Facts and Values* (New Haven, 1963) p. 16.
10.   Rudolf Otto, *The Idea of the Holy* (Oxford, 1923).
11.   D.D. Evans, *The Logic of Self-Involvement* (London, 1963) ch. 3.
12.   Hare, *The Language of Morals*, p. 69.
13.   I.T. Ramsey, *Religious Language* (London, 1957) p. 18.

PART THREE: EPISTEMOLOGICAL CONCEPTS

1.    A.J. Ayer, *The Problem of Knowledge* (London, 1956) p. 31.
2.    Included in A.P. Griffiths (ed.), *Knowledge and Belief* (Oxford, 1967).
3.    Ibid.
4.    R. B. Braithwaite, 'The Nature of Believing' (in Griffiths, *Knowledge and Belief*) p. 31 f.
5.    Included in G. Pitcher (ed.), *Truth* (Englewood Cliffs, N.J., 1964) p. 16.
6.    P.F. Strawson, 'Truth' (In Pitcher, *Truth*) p. 34.
7.    Ibid.
8.    Ayer, *Language, Truth and Logic*, p. 107.
9.    Ibid., p. 88.
10.   Ayer, *The Problem of Knowledge*, p. 57.
11.   R.M. Chisholm, *Theory of Knowledge* (Englewood Cliffs, N.J., 1966).
12.   Norman Malcolm, *Knowledge and Certainty* (Ithaca N.Y., 1964) p. 64.
13.   Ibid., p. 69.
14.   W.K. Clifford, 'The Ethics of Belief' in R.R. Ammerman and M.G. Singer (eds), *Belief, Knowledge and Truth* (New York, 1970) p. 44.
15.   For this concept of proof see George I. Mavrodes, *Belief in God* (New York, 1970) ch. 2.
16.   John Hick, *Faith and Knowledge* (Ithaca N.Y., 1966) p. 208.
17.   Bernard Williams, *Problems of the Self* (Cambridge, 1973) p. 137 f.
18.   W.W. Bartley, *The Retreat to Commitment* (London, 1964) p. 134 f.
19.   For example, Norman Malcolm, 'Is it a Religious Belief that God Exists?', in John Hick (ed.), *Faith and the Philosophers* (London, 1964).
20.   See the articles by Rudolf Bultmann and Artur Weiser on pisteuo in R. Kittel (ed.), *Theological Dictionary of the New Testament*, vol. 8, (Grand Rapids, 1968).
21.   Bultmann in Kittel, *Theological Dictionary of the New Testament*, vol. 6. p. 209.

PART FOUR: ONTOLOGICAL CONCEPTS

1. Paul J. Tillich, *Systematic Theology I* (Chicago, 1951) p. 237.
2. Ayer, *Language, Truth and Logic*, p. 118.
3. W.P. Alston, 'The Ontological Argument Revisited', in A. Plantinga (ed.), *The Ontological Argument* (New York, 1965) p. 89.
4. Bertrand Russell, *The Principles of Mathematics* (London, 1903) p. 449f.
5. Rudolf Carnap, 'Empiricism, Semantics and Ontology', in L. Linsky (ed.), *Semantics and the Philosophy of Language* (Urbana, 1952).
6. Alston, 'The Ontological Argument Revisited', p. 92f.
7. A Flew, 'Theology and Falsification', in A. Flew and A. MacIntyre (eds.), *New Essays in Philosophical Theology* (London, 1955), p. 96.
8. Carl Hempel, 'Problems and Changes in the Empiricist Criterion of Meaning', in Linsky, *Semantics and the Philosophy of Language*.
9. Paul J. Tillich, *The Courage to Be* (London, 1952) p. 184.
10. Paul Van Buren, *The Secular Meaning of the Gospel* (London, 1963) p. 156.
11. Ibid.
12. Ibid., p. 199 f.
13. Ibid., p. 190.
14. Included in J. Hick (ed.), *The Existence of God* (New York, 1964) p. 228 ff.
15. See C.A. van Peursen, *Him Again!* (Richmond Va., 1969) pp. 16−17.
16. D.D. Evans, *The Logic of Self-Involvement* (London, 1963) p. 175 ff.
17. Hick, *The Existence of God*, p. 253 ff.
18. Tillich, *The Courage to Be*, p. 184.
19. Nelson Pike, *God and Timelessness* (London, 1970) p. 29 ff.
20. J.J.C. Smart, 'The Existence of God', in Flew and MacIntyre, *New Essays in Philosophical Theology*.
21. F. Schleiermacher, *The Christian Faith* (Edinburgh, 1968) pp. 203−210. See also Nelson Pike, *God and Timelessness*, pp. 6−8.

# Study Checklist

Philosophy has to be learned as a way of solving problems and answering questions. Hence a checklist of study questions is essential in a textbook on philosophy. Students who are able to answer the questions in this checklist, have mastered the material in the book.

PART ONE: CONCEPTUAL INQUIRY

1.  What is the difference between factual questions, questions of meaning, and conceptual questions, and how are these three kinds of questions related? Illustrate with your own examples.
2.  Which of these kinds of questions are of interest to philosophers? And to theologians? Give reasons.
3.  How would you distinguish between causal acts and conventional acts?
4.  In what sense can a rule be constitutive of an act? Illustrate with your own examples.
5.  What is the difference between locutions, illocutions and per-illocutions and how are they related? Illustrate with your own examples.
6.  What is the difference between illocutions and speech acts?
7.  In what way can locutions, illocutions and per-illocutions go wrong? Is the success of one of these a condition for the success of one of the others? Give reasons.
8.  What kinds of illocutions can you distinguish? In what ways can each of these go wrong?
9.  What is the difference between a constative, a statement, a proposition and an assertion?
10. What is the difference between an expressive and an autobiographical constative?
11. Which expressives always accompany constatives, commissives and prescriptives respectively?
12. Can expressives be reduced to social formalities?
13. What is the difference between a commissive and a promise?
14. What is the difference between being obliged and being forced?
15. How are commissives and prescriptives related to obligations?
16. What is the difference between a prescriptive, an order, a supplication, and a per-illocution?

17. Do prescriptives presuppose that the speaker has authority with respect to the hearer?

18. In what sense are prescriptives always based on 'agreements'?

19. Which factual presuppositions are constitutive for each kind of illocution?

20. Which rules are constitutive for all assertions? Show that we cannot assert anything if we don't keep these rules.

21. What is the difference between a paradox and a contradiction?

22. Is God subjected to the rules of logic?

23. In what ways can the different illocutions in a speech act imply each other? Illustrate with your own examples.

24. Is there a correlation between kinds of illocutions and kinds of per-illocutions?

25. What is a parenthetical instruction and for what purposes are these used?

26. In Plato's dialogue the *Cratylus*, Hermogenes, and Cratylus defend opposing views about the relation between language and reality. What are the main difficulties involved in their respective views, and how does Socrates try to overcome these difficulties?

27. What are the main differences (a) between the views of Plato and Aristotle and (b) between the views of Aristotle and Kant, concerning the relation between words, concepts and things?

28. At what points do Aristotle and Augustine respectively break through the limitations of the names model of language?

29. What is the difference between conceptual realism and conceptualism and which of these two views is to be preferred?

30. Discuss the most important difficulties involved in the names model of language and the ways in which some of the defenders of this model try to overcome them.

31. How does Gilbert Ryle distinguish between speech and language? What, according to him, are the most important elements of speech and language respectively?

32. In the light of this distinction, what is the relation between concepts, words and things?

33. Are concepts skills in using words correctly?

34. What is the relation between conceptual skills and physical skills?

35. How do we acquire conceptual skills?

36. Discuss some of the most important conceptual skills involved in performing a speech act and show why each of these is necessary for this purpose.

37. Which of these conceptual skills can be explained by the names model?
38. What is the meaning of a word according to the model of names and the model of tools respectively?
39. What is the relation between concepts, words and reality according to the model of names and the model of tools respectively?
40. In what way are concepts 'forms of life'? Illustrate this with reference to different kinds of conceptual skills.
41. What is meant by 'classification'? In what way is our classification of reality determined by (a) the reality which we classify and (b) our social, cultural, physical, etc., needs and interests?
42. In what way is classification a skill which we have to acquire?
43. What is the difference and what is the relation between the connotation and the denotation of a classification concept? How is this distinction related to that between describing and referring? Do all words (and concepts) have a denotation and a connotation? Illustrate your answer with your own examples.
44. What role do conceptual skills play in our perception of the world?
45. What is meant by 'mental set'? How does 'mental set' arise and what role does language play here?
46. How do our words and concepts influence each other?
47. Is there a relation between 'mental set' and conceptual realism? Give reasons for your answer.
48. Are all concepts culturally relative or are there some concepts which are fundamental to all thought and culture. Give reasons for your answer.
49. What is the nature of conceptual inquiry on the basis of the names model of language?
50. In what sense is a request for the essential nature of something ambiguous? Discuss some of the most important ways in which this request can be interpreted and illustrate with examples.
51. Show how the definition of class concepts can involve both practical and moral issues.
52. Distinguish between the meaning of words and the meaning of things.
53. Show how the ambiguity of conceptual inquiry on the basis of the model of names can lead to the same philosophical texts being interpreted as dealing with widely different questions. Illustrate with examples.

54. Different metaphors are often used to explain the nature of conceptual inquiry on the basis of the model of tools. Explain the use of the following metaphors for this purpose, and discuss the advantages and limitations of each: (a) conceptual analysis, (b) conceptual geography, (c) conceptual therapy, (d) conceptual grammar, and (e) conceptual codification.

55. Distinguish between historical theology, Biblical theology and systematic theology.

56. Show how systematic theology is a form of conceptual inquiry. Illustrate with examples.


PART TWO: AXIOLOGICAL CONCEPTS

57. Why is 'What are values?' not a satisfactory way of formulating the axiological problem?

58. What is the difference between evaluative and meta-evaluative questions? Illustrate with your own examples.

59. (a) In what sense are colours directly perceived simple characteristics? (b) How does the value of something differ from its colour?

60. Define 'objectivity'. To cope with what sort of difficulties do we distinguish between objectivity and subjectivity? Illustrate with your own examples.

61. Define 'intuitionism' and show why the intuitionist is unable to account for the objectivity of values.

62. How do consequential characteristics differ from non-natural characteristics?

63. Define 'naturalism' and show how this view tries to overcome the difficulties involved in intuitionism.

64. Does naturalism relate the value of something to its factual characteristics in a satisfactory way? Give your reasons.

65. Is one of the following a satisfactory definition of 'good'? Give reasons. (a) Good = approved of by everybody. (b) Good = approved of by me. (c) Good = worthy of approval. (d) Good = according to the will of God.

66. Can we, by seeking agreement about the factual characteristics of something, overcome our differences about its value? Give your reasons.

67. What are the advantages and disadvantages of intuitionism and naturalism in relation to each other?

68. What is meant by the 'emotive theory of value'
69. What is the difference between an expression of feeling and a manifestation of feeling? Give your own examples.
70. How do feelings differ from attitudes and in what respects are they similar?
71. In what sense are attitudes dispositional, intentional and two-valued?
72. Are approval and disapproval (a) expressions of feeling, or (b) expressions of attitude or (c) neither? Give your reasons.
73. What refinements does C.L. Stevenson make to the emotive theory? Are these sufficient to overcome the difficulties involved in this theory? Give your reasons.
74. In what sense are value judgements *vague* as expressions of attitudes? What makes *the specific* nature of the expressed attitudes clear?
75. What are the differences between prescriptive speech acts and attempts at causally influencing someone's behaviour?
76. How are statements of fact, expressions of attitude and value judgements related, and how do they differ?
77. Show how neither intuitionism, nor naturalism nor emotivism can explain how we argue about the value of things. Which of these three do you think comes closest to an adequate explanation? Give your reasons.
78. Show how (a) the fact that value judgements are more than self-referring, makes it *necessary* for us to argue about them, and (b) the fact that value judgements are based on norms makes it *possible* for us to argue about them.
79. On what points can value judgements be open to criticism and how could such criticism be answered?
80. How are the factual characteristics of something relevant to the justification of our value judgements about it?
81. What is meant by 'norms'? Show how the justification of norms, if carried through far enough, must end in an appeal to a view of life. Is it always necessary to go that far? Give your reasons.
82. Describe the illocutionary load of a value judgement and explain the relation between the various illocutionary elements.
83. (a) Are all value judgements prescriptive speech acts (that is, speech acts whose logical form is characterised by a prescriptive)? (b) Is the primary purpose in asserting a value judgement always prescriptive? (c) Are all prescriptive speech acts value judgements? (d) Give reasons for your replies.

84. What kinds of factual characteristics (constative properties) can you distinguish? Give your own examples.

85. (a) What is the difference between constative properties and prescriptive properties? (b) How are these two kinds of properties of something related to the way we act towards it? (c) Do you think that the naturalistic fallacy results from a confusion between constative properties and prescriptive properties? Give your reasons.

86. Are glory and holiness constative properties or prescriptive properties? Give your reasons.

87. What is the difference between value judgements and ascriptions of meaning?

88. What are the most important differences between the ascription of meaning in a gerundive speech act and in a descriptive speech act? What are the advantages and the limitations of each?

89. Under what conditions can descriptive speech acts ascribe meaning? Are these conditions always present and descriptive speech acts therefore always ascriptive of meaning? Give your reasons.

90. What are the differences between analogical and parabolic onlooks? Illustrate with your own examples.

91. In what way could the following speech acts be ascriptive of meaning? Give your reasons.
    (a) Mrs Thatcher is a Tory
    (b) Life is a lottery
    (c) His courage is worthy of admiration
    (d) The Lord is my shepherd
    (e) She looks on her children as her equals
    (f) I look on my children as my personal property
    (g) The Labour Party is in favour of Britain leaving the EEC
    (h) Gambling is against the will of God.

92. What is meant by a view of life? Explain how (a) someone's norms, (b) his ideals and (c) his expectations are related to his view of life.

93. What is meant by a basic conviction? How are basic convictions related to views of life? Does everybody have a basic conviction?

94. What conditions must something fulfil in order to be a primary determinant of meaning? Explain why these conditions are necessary.

95. What is the difference between internal and external criteria for judging a view of life? Which of these are relevant in a discussion between people with different views of life? Give your reasons.

96. Discuss the external criteria for a view of life and show why each of these is necessary?

97. Do the external criteria enable us to decide which view of life is the only true one? Give your reasons.

98. Is the choice of one view of life as the only true one, an irrational and arbitrary choice?

99. Explain how morality is related to religion.


PART THREE: EPISTEMOLOGICAL CONCEPTS

100. (*a*) What are the differences between 'knowing that' and 'being acquainted with', and (*b*) how are they related to each other?

101. Are knowing and believing different attitudes towards true statements? Give your reasons.

102. (*a*) What are the differences between understanding and believing, and (*b*) how are they related to each other?

103. What difficulties are involved in the views which Descartes, Hume and Price respectively hold on the question whether belief is something we could decide to do?

104. (*a*) What view does R.B. Braithwaite defend on the relation between belief and action? (*b*) What difficulties are involved in this view? (*c*) Is Braithwaite able to deal satisfactorily with these difficulties?

105. Explain the limitations of a behaviouristic account of belief.

106. Define the following terms: 'disposition', 'logical possibility', 'empirical possibility', 'technical possibility'.

107. What is the difference between constative beliefs and prescriptive beliefs? How do these two kinds of beliefs respectively determine our actions?

108. Distinguish clearly between two forms of the correspondence theory of truth and explain what difficulties are involved in each.

109. What are the most important differences between the correspondence theory and the coherence theory of truth?

110. What are the most important differences between the two main versions of the coherence theory of truth?

111. Show that the defenders of the coherence theory can only overcome the difficulties involved in the theory by abandoning the theory itself.

112. How does the pragmatic theory of truth try to solve the difficulties involved in the coherence theory?

113. Distinguish clearly between the theories about truth defended by C.S. Peirce, William James and John Dewey respectively. What difficulty do these theories have in common?

114. Distinguish clearly between the views about truth defended by F.P. Ramsey, P.F. Strawson and A.J. Ayer, and list the strong and weak points in these views.

115. (a) What is the difference between saying '$p$', 'I believe that $p$' and '$p$ is true'? (b) how are these three assertions related?

116. Which important aspects of the various traditional theories about truth (correspondence theory, coherence theory, pragmatic theory and performative theory) should be incorporated in any adequate theory of truth?

117. Explain the rationalist ideal of knowledge and show that, if consistently maintained, it must lead to scepticism.

118. (a) What is the difference between analytic and synthetic propositions? (b) What is the difference between *a priori* and *a posteriori* propositions? (c) What is the difference between necessary and contingent propositions? (d) How are these three distinctions related?

119. Show that *a priori* propositions, self-verifying propositions, and propositions about the immediate content of introspection and perception differ from each other in the sense in which they can be said to be 'indubitable'.

120. (a) Explain the way in which we should justify our beliefs according to Carneades. (b) Does this theory provide a way out of the rationalist impasse?

121. (a) How does Norman Malcolm distinguish between a strong and a weak sense of 'knowing'? (b) Is this distinction parallel to that between analytic and synthetic propositions? (c) Does this distinction provide a way out of the rationalist impasse?

122. In what sense is it absurd to require a justification of belief?

123. Which decisions with respect to our beliefs do require justification?

124. In what sense are beliefs open to criticism and in what sense are they not?

125. Are there limits to the extent to which beliefs are open to criticism? Give your reasons.
126. In what sense are proofs 'person-relative'?
127. What is the difference between (*a*) 'I know' and 'he knows', (*b*) 'he knows' and 'he believes', (*c*) 'I know' and 'I believe'?
128. (*a*) What is meant by a 'knowledge claim'? (*b*) What is the difference between acceptable and reasonable knowledge claims? Give your own examples.
129. If truth is a defining characteristic of knowledge, does this not make knowledge something we may have but of which we can never know whether we have it? Give reasons for your reply.
130. Why is it important to include justification in the definition of knowledge? Give reasons for your reply.
131. In what sense is rationalism authoritarian?
132. On what sort of evidence is religious belief based and why must rationalism always reject this sort of evidence?
133. When according to the rationalist, are we justified in believing something on authority?
134. What is the difference between a rationalist theology and an existentialist theology? Give examples of each.
135. Discuss the main steps in a Thomist reply to the rationalist challenge. Do you think this reply is adequate? Give your reasons.
136. What Biblical support is there for the view that religious belief is *fiducia* and not *fides*?
137. What is the difference between 'belief in' and 'belief that' and how are they related? Is 'belief in' possible without 'belief that'? Give your reasons.
138. How would you deal with the rationalist challenge to religious belief?
139. What is the relation between knowledge and religious belief? Is it valid to speak of 'religious knowledge'? Give your reasons.

PART FOUR: ONTOLOGICAL CONCEPTS

140. Explain the differences between the referential question, the epistemological question and the ontological question about a statement that something exists.
141. Explain how the difference between the epistemological and the ontological questions is reflected in the kinds of objections people have against belief in the existence of God.

142. Explain the similarities and the differences between the ontological objections which theologians and philosophers respectively have against belief in the existence of God.

143. Show how Descartes' ontological argument for the existence of God assumes that 'existence' is a predicate.

144. (*a*) What grounds do some philosophers (following Kant) have for rejecting the view that 'existence' is a predicate? (*b*) What difficulties result from rejecting this view?

145. How does Russell distinguish between 'being' and 'existence'? Does this distinction help us to accommodate both the reasons for and the reasons against the view that 'existence' is a predicate?

146. In what sense is the concept of 'existence' systematically ambiguous? Illustrate with examples.

147. Explain Carnap's distinction between internal and external questions about the existence of something.

148. Explain, in the light of this distinction, in what sense 'existence' is a predicate and in what sense it is a condition for predication.

149. Compare the views of Kant, Russell and Carnap on the question whether 'existence' is a predicate or a condition for predication.

150. Explain how the fact that existence is a condition for predication does not exclude the possibility of denying the existence of something.

151. Explain the nature of external questions about the existence of something and illustrate this in the light of Carnap's views about the real-world language (or thing-language, as Carnap calls it).

152. Explain why the real-world language differs from many other language games in the sense that we never *choose* to participate in it.

153. Explain how the real-world language has a primacy in relation to all other language games. Show that the word 'primacy' is systematically ambiguous.

154. Explain how the concepts 'fact' and 'know' are related.

155. How do facts differ from hypotheses and from fictions?

156. Distinguish between states of affairs, things, relations and events.

157. What is the difference between facts and states of affairs?

158. Why can facts only be stated but not described or doubted?

159. What is the difference between facts and questions of fact?

160. Under what condition can a question be a question of fact? Illustrate your reply with reference to Flew's parable.

161. Is it a question of fact whether there are human beings on the planets of some distant star?

162. In what sense can we speak of questions of fact regarding the past?

163. What is the difference between the following two questions and how would you answer each of them? (*a*) Is it a question of fact whether God exists? (*b*) Is the existence of God a fact?
164. Explain how the concept 'real' is ambiguous because its opposite 'unreal' is ambiguous.
165. What is the difference between the concepts 'exist', 'fact' and 'real', and how are they related?
166. What is the difference between the states of affairs to which we have to refer in order to answer the epistemological and the ontological questions respectively? When can these questions be answered by referring to the same state of affairs? Illustrate with your own examples.
167. How is it possible, within the language game of the Christian faith, to say anything about God without thereby denying His unique character as primary determinant of meaning? Explain this problem and discuss critically some of the possible solutions.
168. How is it possible to adopt an attitude towards a transcendent God whom we cannot come across anywhere in the world?
169. Can our attitudes towards God be reduced to attitudes towards the world? Explain and criticise Paul Van Buren's answer to this question.
170. Is it possible, within the language game of the Christian faith, to interpret the existence of God as the existence of a character in a parable or story? Explain and criticise R.B. Braithwaite's answer to this question.
171. Show how talk about God within the language game of the Christian faith, presupposes the factual existence of God.
172. Explain why the statement that something is an act of God cannot be asserted in an existentially neutral way like the statement that the moon revolves around the earth?
173. Is a reference to God's work adequate in order to answer (*a*) the epistemological question and (*b*) the ontological question about God's existence? Illustrate your reply with examples.
174. In what sense are God's works ambiguous as grounds for belief that He exists? What does this imply for the possibility of proving His existence?
175. Discuss the view that every attempt to prove God's existence *per suos effectus*, must be circular.
176. Is a reference to eschatology adequate in order to answer (*a*) the epistemological question and (*b*) the ontological question about God's existence. Give your reasons.

177. Show, with reference to Hick's parable about the two travellers, that the difference between someone who does and someone who does not believe that God exists, is a difference about both a question of fact and a question about the meaning of life.
178. Why is living 'in the sight of the Lord' logically impossible if God does not exist factually? Give your reasons.
179. Can a believing Hindu give thanks to Shiva even though Shiva does not exist in fact? Give your reasons.
180. Do we contradict God's unique character as the Wholly Other, if we ascribe factual existence to Him?
181. In what ways does God's existence differ from the existence of everything else?
182. In what sense is God's existence *necessary*?
183. Is 'God' a proper name or a descriptive term? Give your reasons.
184. In what sense is the existence of Jahweh necessary and not contingent?
185. Does Jahweh exist timelessly? Give your reasons.
186. In what sense is Jahweh eternal and omnipresent?
187. What is meant by the *aseitas* of Jahweh?
188. Why is it absurd for anyone to ask for an explanation why Jahweh exists?
189. How does doubt about the existence of Jahweh differ from doubt about the possibility of human life on Mars?

# Index

*Index*